C000153298

The EU in a Nutshell:

Everything you wanted to know about the European Union but didn't know who to ask

by Dr Lee Rotherham

HARRIMAN HOUSE LTD

3A Penns Road
Petersfield
Hampshire
GU32 2EW
GREAT BRITAIN

Tel: +44 (0)1730 233870
Fax: +44 (0)1730 233880
Email: enquiries@harriman-house.com
Website: www.harriman-house.com

First published in Great Britain in 2012

978-0-85719-231-8

British Library Cataloguing in Publication Data
A CIP catalogue record for this book can be obtained from the British Library.

Printed and bound in Great Britain by CPI Group (UK) Ltd, Croydon, CR0 4YY.

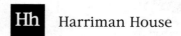

Hh Harriman House

"You come from an island, you can't understand the subtleties of European construction."
FORMER FRENCH PRESIDENT NICOLAS SARKOZY TO BBC REPORTER (NOVEMBER 2011)

of 15 July 2002

laying down the marketing standard for hazelnuts in shell

THE COMMISSION OF THE EUROPEAN COMMUNITIES,

Having regard to the Treaty establishing the European Community,

Having regard to Council Regulation (EC) No 2200/96 of 28 October 1996 on the common organisation of the market in fruit and vegetables (¹), as last amended by Regulation (EC) No 545/2002 (²), and in particular Article 2(2) thereof,

Whereas:

(1) Hazelnuts are among the products listed in Annex I to Regulation (EC) No 2200/96 for which standards must be adopted. To that end and in the interests of preserving transparency on the world market, account should be taken of the standard for hazelnuts in shell recommended by the Working Party on Standardisation of Perishable Produce and Quality Development of the United Nations Economic Commission for Europe (UN/ECE).

(2) Applying these standards should result in the removal from the market of products of unsatisfactory quality, bringing production into line with consumer requirements and facilitating trade relationships based on fair competition, thereby helping to improve the profitability of production. Therefore, it shall apply at all marketing stages.

(3) The measures provided for in this Regulation are in accordance with the opinion of the Management Committee for Fresh Fruit and Vegetables,

HAS ADOPTED THIS REGULATION:

Article 1

The marketing standard for hazelnuts in shell falling within CN code 0802 21 00 and CN code ex 0813 50 shall be as set out in the Annex.

The standard shall apply at all stages of marketing under the conditions laid down in Regulation (EC) No 2200/96.

Article 2

This Regulation shall enter into force on the 20th day following its publication in the *Official Journal of the European Communities*.

It shall apply from 1 January 2003.

This Regulation shall be binding in its entirety and directly applicable in all Member States.

Done at Brussels, 15 July 2002.

For the Commission
Franz FISCHLER
Member of the Commission

I. DEFINITION OF PRODUCE

This standard applies to hazelnuts in shell from varieties (cultivars) grown from *Corylus avellana* L. and *Corylus maxima* Mill. and their hybrids without involucre or husk, to be supplied to the consumer, hazelnuts for industrial processing being excluded.

II. PROVISIONS CONCERNING QUALITY

The purpose of the standard is to define the quality requirements for hazelnuts in shell after preparation and packaging.

A. Minimum requirements (¹)

(i) In all classes, subject to the special provisions for each class and the tolerances allowed, the hazelnuts in shell must be:

(a) characteristics of the shell

— well-formed; shell is not noticeably misshapen,

— intact; a slight superficial damage is not considered as a defect,

— sound; free from defects likely to affect the natural keeping quality of the fruit,

— free from damage caused by pests,

— clean; practically free of any visible foreign matter,

— dry; free of abnormal external moisture,

— free of adhering husk (not more than 5 % of individual shell surface in aggregate may have adhering husk).

(b) characteristics of the kernel

— intact; slight superficial damage is not considered as a defect,

— sound; produce affected by rotting or deterioration such as to make it unfit for consumption is excluded,

— sufficiently developed; shrunken or shrivelled fruit is to be excluded,

— clean; practically free of any visible foreign matter,

excluded,
— sufficiently developed; shrunken or shrivelled fruit is to be excluded,
— clean; practically free of any visible foreign matter,
— free from living or dead insects whatever their stage of development,
— free from damage caused by pests,
— free from mould filaments visible to the naked eye,
— free from rancidity,
— free of abnormal external moisture,
— free from foreign smell and/or taste,
— free from blemishes (including the presence of black colour) or deterioration rendering them unfit for consumption (²).

Hazelnuts in shell must be harvested when fully ripe.

★ **There are 70 words in the Lord's Prayer.**

★ **There are 271 words in the Gettysburg Address.**

★ **There are 313 words in the Ten Commandments.**

★ **De Gaulle's celebrated radio-broadcast call to arms contained 362.**

★ **Commission Regulation (EC) No 1284/2002 laying down the marketing size for hazelnuts in shell runs to 2,509…**

Critics of the European Union sometimes cite figures such as these to show that the EU is a bureaucratic and undemocratic creature.

But are they right?

What is the EU for? What does it do? How does it do it? Why in particular did various countries join it in the first place? Do we need it in the twenty-first century, and does it need us?

'Brussels' remains the most contentious enduring political debate of our times, and the issue has become the assassin of governments. Regardless of your vantage point, you ignore it at your cost.

III. PROVISIONS CONCERNING SIZING

Size or screening is determined by the maximum diameter of the equatorial section. It is expressed either by an interval determined by a maximum and a minimum size (sizing), or by mentioning the minimum size followed by the words 'and over', or the maximum size followed by the words 'and less' (screening). Sizing is compulsory for produce in Classes 'Extra' and 'I' but optional for produce in Class 'II'.

The following classification is laid down:

Sizing (⁴)	Screening (⁴)
22 and above	22 mm and above (or and less)
20 to 22 mm	20 mm and above (or and less)
18 to 20 mm	18 mm and above (or and less)

Contents

About the Author   ix
Acknowledgements   x
Foreword by David Starkey   xi
This Book in a Nutshell   xiv
An EU Timeline   xvi
Executive Summary   xx
A cold war joke from Estonia (1982)   xxii

Part One. Motives and Motivation   I

Part Two. How Brussels Works   81

Part Three. Policies and their Masters   139

Part Four. Beyond the Commissioners   249

Part Five. The Euroquangos   285

Part Six. Recurring Themes and Controversies   313

Part Seven. Aspirations and Directions   361

Part Eight. The View from the Member States   393

Some suggested further reading   486
Helpful websites   487
Déjà Vu   488

About the Author

Dr Lee Rotherham is a research fellow at the TaxPayers' Alliance and one of the country's leading experts on the European Union. Having worked as the researcher to Sir Richard Body and the 'Westminster Group of Eight' Euro rebels who lost the whip under John Major's government, in the wake of the 1997 election he was taken on as a political advisor to three successive Shadow Foreign Secretaries and their Europe spokesmen. Part-based in Brussels, he coordinated a heroically small and nebulous team that provided the basis for a surprising quantity of Britain's media stories on EU proposals at the time – and a spur to spotlighted British MEPs to change the way they had been intending to vote.

During the Convention on the Future of Europe, Dr Rotherham was the advisor and press officer to David Heathcoat-Amory, the Conservative MP delegated to the body drafting the EU Constitution. This placed him alongside the handful of delegates that fought a guerrilla campaign against further integration.

Since then, in addition to work in heritage, in Whitehall, and alongside a children's organisation, he has been widely published, most notably as co-author with Matthew Elliott of the best-selling *Bumper Books of Government Waste* which set the current political agenda on ending public sector profligacy.

He has twice stood as a parliamentary candidate, most colourfully in 2001 in his native St Helens against Shaun Woodward, unleashing a growing platoon of butlers on the nation's TV screens, in addition to the (marginally exaggerated) press reports of him driving across town on election day in an armoured vehicle. He further stood for selection for the primaries to select the Conservative candidate for London Mayor on a heretical platform of cutting pointless budgets and handing power down to councillors.

During the 2011 referendum campaign on the Alternative Vote system, Dr Rotherham was head of opposition research in the successful NOtoAV team.

Acknowledgements

The author would like to thank Matthew Elliott, Malcolm Bracken, the European Commission Representation in the United Kingdom, Hjortur J. Gudmundsson, Helle Hagenau, John Hayes MP, Roger Helmer MEP, Dr Ruth Lea, Ian Milne, Professor Patrick Minford and Sheridan Westlake for their assistance. Thanks also to Myles Hunt, Craig Pearce and Suzanne Tull at Harriman House.

Without the assistance and support my colleagues at the TaxPayers' Alliance, this book would never have gotten off the ground. So a final and gargantuan thank you is reserved for the brilliant TPA team.

Financial support for this book was provided by the Politics and Economics Research Trust (charity number 1121849). The views expressed in this book are those of the author and not of the research trust or of its trustees.

Data referenced in this book is sourced from the relevant EU institution (typically the Commission, EP, or Eurostat) or from the government of the country concerned, unless otherwise noted.

Foreword by David Starkey

Britain – or rather England – has been from the beginning a reluctant partner in the European project. She joined late and reluctantly and almost immediately began to have second thoughts. She has sought and won opt-outs and rebates. Most importantly she stood aside completely from the euro – the currency union which was meant to be the keystone of the arch of political union but now looks likely to undermine it or even overthrow it completely.

Why? For the bienpensant Europhile political elite the answer was clear. England's reluctance was the result of mere Little Englandism. It was petty-minded, backward-looking and destined to be swept aside in the onward march of History.

Actually, my guess is that History herself offers a rather different verdict. For England's semi-detached relationship with Continental Europe is neither new nor an aberration. Instead it is deeply rooted in the political developments of the last five hundred years.

First came the great ideological divide of the Reformation when Henry VIII separated the National Church of England from the Universal Church of Rome. The debate, seen most vividly in the trial of Sir Thomas More, was couched in strikingly 'modern' terms. More argued, like a contemporary Europhile, that the English parliament was a mere parochial assembly, subordinate to the laws and values of a pan-European Christendom. Henry VIII's judges replied, on the contrary, that statute was binding and parliament sovereign. And Henry VIII and his judges won – at least until Britain's accession to the Treaty of Rome.

Second, thanks to the Civil Wars and Revolutions of the seventeenth century, the process of state formation diverged sharply on either side of the Channel, which thence forward became the widest strip of water in the world. In England, power became inductive, rising from the 'people', however defined, who expressed their sovereign will through the representative assembly of parliament. In France, on the other hand, which represented the opposite ideal type, power was deductive. It descended from the king, who ruled through ministerial experts and an ever-expanding bureaucracy.

Representative institutions continued, but were primarily local and consultative.

In a nutshell, the one form of government was parliamentary; the other bureaucratic.

Third, at the beginning of the eighteenth century, the newly consolidated British state embarked on the enterprise of world empire. To facilitate this, it became the axiom of British foreign policy that no Continental power should be allowed to develop a European hegemony that might threaten Britain's backdoor. In the course of the next three centuries, the axiom was applied to defeat the France of Louis XIV and Napoleon and the Germany of Wilhelm II and Hitler.

It should now be clear why Edward Heath's decision to go cap-in-hand to Brussels was so traumatic. For the EU which England joined was a sort of vile antithesis of her own historical development. The EU subordinates national to international law; it embodies in an extreme form the bureaucratic structures of Absolutist France and it aspires consciously to a European Union which, in extent and completeness, exceeds the wildest imperial visions of a Napoleon or a Hitler.

Britain is the extreme case. But she was not alone. Instead, as Lee Rotherham's important and original book shows, each member of the EU had to revolutionise their own historic standpoints. France has embraced European integration after three massively costly attempts to stand up to a united Germany militarily, and several failed attempts to curtail it economically by carving off Germany's industrial heartland on the Rhine. The Benelux states have found a successor policy to failed neutrality. Germans meanwhile are nigh-stereotypically engaged in constant soul-searching and paranoia of what untrammelled power does to them in a unified state. Other countries have found in European integration a measure of medication to historical troubles of their own.

But does that medicine work for all?

Politics is where history is being made today. It is the section of track where the tramlines that have guided us to this moment in time are still being laid down. This book is an extremely useful map to those lines, both tracing their past and pointing to where they face for the future. It provides substantial and often surprising detail of what the EU is actually about, particularly in terms of the nuts and bolts of its institutions (many of which will be unfamiliar to the reader, and probably to many in Brussels itself). It also supplies a context to help the reader understand the original ambition, which in turn allows a proper judgement of the merits – or otherwise – of the whole vertiginous and, it is now clear, immensely risky project.

Take, for example, the tables at the close of the book. These enable the reader to compare and contrast what individual countries put in and get out of EU membership. This is political arithmetic at its most fundamental and vital.

For nothing in politics is inevitable, particularly where history – and Britain's history in particular – offers such abundant alternatives, even to the extent of standing aside from the European project entirely. It was a thought often expressed by that great historian of an earlier generation, A. J. P. Taylor, who wrote newspaper article after newspaper article in the 1960s arguing passionately against Britain's joining in the first place. In his eyes, "The lesson of history is clear: outside Europe we can be more secure and more prosperous than inside."

Testing that hypothesis demands a deep and properly documented understanding of what the institutions of modern Europe and the ever-growing political construct are about. Have we abandoned five hundred years of our history to our cost? The Europhiles of course claimed we were catching the tide of history when we joined. But is the EU proving to be a stagnant and treacherous backwater? Is it time to jump ship? It is a key question of our times.

David Starkey
June 2012

This Book in a Nutshell

WHAT DID COUNTRIES WANT FROM THE EU?

> **In a nutshell...**
>
> See Part One for an overview of the motivations of nations behind wanting to join the EU originally and what they are seeking to get from it today.

HOW DOES BRUSSELS WORK?

> **In a nutshell...**
>
> See Part Two for a look at the main institutions and a list of the ten operating principles behind the European Union.

WHAT DOES THE EU DO?

> **In a nutshell...**
>
> See Part Three for a review of the key policy areas run by and from Brussels and the Directorates General behind them.

WHAT ARE THE OTHER, LESS VISIBLE, PARTS OF THE BRUSSELS MACHINE?

> **In a nutshell...**
>
> See Part Four for an assessment of the lesser-known EU institutions that have to put policies into practice.

WHO ARE THE EU QUANGONAUTS?

In a nutshell...

See Part Five for the EU quangos, the vital cogs that are so small they could fit in a Swiss watch, if only Switzerland were a member state.

WHAT ARE THE MAIN DISPUTED THEMES THAT REAPPEAR?

In a nutshell...

See Part Six for a swift glance at some controversial aspects of how the EU is run.

IS THE EU ON COURSE?

In a nutshell...

See Part Seven for an assessment of what the EU means as seen from an ideological standpoint and what alternative routes exist. These ambitions are not universally shared across the EU countries.

IS THE EU THE RIGHT ANSWER FOR ITS MEMBER STATES?

In a nutshell...

See Part Eight for tables that provide a direct comparison between countries, a concluding appraisal of whether the EU is fit for purpose today and a formula which might be able to answer that question for each member state.

An EU Timeline

Year	Key events
1945	Division of Europe established by frontlines and the Potsdam Conference.
1946	Churchill's Zurich Speech calls for greater European integration (the UK only to be a sponsor).
1947	European Movement founded. Treaty of Dunkirk signed between France and the UK versus any resurgent Germany.
1948	Benelux Customs Union. Dunkirk arrangement expanded to Low Countries. Berlin blockade begins.
1949	Federal West Germany, Council of Europe, and NATO separately founded.
1950	Cold war hots up in Korea. Robert Schuman proposes European co-operation (9 May, later Europe Day). European Payments Union formed for financial transfers and currency movement.
1951	European Coal and Steel Community (ECSC) formed (18 April). Euratom Treaty also sets up nuclear co-operation.
1952	The Six separately sign the European Defence Community (EDC).
1953	Common market for scrap iron.
1954	EDC rejected by French Parliament as too big a sovereignty loss. Western European Union (WEU) established instead. First European trade court ruling.
1955	Saarland rejoins Germany after a referendum rejects French links.
1956	Suez Crisis. Budapest uprising. European Economic Community (EEC) negotiations unstalled.
1957	EEC and Euratom created by the Treaties of Rome (25 March).
1958	Coreper formed for prep work by national civil servants. European Court of Justice (ECJ) established. European Monetary Agreement replaces EPU.
1959	First European Investment Bank loans.
1960	European Free Trade Area (EFTA) formed as 'EEC-lite'. European Social Fund established by EEC.
1961	Bonn summit establishes principle of political union. Berlin Wall erected.

1962	Common Agricultural Policy (CAP) set up. Algeria becomes independent from France and de facto quits the EEC. Nassau Agreement on US-UK co-operation…
1963	…which lead to De Gaulle vetoing the UK joining. All accession negotiations falter. One week later, German-French Friendship Treaty, leading to agreement on aspects of military co-operation. ECJ ruling states' sovereign rights suspended by membership.
1964	Costa/ENEL ruling at the ECJ; Community Law is declared supreme.
1965	France declares it will be withdrawing from NATO.
1966	French 'empty chairs' over major introduction of Qualified Majority Voting (QMV). End deal retains the veto where *national interests* are concerned.
1967	Agreement to harmonise indirect taxes and shift to VAT. Second De Gaulle veto on UK accession. ECSC, EEC and Euratom merge executives.
1968	Common customs tariff applied. Prague Spring.
1969	Hague summit endorses economic and monetary union (EMU).
1970	Treaty of Luxembourg provides for the Community to get its own resources, i.e. direct taxes and VAT take. Davignon Report endorses principle of common EEC positions on the international scene.
1971	Werner Plan endorsed for economic coordination, including exchange rates.
1972	Currency *snake*: a narrow exchange bandwidth. European Monetary Cooperation Fund formed.
1973	First accession wave. EEC-EFTA treaty. Oil crisis.
1974	British Labour government calls for major CAP reform and lower net payments.
1975	Regional Development Fund (ERDF) formed. Lomé Convention with developing countries. Florence University Institute set up. Minor UK change to terms: referendum votes Yes.
1976	Lira crisis.
1977	National fisheries waters extended to 200 nautical miles: this falls straight under Common Fisheries Policy (CFP) management for EEC members.
1978	European Monetary System agreed, with the ECU as the proto-euro.

1979	Exchange Rate Mechanism (ERM) launched. Cassis de Dijon ruling prevents health or environment from use as an excuse to block legal imports. First direct elections of MEPs (replacing delegated MPs).
1980	Death of Tito.
1981	Martial Law in Poland. Greece joins EEC.
1982	Falklands War.
1983	Reagan launches 'Star Wars' research (SDI).
1984	Fontainebleau Rebate agreed: compensates for low per capita income and low CAP receipts. Saarbrucken bilateral agreement on the gradual abolition of Franco-German border checks.
1985	Delors becomes Commission President. Greenland leaves EEC.
1986	Iberian accession. Brussels appropriates the Council of Europe flag.
1987	Single European Act comes into force, aiming to establish a 'Single Market'. EEC institutions become EC institutions.
1988	French-German Security and Defence Council formed.
1989	11 states sign up to Social Charter.
1990	Warsaw Pact crumbles. German reunification. Iraq invades Kuwait. UK joins ERM.
1991	Failed Soviet coup. Yugoslavia disintegrates. French-German brigade becomes operational. Maastricht Treaty agreed, creating the EU. Francovich ruling: a member state must compensate for its breach of Community law.
1992	European Economic Area (EEA) agreement with EFTA countries. Eurocorps formed. Petersburg Declaration puts WEU at EU disposal. Black Wednesday: ERM falls apart expensively. Danish referendum: Nej to Maastricht triggers crisis.
1993	Formal launch of the Single Market. Major global tariff reductions at Uruguay round of GATT.
1994	First meeting of the Committee of the Regions. John Major gains face-saving compromise at Ioannina that marginally tweaks QMV. Nine Tory MPs lose/resign whip over increased contributions to the EU. European Monetary Institute, and Investment Fund, set up.
1995	'Neutral' accession wave. Schengen Agreement comes into force. Europol Convention. ECJ overrides limits on foreign footballers allowed in teams.

1996	Customs Union between EU and Turkey. Factortame ruling overrides UK attempts to avoid quota-hopping by Spanish fishing skippers.
1997	New Blair government immediately drops Social Chapter opt out, though no quid pro quo obtained. Amsterdam Treaty signed.
1998	Decker ruling incidentally endorses NHS health tourism.
1999	Agreeent on the eurozone, with eleven members. ERM II set up. Agenda 2000 agreed with small regional and CAP reform.
2000	Treaty of Nice. Charter of Fundamental Rights.
2001	Greece joins eurozone. Irish No vote against Nice triggers crisis. Danish referendum is ducked. Destruction of Twin Towers on 9/11. Justice and Home Affairs (JHA) agenda reactivated.
2002	Launch of the euro, initially with dual circulation. Galileo GPS programme established. Convention on the Future of Europe begins. EU ratifies Kyoto.
2003	Iraq War. EU police mission in Bosnia. Swedish referendum rejects euro.
2004	Accession of ten new member states. CFSP posts established. Madrid bombings. EU Constitution signed.
2005	EU Constitution rejected by Dutch, triggering crisis. London bombings.
2006	The .eu domain name is created.
2007	Accession of Black Sea states. Schengen also expands into Eastern Europe. Slovenia joins euro.
2008	Malta and Cyprus join eurozone. EU Constitution rebranded Lisbon Treaty. Irish reject Lisbon in a referendum, triggering a crisis. Subprime crisis expands.
2009	Slovakia joins eurozone. Second Irish vote on Lisbon Treaty provides a Yes. High Representative for foreign affairs set up. Treaty of Strasbourg gives Eurocorps legal personality: it now has five members and five associate members.
2010	External Action Service set up. Crisis in the eurozone hits Ireland, premier falls.
2011	Estonia joins euro. Libya crisis (no EU role). Crisis in the eurozone hits Greece and Italy: premiers fall.

Executive Summary

The European Union is the stalker of British politics: however hard Prime Ministers try to avoid the subject, its face ends up pressed against the Downing Street window staring right at them. But what is the EU really about? What did countries expect when they signed up to the process? Do those conditions still apply today, or are national leaders better off looking for some more appropriate deal for the twenty-first century?

The EU in a Nutshell is a book you can dip into, or crack open, now and again, or you can peruse and ponder from cover to cover if you prefer. It combines an array of peculiar statistics and data. These wander the pages, beating up occasional historical facts before forming small mobs to run off into the nearest embassy and burst into ad hoc song-and-dance routines. Well, not quite, but it is a veritable banquet of fascinating, esoteric and often unexpected information, brought together by a Brussels expert with a decade and a half of experience across its institutions. And even he was bewildered by a lot of the peculiar figures and new institutions uncovered!

The book begins with the context and explores the history behind the founding of the European institutions; namely war, decline, trade and fear (sadly, sex only features on MEPs' agendas, and much later on). By understanding what drove politicians into taking their countries into the 'European dream', we better judge the realities that came after.

Next we learn how Brussels works. We discover the main institutions, what they do and how much of a wine allowance they need to do it. Chief amongst these is the Commission and we look at its Directorates-General exploring some of the strange, heroic or plain outrageous spending activities upon which it engages – whether mining consortiums that receive agricultural support, sponsored dinners for visitors to dine with European Commissioners, or the 27-page report on the habitat of a snail (sadly, extinct in Luxembourg).

The Commission isn't the only game in town. There's a huge roll call of players, ranging from the empire of the new Foreign and Security Policy (whose empress is a former CND officer), through such bodies as the European Investment Bank and the Economic and Social Committee, to the

Bureau of European Policy Advisors, which forms an obscure group offering advice on the morality of EU activity. This is even before we get to the hidden world of the Euroquangos. The European Medicines Agency is a key one that lives in London, though it's unlikely most Brits would even be aware of its presence – especially as in 2012 it has been preoccupied with trying to reschedule all of its UK meetings so they happen in Belgium because attendees would otherwise get caught up in traffic jams caused by the Olympics.

Having come to understand what 'Brussels' (and Strasbourg, Luxembourg and Frankfurt) does, it's then time to cover a few of the controversies. What are the facts and figures behind the amount of red tape the EU is said to cause? Just how much are its people paid? What are these reported perks people get, beyond the Uzbek national costume given as a gift (with fetching silk scarf) to Commission President Barroso? Fraud, waste and whistleblowers are also explored, and the dispute over the extent to which EU laws are paramount. With the facts and figures behind these frequent newspaper headlines set out, the book turns to the broad-brush aspirations and backgrounds of those who pushed for a *country called Europe*, a high-minded end goal contrasted with myriad international trade groups around the world that have different styles and objectives.

The book closes by providing the material for the reader to decide whether any country is better off in or out of the EU, setting out some key facts and figures and even a formula that can be used to make up your mind. It is, after all, not enough to understand; with politicians repeatedly trying to escape the stalker, it is important to also have an opinion.

A cold war joke from Estonia (1982)

Brezhnev and his gang are visiting Reagan. They talk about peace and politics and drink vodka. Suddenly, Brezhnev asks:

"Gentlemen, if it's not a secret, then with what money are we drinking here?"

Reagan responds: *"Look out of the window. Do you see a bridge?"*

"Yes."

"The bridge was planned to cost 300 million dollars, but we built it with 150 million. This is the money we are drinking with."

Six months go by and Reagan and his bunch visit Brezhnev. They talk about peace and politics and drink vodka.

Reagan asks: *"Gentlemen, if it's not a secret, then with what money are we drinking here?"*

Brezhnev replies: *"Look out of the window. Do you see a bridge?"*

"No, we don't."

"Well, we are drinking with that."

From: Anecdotes about Soviet Power and their Leaders Collected from Estonia 1960-1986, ed. Juri Viikberg, Punkt and Koma, 2003

P A R T   O N E

Motives and Motivation

MAY CONTAIN TRACES OF
DREAMS, BUREAUCRATS,
WARS AND COAL

18 APRIL 1951

Establishment of the European Coal and Steel Community (ECSC) by the Treaty of Paris, just six years after the close of the second world war.

THE ECSC OBJECTIVE

The European Coal and Steel Community shall have as its task to contribute, in harmony with the general economy of the Member States and through the establishment of a common market as provided in Article 4, to economic expansion, growth of employment and a rise in the standard of living in the Member States.

The Community shall progressively bring about conditions which will of themselves ensure the most rational distribution of production at the highest possible level of productivity, while safeguarding continuity of employment and taking care not to provoke fundamental and persistent disturbances in the economies of Member States.

Article 2

1955

Year of the Messina Conference in which the negotiations for the Treaty of Rome properly began.

VAL DUCHESSE

The Brussels château in which EEC talks continued in 1956. The Suez and Budapest crises in November encouraged an agreement in the following weeks.

THE SIGNATURES ON THE TREATY OF ROME

P. H. Spaak
J. Ch. Snoy et d'Oppuers
Adenauer
Hallstein
Pineau
M. Faure
Antonio Segni
Gaetano Martino
Bech
Lambert Schaus
J. Luns
J. Linthorst Homan

 I leave Messina happy because even if you continue meeting you will not agree; even if you agree, nothing will result; and even if something results, it will be a disaster."

Reported quote from the British observer

FOUNDING PRINCIPLES IN THE TREATY OF ROME

DETERMINED to lay the foundations of an ever-closer union among the peoples of Europe.

RESOLVED to ensure the economic and social progress of their countries by common action to eliminate the barriers which divide Europe.

AFFIRMING as the essential objective of their efforts the constant improvement of the living and working conditions of their peoples.

RECOGNISING that the removal of existing obstacles calls for concerted action in order to guarantee steady expansion, balanced trade and fair competition.

ANXIOUS to strengthen the unity of their economies and to ensure their harmonious development by reducing the differences existing between the various regions and the backwardness of the less favoured regions.

DESIRING to contribute, by means of a common commercial policy, to the progressive abolition of restrictions on international trade.

INTENDING to confirm the solidarity which binds Europe and the overseas countries and desiring to ensure the development of their prosperity, in accordance with the principles of the Charter of the United Nations.

RESOLVED by thus pooling their resources to preserve and strengthen peace and liberty, and calling upon the other peoples of Europe who share their ideal to join in their efforts.

CAMPIDOGLIO

Michelangelo's renaissance palace on the Capitoline where the Treaty of Rome was signed.

OPENING WORDS OF THE US DECLARATION OF INDEPENDENCE

When in the Course of human events it becomes necessary for one people to dissolve the political bands which have connected them with another and to assume among the powers of the earth, the separate and equal station to which the Laws of Nature and of Nature's God entitle them, a decent respect to the opinions of mankind requires that they should declare the causes which impel them to the separation.

OPENING WORDS OF THE TREATY OF ROME

His Majesty The King of the Belgians, the President of the Federal Republic of Germany, the President of the French Republic, the President of the Italian Republic, Her Royal Highness The Grand Duchess of Luxembourg, Her Majesty The Queen of the Netherlands ...

PRESIDENTS OF THE ECSC AND THEN THE COMMISSION, BY NATIONALITY (TO DATE)

French	4	German	1
Italian	4	Dutch	1
Belgian	3	British	1
Luxemburgish	2	Portuguese	1

Parallel Treaty set up alongside the EEC, to secure access and co-operation with regard to civilian nuclear power. Run by Euratom.

234	Number of articles in the Euratom Treaty
300	Number of inspectors the EU employs to guarantee the clauses relating to the non-military application of civilian nuclear fuels
1965	Year Euratom Executive was merged into the European Communities
French	Nationality of the Presidents of Euratom during its administrative independence
1981	Year the Euratom Cricket Club "reached critical mass" (yes, really)

In a nutshell...

The establishment of the foundations for the later EEC and EU are set in the context of centuries of struggle to dominate the continent of Europe, and as often the struggle to avoid the domination of others.

The scars of history run much deeper than the tank ruts of Guderian or the trench lines of Verdun. Motives stretch back to the volley fire at Jena and the ambush at Yellow Ford. They equally reach to the pulpit at Geneva and the Reading Room at the British Library, to the Council of Trent and to the Tennis Court Oath.

A united Europe today is to its adherents an ideal, if not verging on an actual religion.

AD 212

Edict of Caracalla: last successful attempt to forge a common social identity in Europe, as Roman citizenship is granted to all free men (partly for tax reasons).

UNAM SANCTAM

Papal Bull of 1302, the high-water mark of the Catholic Church as it attempted – and failed – to assert supremacy.

ROTA ROMANA

The mediaeval Church's highest law court, a proto-ECJ.

COUNCIL OF CONSTANCE

Meeting of national Church leaders to end the Western Schism in the early fifteenth century: there were three concurrent popes.

Germans (including a handful of Scandinavians and Eastern Europeans), English, French and Italians voted on a national position, then voted nationally to find a communal position, with three national votes making a decision. Possibly the earliest example of QMV in European politics.

CHRISTMAS DAY, AD 800

Coronation of Charlemagne as Holy Roman Emperor, a state harked back to by supporters of European integration.

ALCUIN

Celebrated English monk sent to the court at Aachen as an adviser. With his assistants, formed an early UKREP.

HANSEATIC LEAGUE

The first EEC, covering the important North Sea and Baltic ports under trade agreements, from the twelfth century to the rise of the nation states and the discovery of the New World.

MEZZOGIORNO

The only part of the EEC that lay outside of Charlemagne's original European Empire.

I speak Spanish to God, Italian to women, French to men and German to my horse."

Quote attributed to Holy Roman Emperor Charles V

"United Europe has seldom been so nearly realized as it was after the Peace of Aix-la-Chapelle, in 1748. The King of England was a German, the King of Spain was French. The Empress of Austria was married to a Lorrainer with a French mother, the King of France was half Italian and his Dauphin was half Polish with a German wife. Scottish and French architects were at work in Russia and Germany, Italian cabinet-makers in France, French painters in Rome, Venetian painters in London, Dutch painters in Paris. Internationalism even extended to the armies of the day. During the last campaign of the War of Austrian Succession in 1747 […] it so happened that none of the generals engaged was a native of the country for which he fought."

Nancy Mitford, Madame de Pompadour (Clay, 1955)

CULTURE FORGED BY DIVERSITY

1756	72 years
Invention of Mayonnaise during the Siege of Fort St Philip, Minorca.	Duration of the reign of Louis XIV (1643-1715) – in English terms, from Charles I to George I.
The cook of Marshal Richelieu had run out of butter and cream for sauces.	

WAR OF THE SIXTH COALITION

Alliance that finally defeated Napoleon, only for him to return in 1815. This was a pointer to the amount of diplomatic and military effort required in such an alliance.

UK SHARE OF EUROPEAN INDUSTRY IN 1870

21% Food/drink/tobacco

29% Textiles/clothing

43% Utilities

45% Metals

70% Mining

30% UK share of total European industry

Source: *An Economic History of Modern Europe*, Broadberry/Fremdling/Solar

99 DAYS

Duration of the reign of Kaiser Frederick III. He was the liberals' great hope for Prussia but his reign was cut short by cancer.

He was succeeded by his son, Kaiser Wilhelm II, in 1888.

1900

German steel production, profiting from the seizure of Lorraine and revolutionary new processes, surpasses that of Britain

1910

German steel production approaches double that of Britain. It dropped massively after the war

1935

German steel production overtakes UK again

"FROM SEA TO SHINING SEA"

Abridgement of the Manifest Destiny of the United States

"FROM THE ATLANTIC TO THE URALS"

Stated European aspirations of de Gaulle (1962), until an angry Khrushchev despatched a letter seeking clarification

EU: NON-COMPATIBLE OBJECTIVE 1

Ending war in Europe, and Franco-German strife in particular, by establishing a common federal European state

EU: NON-COMPATIBLE OBJECTIVE 2

Fostering friendship in the EU by having closer trade ties between countries and greater co-operation, without creating a common political identity

"A KIND OF UNITED STATES OF EUROPE"

Churchill's aspirations for European co-operation... from which the UK stood apart

AN INTERNATIONAL CULTURE

Five European composers who worked in another country

Beethoven

Handel

Chopin

Wagner

Mercury

A SHARING OF CULTURE

Five European artists who worked abroad

Da Vinci

Holbein

El Greco

Canaletto

Picasso

A CONTINENT OF ALTERNATIVES

Five twentieth century European exiles

Dietrich

Einstein

Bartok

Freud

Mann

NATURAL INTEGRATORS?

Year of a country's adoption of the Gregorian calendar

1582	Belgium and Southern Netherlands, France, most of Italy, Luxembourg, Poland, Lithuania, Portugal, Spain
1583	Austria, Southern Germany, half of Switzerland
1584	Czech Republic (Bohemia), Slovakia (Moravia)
1587	Hungary
1590	Transylvania
1610	Prussia
1700	Denmark, Norway, North West Germany, Northern Netherlands, half of Switzerland
1724	One remaining Swiss canton
1752	UK including Ireland
1753	Sweden (had tried 1700-40 to change gradually, but also ran confusing leap years that were out of synch internationally), Finland (which partially used Julian on the Russian Conquest)
1912	Albania, Bulgaria
1915	Latvia, Lithuania (restored)
1918	Estonia
1919	Romania, centrally recognised in Yugoslavia
1924	Greece

EARLY EUROCONFUSION

23 April 1616

Traditional date of the deaths of both Shakespeare and Cervantes

Though as different calendars were in use, Cervantes had already been dead for a week and a half when the Bard shuffled off this mortal coil

Sources: Calendopedia, UNESCO et al.

SOME SUGGESTED DYNAMICS IN THE HISTORICAL DEVELOPMENT OF STATES

 Entropy. Inherent conditions for a nation's own destruction as it returns to its lowest devolved geographic state: "Lo, all our pomp of yesterday/Is one with Ninevah and Tyre!" (Kipling).

Natural Selection. From Type A, Type B state emerges and fails, while its competitor Type C survives. Some states thus escape entropy by adapting. Competition generates innovation, invention and enterprise, extending even to the arts.

Microcompetition. The concept that smaller states are better suited for natural selection, particularly where there is no large external threat or no prospect of a single state holding strategic resources. Examples include Renaissance Europe, especially the microstates of Italy and Germany, and classical Greece. Relies upon freer forms of government, otherwise technological superiority is not maintained and larger states cannot be defeated.

Founding imperialism. States accumulate territory through defensive imperialism (securing the next mountain pass or ford over the horizon), trading acquisitions, or outright colonial aspirations. Can swiftly generate larger states, ultimately accelerating the effect of entropy (for instance, Ming China or the late Ottomans).

Gravity. Large or powerful states pull lesser states into their political or economic orbit (e.g. unified Germany in Eastern Europe).

Collectivism. Political leaders seek communal betterment through joint activity and an aspired common identity (e.g. Communism, pan-Europeanism, the federal states of North America).

Redactionism. Through revisionism (righting perceived wrongs or correcting past mistakes), or restoration (nationalism or past imperialism revisited), founding imperialism is retriggered, though the conditions that initially encouraged it may well have passed.

What did the Founding Six member states get out it?

In a nutshell...

A secure trading establishment which kept out unwanted competitors, largely subsidised by the German taxpayer, that anchored a reformed West Germany, protected long-declining French interests, and provided food security after terrible wartime privations.

8

Number of recognised governments-in-exile in London during the second world war. The figure excludes countries such as France that had free forces under an alternative government.

2 AXIS POWERS, 6 DEFEATED AND OCCUPIED STATES

Wartime status of the EEC founders

A LITANY OF FAILURE

Previous French attempts to control German production in the Rhineland

1919   Rhineland demilitarised after the Treaty of Versailles. Saarland falls under a committee

1923-4   French support to a Rhineland separatist movement fails. Military occupation occurs in response to loan defaults and political instability. Civil disobedience. Troops later withdrawn

1935   Plebiscite in Saarland supports rejoining Germany

1936   German forces test French policy and occupy the Rhineland militarily

1945   French awarded an Occupation Zone

1946   French detach Saar from their Occupation Zone and try to Gallicise it

1949   Western Zones downgraded

1955   Occupation zones end. Saar referendum – French proposals defeated

23 OCTOBER 1955

Date of the Saar referendum, which resolved that French policy of hobbling Germany by detaching key areas of production was not going to work

67.7%

Percentage of Saar voters that rejected the proposal of creating a special status for them

WHAT SPECIFICALLY DID FRANCE GET OUT IT?

In a nutshell...

European integration reassured a France in relative decline that its stronger neighbour Germany would be restrained, while supporting a countryside which Paris has long seen as the source of its national strength. The EEC was a new approach after 36 years of failed occupations and 85 years of failed confrontationalism.

Geo-strategically, joining the EEC made sense for France. Its concerns over its declining countryside were covered by the central plank of the CAP, funded by German gold, which were old reparations in a new format. German war output was covered by treaty, while France's relative decline with respect to the Superpowers was countered by forming a European entity in which France, with a European Commission run on essentially French lines, would project its own authority globally once more. Since the form of the agreement would take that of a customs union, French politicians hoped that the nation's economy would be protected as and when required. The country's default setting is protectionist, and has been since Colbert's regulatory and interventionist policies in the time of Louis XIV.

118

Number of huge paintings of celebrated French victories and heroes in the Gallery of Battles in the Palace of Versailles

11 CENTURIES

Period of French history covered by this artwork, concluding with Napoleon

5

Military victories over England or Britain specifically commemorated

12

Commemorative paintings of generals lost in the process

1328

Death of Charles IV of France. Crown jumps to a nephew rather than his daughter, who was married to the King of England

1420

In the Aftermath of Agincourt, the Treaty of Troyes provides for the English monarch to inherit the French throne on the death of its incumbent. But the French heir abrogates the treaty.

GEORGE III

Monarch who finally dropped the English claim on the French throne

A MATTER OF NUMBERS

4 million

Population of England in the Elizabethan age

20 million

Population of then now-united France

10 million

Population of France's rival, Spain

ALL THE 3S – KEY DATES IN FRANCE'S RISE

1453

Defeat of English rivals at Castillon

1643

Defeat of Spanish at Rocroi smashes Habsburg threat

1763

French supremacy curtailed by Treaty of Paris

1813

After failure in Russia, the tide starts to turn against Napoleon in Germany and Spain

1866

Date at which the population of Prussia and its confederates exceeded that of France.

The historical backbone of France's power – a massive rural population – has been eclipsed.

CONSEQUENCES FOR FRANCE OF THE THREE GREAT FRANCO-GERMAN CONFLICTS

1871 – Loss of Alsace-Lorraine, the Rhine border, and the fall of the Second Empire

1918 – Devastation across much of Northern France, huge loss of life, les Gueules Cassées (war injured), diminished finances, social unrest, minor territorial gains

1945 – Diminished prestige, broken military, war damage, large loss of life, fatally-weakened Empire, but near-parity in population with West Germany until reunification

FIVE

Number of different French or German passports an OAP in Alsace would have had over his lifetime by the time of the ECSC

ONE EVERY TWO HOURS

Average rate of Frenchmen being shot during the occupation – still light compared with occupied territories on the Eastern Front

44 DAYS

Duration of the Battle of France in 1940

1528 DAYS

Duration of German occupation of Paris

FORCED ABSENCE

A million forced deportees to Germany

One and a quarter million prisoners of war

150,000 sent to prisons or concentration camps

> **"** *And whereas we have the sea as our frontier all round, France has nearly 2,000 miles of coast and almost the same length of land-frontiers. These land-frontiers make France a far more continental than a maritime Power. Neither the French navy, nearly as large as our own and thoroughly efficient in 1939, nor the fine French mercantile marine and fishing fleets, nor the possession of an Empire overseas second only to the British Empire, has made Frenchmen in the mass think of the sea as a really important element in the nation's existence. For it is only over the land-frontiers that any direct threat to the nation has come in recent centuries."*
>
> Instructions for British Servicemen in France 1944

WHAT SPECIFICALLY DID GERMANY GET OUT IT?

In a nutshell...

Membership of the European club expunged national war guilt, allowed the country a legitimate place on the international stage and provided a larger home market for its competitive economy.

German economic recovery was not matched in most other postwar economies, which remained high tax and highly regulatory in comparison. This provided German exporters with an opportunity. The establishment of the EEC would expand the German home market across the founding six. It would also guarantee that states liable to slap punitive tariffs on competitors, particularly the French, would themselves be treaty bound not to do so on German goods.

The EEC was therefore a tool to protect Germany's economic growth, rightly seen as a precondition to the country's longstanding stability and security. East Germany of course still lay within the Soviet sphere of influence, and the Russian bear was a constant and very near threat to the country's independence. A strong economy based on good links to the West would be harder for Moscow to undermine.

CIMBRI AND TEUTONES

First appearance of the Germans in Western literature, at the close of the second century BC, when these two huge tribes nearly annihilated two Roman armies, and triggered a constitutional crisis that ultimately destroyed the Roman Republic. A bad start.

BUILDING BRIDGES

Second main appearance of German tribes was when they threatened to cross the Rhine and settle in Gaul (France). Julius Caesar built a bridge and crossed the Rhine to impress upon them the error of their ways – a tactic that still had to be followed by Emperor Julian four centuries later.

TEUTOBERG

Third main historic appearance by the Germans. Roman success in colonising Germany was undone by Arminius, who in AD 9 ambushed and destroyed three Roman legions. The trend continues.

3

Number of German tribes who went on to successively sack Rome, cementing a poor reputation.

DO YOU SPEAK OLD GERMAN?

For a brief while, the lingua franca of Europe – so that travellers from Essex, Tongres or Arles were able to understand each other's German dialects in a tavern in Milan.

60

Number of rulers of the Holy Roman Empire, which by the end was mostly just Germany

1006 YEARS

Actual duration of the first 1000-year Reich

WHY PRUSSIA?

Of Prussia's competitors to lead Germany:

★ Austria had lost its moral ascendancy with Napoleon ending the Holy Roman Empire

★ Bavaria was under-industrialised and with a distinct regional identity that set it apart

★ Saxony had already lost territory to Prussia in 1815

★ Hanover had ended its personal union with Britain thanks to Queen Victoria and Salic Law splitting the two thrones

★ Prussia was large, had an effective military, quality armaments factories and a good rail network when the decision was finally resolved by wars

FIVE BILLION FRANCS

French war reparations to Germany in 1871

226 BILLION REICHSMARKS

Original level of German war reparations after the Treaty of Versailles in 1919

OCTOBER 2010

Date of final payment of German war reparations, £59.5 million

WHY GERMANS ARE STILL WORRIED ABOUT THEIR ECONOMY TODAY

1:4.20

US Dollar exchange rate with the German Mark in 1914

1:4.2 trillion

US Dollar exchange rate with the German Mark in November 1923

Source: *Der Spiegel*

140 billion Marks

Price of a loaf of bread in November 1923

Source: *Economist*

" Few people understood what had happened. Even today, three generations later, much of it sounds pretty incredible. Take for example the family that sold its house to emigrate to America. On arrival at the port of Hamburg, they found that the money wasn't enough to pay for their crossing – in fact, it didn't even pay for their tickets back home. Then there was the man who drank two cups of coffee at 5,000 marks each, only to be presented with a bill for 14,000. When he asked why this was he was told he should have ordered the coffees at the same time because the price had gone up in between. And then there's the story about the couple that took a few hundred million marks to the theatre box office hoping to see a show, but discovered it wasn't nearly enough. Tickets were now a billion marks each.

"The hyperinflation left behind a national trauma that can be felt to this day. The experiences of 1923 have etched themselves into the German psyche. Fear of inflation is widespread, and German economists feel more duty-bound than others to vouchsafe economic stability."

Source: *Der Spiegel*

" Here were all the horrors of galloping inflation. The more expensive bars were filled with fat profiteers and their hard-faced, brassy mistresses who drove around in huge cars and seemed to batten on the wretched, starving, professional classes.

"I was horrified to meet a distinguished German professor and his family who never saw meat at all and could only afford potatoes for their one meal of the day. Prices in the shop windows were altered four or five times a day, but owing to protests from the British garrison, the N.A.A.F.I canteen promised to keep their prices stable for a week. By the end of the second day some wonderful bargains were available because the mark had continued to fall.

The result was fantastic. The whole garrison descended on the N.A.A.F.I like a crowd of vultures. There were lorries and cars blocking all the streets round their premises, and women were diving for the counters and seizing anything they could lay their hands on, golf balls, bottles of whisky, fruit, it didn't matter, it was a bargain. I don't think anyone who has not witnessed at first hand the real horrors of inflation can understand what it means."

Lt Gen Sir Brian Horrocks, A Full Life, writing from the viewpoint of the first
BAOR (British Army of the Rhine) in occupied Germany after the first world war

65%

Tax shortfall of the German exchequer between 1919 and 1923 made up by printing money

Source: *Economist*

29.2 BILLION MARKS

Value of notes in circulation in November 1919

497 QUINTILLION MARKS

Value of notes in circulation five years later

18

Number of zeroes in a quintillion

Source: *Economist*

LEVELS OF HYPERINFLATION

Austria x 14,000

Hungary x 23,000

Poland x 2.5 million

Russia x 4 billion

Germany x 1 trillion

Source: Professor J. Bradford DeLong, University of California

70%

Proportion of inner Berlin in ruins in 1945

TWO MILLION

Estimated number of rapes by Soviet soldiers of German women during the last six months of the second world war

1955

Year when the small number of survivors who had capitulated at Stalingrad were allowed home from Soviet camps

ONE IN SEVENTEEN

Estimated level of German war dead, 4 million out of 68 million

16 MILLION

Number of Germans classed as refugees in 1945

4.5 MILLION

Additional number of displaced persons in Germany, over half as forced labour and most of the remainder as prisoners of war

CAUSE TO REMEMBER

2 WEEKS

Time it took for Soviet war dead in 1941 to exceed the total number of British dead across the entire war

6 MILLION

Number of slave labourers released by German capitulation

1,500

Average daily calorie intake by Germans in late 1945, one third of that of US soldiers in the occupying force

12 MILLION

One estimate of number of ethnic Germans forced out of Eastern Europe following the end of the second world war

ONE-THIRD

West German economic output in 1947 compared with that of a decade earlier

1 MILLION TONS

Food aid delivered by Britain into its occupation zone between June 1945 and April 1946, despite rationing at home. The winter of 1947 was particularly terrible and triggered more UK rationing in order to provide support

2,323,067 TONS

Quantity of material delivered during the Berlin airlift

$10 BILLION

Soviet war reparations demanded from Germany, largely achieved by stripping East German factories and rail yards

NINE

Number of years after the war that Angela Merkel was born

We have a historical obligation to protect by all means Europe's unification process begun by our forefathers after centuries of hatred and blood spill. None of us can foresee what the consequences would be if we were to fail."

Angela Merkel on the 2011 eurozone crisis

CREATING THE DEUTSCHE MARK AND THE GERMAN ECONOMIC MIRACLE

Given the excess of money in circulation compared to actual products in the marketplace, the solution that emerged was to end controls both on the currency and on prices. Thus the Deutsche Mark was born.

On top of this, there was a new simplified tax system set at a lower rate, all in marked contrast to the domestic policies of Britain's socialist government.

Shops filled with goods, factories filled with workers, and the German economic miracle had begun.

German racket designed to take over the whole of Europe."

The comment by Trade Secretary Nicholas Ridley on monetary union in 1990, that triggered his resignation. He added insult to injury by claiming the French were acting like poodles in the rushed process and that the Commission comprised a number of unelected reject politicians so that one might as well hand sovereignty over to Adolf Hitler.

In a nutshell...

Reliable government.

Italy did not come out well from the second world war. Only four Italian divisions were deemed credible by the time of the Italian defection to the Allied cause. Unfortunately, two of these were fighting for the Germans.

After ridding themselves (with help) of Mussolini, no enduring stable government emerged, other than a series of alliances covertly propped up by outside support. The colonies were lost, with a sliver of Trieste retained. The monarchy was abolished. The South fell back into the sway of organised crime. Politics was dysfunctional: the films of Don Camillo, the countryside priest battling the Communist mayor Peppone, were funny and popular since they were recognisable and topical.

As Kew archives today reveal, British diplomats during the war had even fancifully toyed with the idea of breaking the country up in to three. Italy was only three generations old: anything was possible.

600,000

Annual number of Italian emigrants during the Great Emigration

23

Number of years of fascist government in Italy

1976

First year in which Italy's immigration figures matched emigration. Over 7% of the population is now foreign born

1943

Date at which Mussolini thought Italy would be militarily prepared to enter the second world war (given the chance)

SEPTEMBER 1943

Italian Armistice and change of sides

D DAY MINUS 1

Date of the capture of Rome by the Western Allies (5 June 1944)

ONE-THIRD

Italian steel production compared with France's before the outbreak of war

ONE-HUNDREDTH

Italian coal production compared with Britain's before the outbreak of war

ONE-THIRD

Fall of farm production during the War

950 CALORIES

Italian daily ration intake in 1942, less even than the Poles

1941   Sale of coffee and making of pastry prohibited. Clothing rationed. Petrol banned for private cars, leading to the forced scrapping of all cars over 12 years old

1942   Restaurants only allowed to serve soup, vegetables and fruit. End of Sunday bus services and first class train services

1943   Beer production banned except for armed forces

 Curiously, or perhaps typically, electricity for industry was reduced a year before electricity for domestic users was cut by 25%. The latter restriction resulted in long queues for candles, a problem neatly solved three months later when their manufacture was prohibited."

Daily Telegraph, experience of a second world war eyewitness

66%

Amount of state highways unusable after the War

40%

Level of destruction of state railways

TWO MILLION

Unemployment level at the close of hostilities

12

Number of Italian governments between 1945 and the signing of the EEC treaty, with two not even lasting a fortnight.

ITALIAN CRIMINAL GROUPS

Mafia/Cosa Nostra (Sicily)

Camorra (Naples)

'Ndrangheta (Calabria)

We are all taught from childhood that, while Italy is the best country in the world, with the finest cuisine, the greatest art, the most beautiful music, we are also brought up to believe it should never be run by Italian politicians. That's why we're happy to let the EU take charge. You English think of Eurocrats as lazy and corrupt, you think of them as Italians. But we imagine them turning up to work on time and refusing bribes, we think of them as English.

Italian Senator quoted by Daniel Hannan MEP

In a nutshell...

Trade with an economically-resurgent neighbour, German democratic stability and guarantees of food security.

Economic and political union in Europe began here. Seeking a replacement to customs union with Germany, Luxembourg failed with France, so went for economic union and a common currency with Belgium in 1921 instead. Having repeatedly seen the cost of failure when trying neutrality, the three governments in exile agreed to closer economic, political and military co-operation after the war.

So, for the Benelux states joining the EEC was not only a response to failed attempts to stay out of European politics in the past; it was the extension of Benelux policies on to a larger continental scene.

1572

Revolt of the Northern Netherlands ends a thousand years of relative unity under Frankish, Burgundian and Hapsburg monarchs

80 YEARS WAR

The resulting conflict; settled as part of the general peace-making in war-torn Europe in 1648

1795-1806

Batavian Republic (occupied by, then allied to, France)

1815

United Kingdom of the Netherlands reunites the countries

1830-1831

Belgian Revolution

1839

Independence of the new Belgian state recognised

BELGIUM: A FORCED MARRIAGE

Wallonia – French-speaking South, wanted to join France

Flanders – Dutch-speaking North, wanted to remain Dutch

Result: to avoid giving Paris control of the seceding Channel coastline and to neutralise the great port of Antwerp. A joint entity was forced on two unwilling participants.

Consequence: a government reliant upon maintaining the support of the Walloons, at the cost of the interests of the Flemish

There are only two things I hate in this world.
People who are intolerant of other people's cultures.
And the Dutch."

Nigel Powers (Sir Michael Caine), *Goldmember*

LUXEMBOURG'S NEW STATUS

Dutch sovereignty

Prussian garrison

Customs union within the German Confederation

1890

Luxembourg's dynastic link with the Dutch Crown broken, and it gains full and guaranteed independence.

"THE GIBRALTAR OF THE NORTH."

Luxembourg's nickname, thanks to its geography and its fortress.

TREATY OF LONDON 1867

Defortified and neutralised Luxembourg, and reaffirmed British involvement in guaranteeing the independence of the Low Countries

1 OUT OF 3

Number of Low Countries that retained their neutrality during the first world war

WWI BATTLEFIELDS ASSOCIATED WITH BELGIUM

Ypres

Passchendaele

Zeebrugge raid

Ostende raid

Flanders Fields

SO MUCH FOR EUROPEAN REFERENDA

27%

Share of the population in a referendum in Luxembourg after the Great War that voted for economic union with Belgium. France was the popular choice.

A PAMPERED SOUTH, A SPITED NORTH

68%

Share of state spending on Belgian railroads in the south, from 1832-1912

38%

Share of south's population

30%

Share of indirect taxes raised in the south, Wallonia, over this period

The Belgian system has a built-in tendency towards corruption: the more a politician submits to the system, the better off he and his family will be."

Paul Belien, *A Throne in Brussels*

5 DAYS

The time it took for German forces to overwhelm the Netherlands in 1940

85,000

Number of homeless after the bombing of Rotterdam

400 INFANTRY AND 12 CAVALRY

The forces supposedly available to Luxembourg to resist

"Mir welle bleiwe wat mir sin"

"We want to stay what we are"

Luxembourgers' call to resist assimilation by Nazi Germany, including conscription and dispatch to the Eastern Front.

1943

The three governments-in-exile agree to the postwar establishment of a monetary association

1944

They agree to a customs convention also

Before the Coal and Steel Community was even in force, the three countries were already advanced along the route of forming a trade association, with:

★ a joint body for parliamentary delegations

★ a committee of ministers

★ a coordinating economic council

★ a secretariat

★ a judicial body

20,000-30,000

Estimated number of Dutch civilians who starved to death in the Hongerwinter of 1944-5. The CAP is more logical with such a terrible backdrop

1949	1960
Year in which The Hague formally recognises the loss of its East Indies empire	Belgium gave independence to its colonial possession the Congo

ARE THE ORIGINAL MOTIVES OF THE FOUNDING SIX THE SAME TODAY?

In a nutshell…

 The ECSC has changed massively over the years, with the EU becoming a very different creature engaged in a massive range of policy areas not originally listed, employing a large number of quasi-governmental departments and agencies and a small army of staff (indeed, this is a staff that approaches the size of the Belgian army).

The economic benefits of membership for many countries weaken once trade deficit dynamics are factored in. Major trading imbalances have been in play between northern and southern Europe, seeing the very economies most in debt today undertaking significant levels of private borrowing to support consumer spending. The key problem is that these loans have largely been for products manufactured abroad. The German economy did very well out of this in recent years, with a massive export surplus across the EU.

A massive problem now is the juddering euro itself. The euro was once pushed as the solution to German unification, and the means to avoid the continent's domination by that power; complaints about the central role Germany plays in deciding the Euro's fate increasingly, however, suggest that this supposed answer to a unified Germany has paradoxically merely replaced Berlin with Frankfurt as the "German issue" in peoples' minds. At least, graffiti in Athens seems to suggest so.

4.9%

West German average annual GNP per capita growth rate up to 1980

EIGHTH

West Germany's world ranking for per capita GDP in 1991 (the US was ninth)

6,900

Number of German troops in 2010 actively deployed on peacekeeping missions

380,000

Number of Soviet troops stationed in East Germany by the 1980s

331 MILES

Distance from Berlin to the nearest outpost of Russian troops today, in Kaliningrad

1994

Date of withdrawal of last Russian troops

66 *The European Union and the European project has been a peacemaker for over half a century. Peace was the overarching objective of European integration from day one. In the mind of Jean Monnet, Robert Schuman, Konrad Adenauer, Alcide de Gasperi and many others, the idea was to make it through economic integration. But economic integration was a means to an end: peace. You are all experts in peace, so I don't need to persuade you. But we must never stop recalling to our citizens and notably the young generation that peace is and will remain, not the only one, but Europe's most fundamental raison d'être."*

Commission President Barroso, 2009

47

Cold war bases maintained by the US in Germany

251,997

Average number of US troops in Germany, 1981-5

Source: Heritage Foundation

BAOR

Frontline UK contribution to German defence, the British Army of the Rhine. The title was first used by British garrison forces in Western Germany in the decade after the first world war

WATERING CAN

Possibly the most ingenious surveillance camera in the Stasi museum in Berlin, it allowed someone watering their plants to covertly photograph their neighbour, while facing at right angles

1985

First time allegations appear in press of links between an MEP and an Eastern Bloc intelligence agency.

Things are simpler today. Nowadays, despite laws in several states banning Communist-era secret servicemen from standing in national elections, parliaments have been reticent about banning them from standing as MEPs, owing to European human rights law.

> *French technocrats see in 'Europe' a way of preserving their power against the free world market in which competition, not state diktat, decides what gets produced, where and by whom. They are prepared to give the appearance of ceding some degree of French national sovereignty to do this, confident that their expertise and ruthlessness will ensure French international sovereignty instead [...]. Similarly, the Bundesbank under Tietmeyer might in the end be prepared to give the impression of sacrificing its own national monetary policy autonomy via the creation of an ECB, in order to protect central-bank prerogatives from the encroachment of globalized 'Anglo-Saxon' financial markets – if the ECB is set up to behave exactly like the Bundesbank."*

Bernard Connolly

Amount of France's foreign trade that it conducts with EU states

SECOND

France's position today as world exporter of agri-goods, after the US

€700 BILLION

Value of Germany's exports, dominating the Single Market, generating a longstanding surplus and reinvested in the Mediterranean economies.

WHAT DID THE 'ATLANTIC' JOINERS GET OUT OF IT (1973)?

In a nutshell…

The first wave of applicants were the UK, Ireland, Denmark and Norway (which pulled out after a referendum said No). They were mostly seeking the trade benefits.

WHAT WERE THESE COUNTRIES?

One major European state with a large population, a big economy, an imperial tradition, a world language and a successful (though costly) wartime experience (UK).

One socially conservative small rural economy on the edge of the Atlantic, attempting to assert its economic post-colonial independence (ROI).

Two countries that had both been occupied during the war, now increasingly a distant memory. One had a significant agricultural sector and was locked into the German economic orbit (Denmark).

All were peripheral European countries, with strong democratic traditions and with a significant interest in freer trade.

★ ★ ★ ★ ★ ★ ★ ★ ★ ★ ★ ★

VIKING STATES

Another way of looking at them, with traditions of individualism, personal freedom, mercantile adventurism, and a view looking out at the Atlantic and beyond forced from being residents of the outskirts of the continent.

Their legal and parliamentary traditions combine with their 'peripheral vision' to make them comparatively outward looking, with an eye beyond simple integration with an angry neighbour.

Their geography, location and even climate have helped protect them against aggressors and forced assimilation by dominant cultures.

1971

Discovery of major oil reserves off Norway's coast

A CASE OF 6S AND 7S

The 6: the EEC

The 7: EFTA

3: EFTA countries (UK, Denmark, Norway) looking at moving from the latter to the former

51/90 MILLION

UK population share of the EFTA market, hence why its leaving was a spur to the others

170 MILLION

EEC population at that period, hence UK government interest in leaving EFTA

FINLAND

Member state of the Nordic Council that stalled improvements in free trade through that organisation, in order to avoid triggering Soviet concerns.

Attempts to increase free trade through EFTA had not progressed as quickly as had been hoped and slower than tariff reductions within the EEC

1979

Year Ireland ended its currency parity with Sterling.

It maintained, and maintains, the Common Travel Area – making migration an area of continuing common concern

FISH

The other factor all four applicants shared in abundance and thus an interest in the hungry ports of the existing EEC

WHAT WAS THE BRITISH EXPERIENCE?

In a nutshell…

Britain saw EEC membership as a sick man's prop. Meanwhile, Prime Minster Ted Heath was a European integrationist with a dominant ideological interest.

AD 410

Sum previous British experience of leaving a European Union

" *The barbarians beyond the Rhine made such unbounded incursions over every province, as to reduce not only the Britons, but some of the Celtic nations also to the necessity of revolting from the empire, and living no longer under the Roman laws but as they themselves pleased. The Britons therefore took up arms, and incurred many dangerous enterprises for their own protection, until they had freed their cities from the barbarians who besieged them. In a similar manner, the whole of Armorica, with other provinces of Gaul, delivered themselves by the same means; expelling the Roman magistrates or officers, and erecting a government, such as they pleased, of their own."*

Zosimus on the events of that time

116 YEARS

Duration of the (for the English, frequently self-funding) Hundred Years War

ONE-TENTH

Proportion of English people in 1377 who were born in Yorkshire

BEYOND THE PALE

Continental cities owned by England after the end of the Hundred Years War

Tournai (1513-1519)

Boulogne (1544-1550)

Calais (to 1558)

Dunkirk (1658-1662)

A GERMAN MONARCHY

Royal Family names

Brunswick-Lüneburg
House of Hanover

Saxe-Coburg-Gotha
Prince Albert

Schleswig-Holstein-Sonderburg-Glücksburg
**a.k.a. Mountbatten;
Prince Philip**

ONCE EVERY 43 SECONDS

Average rate of fire of 25 pounder shells by the British Army over the duration of the second world war (hence the national debt)

Source: Imperial War Museum

CHURCHILL'S VIEW IN DECEMBER 1940 OF THE FUTURE SHAPE OF POST-WAR EUROPE, FROM THE COLVILLE DIARIES

Talking of the future he sketched the European Confederations that would have to be formed ('with their Diets of Worms') and shuddered at the thought of the intricate currency problems, etc. He did not understand such things and he would be out of it."

In addition to the UK, France, Italy, Spain and Prussia, there would be four confederations:

★   A Northern, based at the Hague

★   Mitteleuropa, at Warsaw or Prague

★   A Danubian, including Southern Germany, at Vienna

★   A Balkan, at Constantinople

HOW IT WOULD FUNCTION

The nine powers would meet at a Council of Europe.

There would be:

★   A supreme judiciary

★   A supreme economic council for currency questions

★   Joint contributions to an internationally-controlled military and civilian aviation

★   National militias, excepting Germany for 100 years

The Council would be restricted in its methods of dealing with a Power condemned by the remainder in Council."

CHURCHILL'S VIEW ON BRITAIN'S ROLE

> *The English speaking world would be apart from this, but closely connected with it, and it alone would control the seas, as the reward of victory. It would be bound by covenant to respect the trading and colonial rights of all peoples, and England and America would have exactly equal navies. Russia would fit into an Eastern re-organisation, and the whole problem of Asia would have to be faced. But as far as Europe was concerned, only by such a system of Confederations could the small powers continue to exist and we might at all costs avoid the old mistake of 'Balkanising' Europe."*

100 YEARS

How long Churchill thought it might take for this Grand Design to work

1960

UK ends Blue Streak missile programme, but takes it to the European Launcher Development Organisation for civil use

1971

UK pulls out of ELDO (European Launcher Development Organisation)

1965

Canada drops the Red Ensign and adopts a national flag with no incorporated Union Flag

> *The move into the Common Market has been, from first to last, a confession by British Ministers that they did not know what to do. Originally it was a scheme for smuggling through devaluation of the pound, and hence reduction of wages, without anyone noticing. Now it is not even that. Entry into the Common Market is not a policy. It is a substitute for a policy. Its consequences, its implications, are never explained."*

AJP Taylor, writing in the *Sunday Express*, 1962

1972

Britain's first official miners' strike, a dockers' strike in which the use of troops is threatened, and first official building workers' strike since the 1920s

23,909,000

Number of strike days reportedly lost in Britain in 1972

17 DAYS

Average length of these British strikes

1919

Last year in which strike days had exceeded this total

★ ★ ★ ★ ★ ★ ★ ★ ★ ★ ★ ★

300,000

Number of shop stewards in the 1970s

1.9 MILLION

Number of British-made cars in 1972, which was the high-water mark. The figure today is three-quarters that

★ ★ ★ ★ ★ ★ ★ ★ ★ ★ ★ ★

WHERE DO THESE COUNTRIES STAND TODAY?

In a nutshell...

The populations of the 1973 applicants are today amongst the most EU-critical. These countries joined some decades after wartime considerations were preeminent and decades before the EEC ceased to be primarily an economic association. They are caught in a middle ground where there is a notable lack of consent on the organisation's ambitions.

FIVE

Number of rejections of European proposals in referenda, in countries that applied to join together in 1973

ONE

Number of 1973 wave applicant states that have adopted the Euro

100

Number of additional customs officials reportedly sent by Copenhagen to the German border in 2011 despite Schengen obligations

49:40

Percentage of British electorate who would vote to leave the EU as opposed to stay in, according to a *Guardian*/ICM poll in October 2011

19:68

Results from a similar ICM poll a decade earlier

ONE MILLION

Reported number of words used in the EEC accession debate in the House of Commons

12

Number of days allotted to MPs to debate the Lisbon Treaty

€17 BILLION

Regional and structural aid given to Ireland up to 2006 since joining the EEC

€751 MILLION

The reduced grant now given to Ireland over a six-year period

1975

Last occasion where UK voters had a specific choice on national policy towards Brussels, other than voting on a party's complete manifesto

2:1

Ratio of the vote for staying in the EEC

10:1

Reported ratio of funding available between the two respective sides

OTHER BACKING THAT MAY HAVE INFLUENCED THE RESULT

- ★ Two secret services
- ★ State broadcasting bias
- ★ Corporate bankroll
- ★ Co-operating parties
- ★ Media unanimity

6

Number of referenda held in Denmark

| Number that led to a revote

2

Number that ended in a Nej

★ 1992 Maastricht
★ 2000 euro membership

SEAHORSE AND EXODUS

Incident off Bantry Bay, where a large Spanish quota-hopping fishing vessel collided with a smaller Irish boat, resulting in a fatality

7

Number of Irish referenda

OPT OUTS

Euro (UK and Denmark)

Schengen (UK and Ireland)

2

Number of Noes (Nice and Lisbon)

Justice and Home Affairs (UK and Ireland and in some aspects Denmark)

|

Number that led to a revote

Defence (Denmark, plus in some aspects the UK)

Charter of Fundamental Rights (UK)

Policing and Criminal Justice (all three)

A DROP IN TRADE IMPERATIVES

Over the period 2001-2010, Germany's share of all EU trade rose, from 21.7% to 22.8%.

The Netherlands, meanwhile, went up from 11.2% to 13.1%, and Belgium's went up marginally.

This was during the period of expansion to an EU of 27, with a larger communal economy.

But Denmark's went down from 2.1% to 1.9% despite being closely affiliated to the German economy, while Ireland went down from 3.2% to 2% and the UK's from 9.7% to 6.5% – actually half that of the Dutch intra-EU trade levels.

France's share in the meantime dropped by a quarter. Its political tranquillity suggests national interests in EU membership are not purely focused on the economics.

ROTTERDAM AND ANTWERP EFFECT

The situation whereby some exports to the Low Countries are statistically counted as EU trade, when in fact the products are being transhipped to the two huge container ports for distribution globally

BALANCE OF POWER

The underlying principle of English diplomacy for 500 years, seeking to ensure that no one power dominated the continent. Overturned with support for Franco-German unity

1994

Year the German Supreme Court ruled that German forces could serve overseas. However, the Rules of Engagement, and significant prospect of trial for any fatal engagement, have severely limited effectiveness

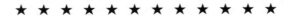

WHAT DID GREECE GET OUT OF IT (1981)?

> **In a nutshell...**
>
> The marble shards of ancient temples remind locals and visitors of the country's past contributions to European politics. But more pressing was stability after a military junta, plus some sense of security given its Warsaw Pact and Turkish neighbours.

SOME MODELS BEHIND THE CITED 'GREEK LEGACY'

Demosthenes, politics

Apelles, art

Praxiteles, sculpture

Pythagoras, science

A RE-ESTABLISHED AND EUROPEAN IDENTITY

1071 – Byzantines smashed at the Battle of Manzikert

1204 – Constantinople sacked by Western European crusaders

1461 – Mistra submits to the Turks

1829 – Re-emergence of an independent Greek state

A COINCIDENCE IN TIMING

1453

Fall of Constantinople marks eclipse of Greek East

Battle of Castillon marks confirmation of French primacy in the West

★ ★ ★ ★ ★ ★ ★ ★ ★ ★ ★ ★

FIRST BALKAN WAR

1912

Serbia, Bulgaria, Greece, Montenegro, and Ottoman Empire, over Macedonia, while the Porte was busy fighting Italy in Libya.

SECOND BALKAN WAR

1913

War resumed after a coup. Macedonia partitioned, Albania granted independence

1920

Treaty of Sèvres cedes Smyrna to Greece

1922

Turks win bitter war with Greece, ending the Greek presence in Asia Minor that had survived Darius the Great

150,000

One estimate of the number of people killed during the sack of Smyrna by the Turks

4½ YEARS

Duration of the Greek civil war

7½ YEARS

Duration of the government of the Greek Colonels

£9 BILLION

Pre-adjusted value of forced loan Greece was required to pay to its wartime German occupiers, which some Greeks have started to ask for back

250,000

Red Cross working estimate of the number of Greek civilian dead during the great famine in the second world war

500

Number of Greek children dying daily of malnutrition at its height

€20.4 BILLION

Current six year EU grant to Greece for development projects

1947

Greece obtains the Dodecanese, formerly an Italian colonial possession

IMIA/KARDAK

Greek and Turkish names for the islet group that in 1996 was the focus for military tension

2,383

Number of Greek islands in the Aegean, whose airspace, territorial waters and marine mineral rights remain a flashpoint with Ankara

FOUR

Number of NATO states that have maintained defence expenditure above the recommended baseline level. Greece is one of them

€618 MILLION

Funds dedicated to the 2008 budget to support farming in outlying areas – the Azores, the Canaries and French overseas departments. The Aegean islands are bolted on to this funding and combined make up the *specific measures*.

OLIVES, MASTIC AND HONEY

Greek producers supported.

55% TO 70%

Amount of beekeepers' income on Chios that comes from these grants

2.35%

Value of EU grants as a share of
GDP over the last twelve years

€3.5 BILLION

Value in real terms

2013

Likely cut-off date for this level of largesse

★ ★ ★ ★ ★ ★ ★ ★ ★ ★ ★ ★ ★

WHAT DID THE IBERIAN JOINERS GET OUT OF IT (1986)?

In a nutshell…

Democratic stability after dictatorships; end to isolation as backwaters; the prospect of regional aid and CAP support; and access to British and Irish fishing grounds.

1479

Unification of Spain

1898

Spanish-American war. Defeat expels Spain from its last main imperial holdings, and triggers both a cultural revival as well as clerical and anti-clerical extremism

★ ★ ★ ★ ★ ★ ★ ★ ★ ★ ★ ★ ★

POLITICAL VACUUM

8 MONTHS
Average duration of a Portuguese government over the ten years preceding Salazar

35 YEARS
Duration of Franco's personal rule (dies in 1975)

36 YEARS
Duration of Salazar's personal rule (dies in 1970)

Domestically at least, the Portuguese approach was more low-key, traditional and autocratic than militaristic, ceremonial and dictatorial.

450 FEET
Height of Franco's monumental cross in the Valley of the Fallen

20,000
Number of defeated Republican prisoners used as forced labour to construct it

1974
Carnation Revolution

Left Wing coup seizes control in Portugal

RETORNADOS
The quarter of a million colonial settlers who fled Moçambique after its rapid independence

25 YEARS
Duration of occupation of East Timor, after the Indonesians took advantage of a hasty Portuguese retreat by invading.

AN ISSUE OF IDENTITIES

1716 Prohibition of Catalan in the administration of justice

1768 Prohibition of Catalan in public education

1772 Prohibition of Catalan in accounts books

1801 Prohibition of Catalan in theatrical performances

1862 Prohibition of Catalan in documents drawn up by notaries

1896 Prohibition of Catalan in telephone conversations

1923 Prohibition of Catalan as an optional taught subject

Source: Conviviencia in Catalonia by Jacqueline Hall

133,708	90 MINUTES
Number of missing people in a census submitted by a Spanish human rights judge in late 2011 seeking to open their cases	Amount of time for which coup leaders, who took hostage MPs, were able to seize Madrid TV and radio stations in 1981

★ ★ ★ ★ ★ ★ ★ ★ ★ ★ ★ ★

WHAT DID EAST GERMANY GET OUT OF IT (1990)?

In a nutshell…

East Germany joined the Community as a by-product of reunification. It got grants plus markets for products that were cheaper to produce at a cost of having to enforce higher standards which removed that competitiveness.

10 YEARS

Duration of Soviet programme of war reparations from East Germany, basically lifting any assets not bolted down

HALF

Amount of pre-war production transported to other parts of Germany; after 1945, this was obstructed by the Soviets

18 HP

Engine power of the Trabant, a fibreglass car with no petrol gauge but a reserve fuel tank in case the driver was caught short

THE GENERAL'S CANTEEN

Current temporary site of the Stasi museum in Berlin

20 HECTARES

Size of the Ministry for State Security

8,000

Number of Stasi personnel employed within the main office complex alone

37

Number of East German Golds at the 1988 Olympics, as opposed to West Germany's 11

39%

Soviet share of East German export market by mid-1980s, nearly five times ahead of the next listing, West Germany

THREE-QUARTERS

Proportion of Soviet oil as a share of total imported GDR oil

COMMUNIST EAST GERMANY'S SPECIAL BACK DOOR DEAL WITH THE EC

★ Free entry of agricultural products, with prices at above world market levels under the CAP

★ No tariffs for non-agricultural finished products sold to the FRG

★ Grants for road and rail improvements to West Berlin

★ VAT exemptions

1:1	RESULT
Rate at which Ostmarks from the GDR were swapped for DM from the FRG	Initially good for people in the East, as their currency was overvalued.
	However, it came with wage parity, so East Germany lost its economic competitiveness, resulting in enduring high unemployment and welfare dependence. The timescale for mass privatisation may also have contributed to a property crash

DOUBLE

Enduring rate of unemployment in the East, compared with the West

WHAT DID THE NEUTRALS GET OUT OF IT (1995)?

In a nutshell...

 Post-cold war, membership of the European Club was less of an issue to neutrals – countries such as Austria, Finland and Sweden – whose proximity to the USSR had restricted their engagement with other Western powers. EFTA was seen as unsatisfactory given the small home market. The 1995 entrants were again a group of peripheral states with an interest in improving their export access, but also realigning themselves after the fall of the Soviet threat.

SEVEN

Number of EFTA remaining countries in 1994

SIX

Number of countries that have left EFTA for Brussels

23.6 MILLION SWISS FRANCS

The current staff budget to operate EFTA

100

Approximate total number of EFTA staff

THREE YEARS

Duration of standard terms of employment for EFTA staff. Contracts may be renewed once

EFTA OFFICES ARE AT THESE LOCATIONS:

★ *Brussels*

★ *Luxembourg*

★ *Geneva*

126 YEARS	2
Duration of the Union of Kalmar that last united (mediaeval) Scandinavia	Number of cold war national capitals in range of Communist artillery. Vienna shared this distinction with Seoul
1905	
Year of Norwegian independence, from Sweden	

FINLANDISATION

A country that is independent but in thrall to Soviet geopolitics.

The corollary was that had Finland not fought the Soviets in the first place, it would instead have been Sovietised.

80KM

Distance between Helsinki and Tallinn, then in the Soviet Union

1814

Last date of Swedish military intervention

A MILLION BAYONETS

Home guard policy during the second world war, attempting to dissuade occupation as Norway had seen. The other element was continuing to trade with belligerents, which meant Germany.

22 YEARS

Length of time by accession that a neutral country (Ireland) had already been an EC member. France was also hardly a NATO enthusiast

VON MISES AND HAYEK

Celebrated free market theorists from the Vienna School

2:1

Margin to join, in the Austrian referendum

11:9

Margin in Finland

21:19

Margin in Sweden

Norway voted narrowly against.

WHAT DID THE MEDITERRANEAN ISLANDS GET OUT OF IT (2004)?

In a nutshell...

More integration for the small economies of Cyprus and Malta with their main trading partners on distant mainland Europe; assistance over migration via Malta; and North Cyprus kept on the agenda.

413,000

Population of Malta

1.12 MILLION

Population of Cyprus

112 MILES

Length of the partitioning Green Line in Cyprus

3:1

Ratio of annual tourists to Malta's population

22 MILLION TONNES

Amount of goods transiting Maltese ports at the time of accession

1636

Distance in miles between Larnaca and Frankfurt

COMMON LINKS

★ Mediterranean islands

★ Peripheral

★ Small populations

★ Gained their independence from Britain forty years before

★ Spared occupation by the Germans (though Malta's George Cross indicated at what price)

CHANGING DIRECTION

As UK seeks to join EEC, Malta seeks an association deal

1970s: policy reversed, with a non-aligned policy under Dom Mintoff's hard Left

A split thus develops between the Nationalists (ironically, pro-EU) and the Socialists (nationalist). The EU vote mirrors this divide today.

46.3%

Maltese who voted No to accession

AID TO SHIPBUILDING

Major issue against Maltese accession

EU AID IN ILLEGAL IMMIGRATION

Major issue supporting accession

LAMPEDUSA

Italian island off Sicily used as a holding area for its illegal immigrants. Malta doesn't have a Lampedusa – it is one

TWO-THIRDS

Share of Malta's imports that come from the EU

43%

Share of its exports that go there

DIRECTLY

Manner by which the *acquis communautaire* is applied to Northern Cyprus.

The South's successful application to join brought in the whole island, though in the North a shadow membership effectively operates, applicable only so far as the courts reach.

NO RHINELAND DOMINANCE

One-fifth

Share of Cyprus's exports that go to the UK

One-fifth

Share that goes to Russia and Greece between them

2008

Year both Cyprus and Malta joined the Euro

40%

Share of loans by Cyprus's three largest banks to customers in Greece.

With a population of just over a million and an economy the size of a German city, perhaps the gamble is still that the country will also get major bailout when the bankers' enosis goes horribly wrong and there is nothing left to count on from Athens but the Eurovision vote.

WHAT DID THE POST-COMMUNIST JOINERS GET OUT OF IT (2004 AND 2007)?

In a nutshell...

Security from Russia and a realignment of trade towards the West.

VISTULA

Furthest point of advance of Soviet Revolutionary forces aiming to sweep across Europe in 1920, halted by General Pilsudski on the river than runs through Warsaw.

FIVE

Number of times Warsaw was wrecked during the second world war

1. Battle for Warsaw, September 1939
2. Warsaw Ghetto Uprising, mainly April-May 1943
3. 63 days of Warsaw Uprising, August 1944
4. Thorough German dynamiting after Warsaw Uprising
5. Soviet occupation of Warsaw, January 1945

85%

UNESCO estimate of the amount of historic Warsaw destroyed by the Germans

21,857

Number of Polish officers executed at Katyn according to Soviet-era documents

13.4%

Collapse in Polish industrial production between 1978 and 1982 resulting from unsustainable trade deficits

SIX

Total number of Czech academic institutions in 1989 that taught any economics

42%

Rise of Hungary's GDP between 1995 and 2009

€25.2 BILLION

Amount of EU money for Romania to improve its transport network over seven years

39.8%

Slovakia's national debt level today

SENT TO SIBERIA

Latvia's first European Commissioner was born in Tomsk, whence her family had been deported by Stalin

FINANCE MINISTRY

The place of work of Estonia's first Commissioner during the 1970s, as a member of the Communist Party of the Soviet Union

PRESIDENT

Lithuania's first Commissioner studied at Leningrad and Moscow, and is now the country's head of state

GROUPING THE WAVE

Alongside Cyprus and Malta, a large group of East European states also successfully applied for membership at the same time.

★ The Baltic Three (Estonia, Latvia and Lithuania)

★ The Sceptic Two (Poland and the Czech Republic)

★ The central European trio (Slovakia, Slovenia and Hungary)

★ The Black Sea pair of Bulgaria and Romania (admitted two years later)

Although the histories of these countries are fascinating, not least how for many of them the West first reached out via German swords and Christian missionaries, the drive for EU membership comes from a much simpler historical fact. Following the second world war, these countries ended up on the wrong side of the Iron Curtain. Slovenia, as part of Yugoslavia, managed to remain outside of Stalin's grasp; but for the rest the next forty years saw oppression, totalitarianism and foreign domination.

The Baltic Three had won their independence after the Russian Revolution. They were not as fortunate as the Finns during the second world war, though partisans continued a lonely fight in the woods against the Soviets for a surprising number of years. They were formally annexed into the USSR and saw large numbers of settlers arrive as part of a Russification programme. This left several legacies on independence.

One legacy was a large ethnic Russian-speaking minority in each country. A second was a handful of potentially dangerous border disputes, resulting from territories carved off after occupation. A third was a handful of Soviet-era monuments which were flashpoints for protests, whether removed or allowed to stay. Then there was the issue of national defence, since they shared a common border with Russia with minimal military manpower or resources to defend it, and it was unclear whether they could join NATO without provoking Moscow. On top of that, despite successfully reorienting themselves towards Western markets, they were still heavily trade-dependent on Russia for their imports (in the case of both Estonia and Lithuania, for around a quarter of their supplies). Joining the EU made sense, as with many other Russian border states, as a back door to gaining a security commitment from a West nervous about expanding NATO to the Russian border. It also promised guaranteed markets and potential new sources of resources, which could be useful if a petulant Moscow resorted to its off switch, or failed to pay its debts.

Poland and the Czech Republic had an interest in joining that also matched that of Paris. Both suffered as neighbours of Germany. They also had residual concerns over their annexation of German territories after the war. Both countries have proved on occasion to be as Euro-critical as the Scandinavians. Realpolitik, however, is a determining factor. One-third of Czech exports go to Germany alone, quite aside from the figures for the rest of the EU. One-quarter of Poland's exports are German-bound. Even though both countries are sceptical of EU integration (the pair were the last to hold out over the Lisbon Treaty), there is a sense of inevitability about a need to be part of the trading club.

But so far, despite more pro-Brussels governments lately being in place, Poland and the Czech Republic have avoided entry into the euro. So long as they do, Centrist leaders in both countries will likely continue to assess EU membership as basically positive. This could change drastically if key practicalities change, not least over how CAP changes affect Poland's part-time farming community, or how human rights material affects the social teachings of the Catholic Church, or in Prague's case if in any further European treaties there is a revision of German property rights. The eurozone crisis has further stiffened resistance to European integration, which had for a time been wavering. As Czech Prime Minister Petr Necas put it in late 2011, his country agreed to join a currency union, not a debt union.

Slovakia, Slovenia and Hungary are the other three states from central Europe, united more by geography than anything else. All three are breakaway states, albeit Hungary's genesis now lies some distance in the past. Slovakia split amicably from the Czech Republic in 1993, though remained linked in a customs union. Slovenia was the first of the Yugoslav successor states to successfully join the EU. They all sought to re-orientate themselves economically. As new states and countries seeking affirmation after years of submerged identity or foreign domination, the threat of losing power and identity to the EU did not seem in the same league as the circumstances from which they had come.

The Black Sea pair of Bulgaria and Romania joined in 2007. Soviet interest in the Dardanelles had previously made them frontline states. Both were now economically peripheral states and not very wealthy ones at that. Romania's condition was particularly exposed thanks to its northern border. Ethnically Romanian Moldova had been sliced off by the USSR, and Trans-Dniestr sliced itself off from that. That left Romania with an unresolved frontier issue to the North that has a large Russian army sitting on it, while to the west lay Balkans warzones. So the EU was again appealing as a back door to NATO protection. As poor countries, and with Romania in particular having a large and underdeveloped agri-sector, both also faced the prospect of receiving significant amounts in grants. Merely taking measures to accelerate change in their economies had qualified both for huge development grants. It also generated new possibilities for an impoverished ruling class...

WILL EU MEMBERSHIP ALWAYS PROVE SO ATTRACTIVE TO EASTERN EUROPE?

In a nutshell...

Membership is attractive until the grants stop and the effects of regulation on competitiveness become noticed.

SOME KEY FACTORS AROUND JOINING

★ 2004 entrants had a clearer idea of the EU's political ambitions

★ States began with first-hand experience by having been included in the Convention on the Future of Europe

★ The elite dealing with the EU shared (or feigned) European idealism

★ The less developed of the applicants had to put on a better show of their European credentials

★ Psychological draw of "reunifying the continent"

★ Appeal of a one-off counter of European decline by expanding to a market of half a billion

CHANGED FACTORS TODAY

★ Changed level of military threat from Russia

★ NATO membership

★ EU policy on Russian energy imports and the extent to which border states or Berlin direct it

★ Questions over the duration and extent of development aid

RESULTS OF THE METHODS USED

EAST GERMANY II

Basic industries in which Eastern Europe had potential – due to low costs, low wages, enduring state subsidy and weaker regulations – now fell under EU law.

By making the east join the club, it made their steel, coal, cloth and protected domestic manufacturers more expensive.

Those industries would adapt (or die) thanks to authorised state support – much of it from Western taxpayers – and foreign investment, but they secured a smaller niche in the Single Market at the cost of lost competitiveness, better working conditions, but fewer jobs. The winners were their Western competitors with room to export to these new markets.

OTHER ROUTES

1992

Central European Trade Area (CEFTA) created

VISEGRAD GROUP

Poland, Hungary and the splitting Czechoslovakia

A joint population roughly equivalent to that of the British Isles and a combined GDP of $130 billion

10 YEARS

Duration of Baltic Free Trade Area.

Membership of these free trade areas was incompatible with EU membership and had to end on joining the EU as a tariff block

WHAT IS AN OCT AND HOW DO THEY FIT INTO THE EU ARRANGEMENT?

In a nutshell...

Overseas Colonies and Territories (OCTs) are the remaining fragments of the European Empires. They gained different deals when their parent countries joined.

CHANGING CONDITIONS

St-Bartholémy, 2010

Became self-governing from Guadeloupe.

At this point it stopped being classified as an ultra-periphery region (since Guadeloupe and Martinique are considered as part of the French mainland) and became an associated overseas territory, in order for it to be subject to less EU regulation.

OCT-EC FORUM

Brings together all the interested parties once a year.

There are budgets specifically available for development purposes.

The number of Commission officials attending outnumbers the number of delegates from the islands.

FORUM MEMBERSHIP

The (mostly empty) French Territories in the south west Pacific, New Caledonia, the Dutch Antilles, Mauritius, Montserrat, St Helena, Tristan da Cunha, Anguilla, Greenland, the Falklands, the Turks and Caicos, the British Virgin Islands, St Pierre and Miquelon, Cayman Islands, Wallis and Futuna, Aruba, French Polynesia, and Mayotte.

These are predominantly British and French territories, though Denmark, the Netherlands, Belgium and Spain also attend.

OTHER FORMS OF ASSOCIATION

Gibraltar

Membership without the CAP (since the Rock is, well, a rock) and key trade elements

The Channel Islands and the Isle of Man

Under Protocol 3 of the Accession Treaty, residents of both retain movement rights with the UK but not free movement across the EU; trade and agricultural preferential tariffs are applied; but they retain the status control of their offshore banking systems.

FURTHER AFIELD

Other examples of territories that fall outside of full EU membership include the Faroe Islands, the African territories of Ceuta and Melilla, and Britain's Sovereign Base Territory in Cyprus

RESULT

The various agreements and treaty clauses covering the surviving colonial territories are such that a Caribbean island hopper could jump in a series of short flights from land which is part of the European Union, to a territory which has an OCT arrangement, to an island which is sovereign and part of the EU's ACP development aid treaties.

EU association does not take a uniform shape.

★ ★ ★ ★ ★ ★ ★ ★ ★ ★ ★

WHICH ARE THE CANDIDATE STATES TODAY AND WHY DO THEY WANT TO JOIN?

> **In a nutshell…**
>
>
>
> Croatia, Montenegro and FYROM (Macedonia) have ongoing applications as they emerge from Yugoslavia's shadow. Turkey's is on slow burn and the intent to anchor to the West may have faded. Iceland seems to have changed its mind on realising the public reaction was more hostile than its government anticipated.

TYPES OF ACCESSION COUNTRIES

★ Countries which have declared an interest in joining

★ Countries which have been identified as potential candidate countries, such as Serbia

★ Countries which have actual designated candidate status

3	I
Candidate states that are Yugoslav successor states.	Candidate that 'made it' in 2011/12: Croatia (votes permitting)

MONTENEGRO AND MACEDONIA

The other two

> *Dragan [x] managed to escape his captors by jumping out of the boot. There was another person in the boot who identified himself as a police officer."*
>
> Serbian government report of a reported kidnapping in Kosovo during the insurgency

THE OTHER BALKANS RUNNERS

Serbia

Signed a Stabilisation and Association (SAA) agreement with the EU in 2008

Albania

An SAA came into force in April 2009, the same month it formally submitted its membership application

Bosnia

Had an SAA and an interim trade agreement in 2008, and in 2010 citizens obtained some additional limited Schengen access

Kosovo

Remains a case apart; it has effectively been under the tutelage of an EU Special Representative with peace guaranteed by NATO and European police operating under a UN mandate. Its sovereign legal status remains internationally disputed: as such, it cannot apply in its own right for EU membership

★ ★ ★ ★ ★ ★ ★ ★ ★ ★ ★ ★

REASONS WHY ICELAND'S BID WAS UNEXPECTED

★ Its key industry, fishing, would lose out under the CFP

★ The public doesn't appear to support it

★ The move has minority political support

REASONS WHY TURKEY SHOULD NOT BE OPTIMISTIC ABOUT ITS BID

★ Germany is home to around three million people of Turkish extraction, or perhaps three-quarters of the European diaspora, suggesting it would be the location of first choice were the free movement of workers to kick in.

★ A number of intellectuals in some Catholic countries play on the idea of Europe as a Christian (by which they mean Catholic) continent.

★ France appears to be preoccupied with Turkey's population. At around 79 million, Turkey would join Germany in outgunning it in MEPs and at the Council of Ministers.

★ France was also a preferred place of exile for fugitive Armenians, which also seems to have sunk into the intellectual psyche in Paris.

★ Turkish farmers and Kurdish villagers taking money from a pot once destined for the French countryside is a more practical consideration.

REASONS WHY THIS MAY NOT BE AN ISSUE ANYWAY

★ Having been quite obviously rebuffed by reticent EU members, the Turks have elected an Islamist, though secular, government.

★ Ankara's focus has shifted away from the West and towards the traditional Arab hinterland, and to Iran.

★ With a fast growing economy running at nearly double figure growth, and a banking system that having learned lessons five years ago has not needed state bailouts, who needs the eurozone anyway?

Εδω δεν ειναι παιξε γελασε
Εδώ ειναι βαλκάνια

WHICH COUNTRIES HAVE SAID, 'NO, THANKS'?

In a nutshell...

Norway has rejected joining twice; Iceland has lately backed off; Switzerland twice rejected economic integration but agreed to other arrangements; the Faroes excluded themselves from Danish accession; Greenland and Algeria left.

97%

Fish as a share of the Faroes' exports volume

77,063 TONNES

Total catch of Iceland's fishing fleet just in October 2011

930

Year of the establishment of Icelandic parliamentary democracy

2,300 PAGES

Length of the Parliament's commissioned report on the Icelandic banking collapse

SIDES OF THE POND

The capital of Greenland – Nuuk – is closer to Washington, D.C., than it is to Brussels

1976

First post-independence agreement between Algeria and the EEC, prior to which both parties partially and informally retained some privileged access

TWO

Number of times the Norwegian government has tried to join the Community

Number of times it has been defeated in a referendum

Number of key industries at risk from Community membership (oil and fish)

KNUT HOEM

Norwegian Fisheries minister who resigned over the terms of Norwegian accession and their impact upon their industry

THREE

Number of Cod Wars between Iceland and Britain, each over the extension of territorial waters

200 NAUTICAL MILES OR TO A MEDIAN LINE

Fisheries limits after the third extension.

Similar limits were extended to UK waters, though under the CFP the British extension now fell under the jurisdiction of the CFP and were not for national exploitation

TURBOT WAR

Fisheries conflict in 1995 between Canada and Spain over allegations of illegal Spanish overfishing. The UK and Ireland, and in particular their fishermen, supported Ottawa (hence the proliferation of Jolly Rogers at British ports)

2002

Switzerland joins the UN

... BUT OUTWARD LOOKING

International organisations and campaigns hosted by Switzerland

★ International Committee of the Red Cross

★ International Telecommunication Union

★ Universal Postal Union

★ Intergovernmental Organization for International Carriage by Rail

★ International Olympic Committee

★ League of Nations, and today the United Nations Office at Geneva (UNOG)

★ Eight United Nations agencies, including the World Intellectual Property Organization (WIPO), the International Telecommunication Union (ITU) and the World Meteorological Organization (WMO)

★ International Labour Organization

★ European Broadcasting Union

★ World Conservation Union

★ World Wide Fund for Nature

★ Bank for International Settlements

★ European Organization for Nuclear Research (CERN)

★ World Trade Organization

★ International Air Transport Association

★ International Organization for Standardization

35

Number of international organisations enjoying headquarter or special fiscal arrangements or immunities in Switzerland

1992

Rejects accession to the EEA and settles for a looser bilateral deal

2001

By a margin of over two to one, voters reject moves towards EU membership. Referenda did, however, consent to some Justice and Home Affairs co-operation.

70.8%

Greenland's No vote on accession to the EEC in 1972.

The territory was outvoted by polls in mainland Denmark

1982

Greenland-only referendum provides a clear, but reduced, vote supporting withdrawal from the EEC, which occurs in 1985. It gains OCT status instead.

 Like other fisheries dependent communities, the Faroese have not found it their interest to become subject to the Common Fisheries Policy."

Current line from the Faroese government, which has rejected accession. Bilateral agreements and free trade agreements with other countries are in place instead.

If we implemented all the EU regulations, we would need 56,000 people just to govern 56,000 people."

Minninnquaq Kleist, head of office at Greenland's department of foreign affairs, reacting to renewed Commission interest in mineral-rich Greenland.

Source: Public Service Europe

HOW HAVE REFERENDA FIT INTO THE CHANGING FACE OF THE EU?

In a nutshell...

Referenda have become a key part of EU politics across the continent.

6

Referenda held by Denmark. Two had negative results, rejecting Maastricht (first time around) and saying No to joining the euro in 2000.

The count party for the latter at Brussels was a wake for all but one table in the room.

2

EU referenda in Finland

3

EU Referenda in France

Maastricht was a very close run thing. Its voters rejected the EU Constitution by a wider margin, but were not allowed a revote. The same was true of the Dutch voters who also voted against.

7

Irish referenda.

It rejected Nice in 2001 and was obliged to vote again, amidst threats of general economic cataclysm.

SKOL

Sweden voted marginally to join the EU, but more clearly against adopting the euro in 2003, both on high turnouts.

10

Other countries that have had votes on accession

LUXEMBOURG AND SPAIN

Countries that had votes on the EU Constitution that are today generally forgotten.

For observers, Spain's was a foregone conclusion, though surprisingly nearly a quarter of the voters said No or left the ballot blank, on a 42% turnout. More unexpectedly, Luxembourg's Yes was only 56.5% in a founding member state on a compulsory vote.

SO, DO NATIONAL PRIORITIES STILL REVOLVE AROUND THE EU TODAY?

In a nutshell...

The motives for many countries when they joined the EU are considerably different from the realities facing them today. A reassessment would be useful in many national capitals.

DEMOCRATIC AND FREE – ESPECIALLY THE NORTHERN PERIPHERY

Democracy Index 2011: European countries in the top ten world rankings

1	–	Norway (overall score, 9.8)
2	–	Iceland (9.65)
3	–	Denmark (9.52)
4	–	Sweden (9.5)
5	–	(New Zealand, 9.26)
6	–	(Australia, 9.22)
7	–	Switzerland (9.09)
8	–	(Canada, 9.08)
9	–	Finland (9.06)
10	–	Netherlands (8.99)
...		...
12	–	Ireland (8.56)
18	–	UK (8.16)

FOURTEEN

Number of EU countries controversially classed as "flawed democracies"

Source: Economist Intelligence Unit

Time marches on

The influences that drove countries to seek to join the EEC, and its successor organisations the EC and EU, are therefore manifold. While the idealism behind European integration acts as a personal magnet for some key figures, the key motors were historical, economical and geographical.

For periphery states, membership of the Community was a way of integrating with the nearest large and developing market, and therefore securing long-term trading interests rather than risk stagnation. The examples of peripheral states such as Norway and Iceland that declined to join suggest that this option is not the only valid one.

For continental states bordering Germany, European integration is an attempt to answer the old conundrum of what to do with a powerful, large and ultimately dominant mass of Germans at the centre of the continent. A common national identity has made a return to partition implausible. Demilitarisation has part worked, making panzer commanders proud of their pink berets but equally now incapable of shouldering a major part of the West's burden on the world stage. So, today, there is still the problem of how to incorporate a German military in a way similar to German war production (coal and steel), and the recent answer has been to expand the remit of the EU into defence and other areas.

The EEC took the form of an economic association and everything else is a bolt-on (calling it an 'app' would be too generous, given some serious software incompatibilities). The central motive for most states has been access to the Community's consumers without being hit by punitive tariffs. This was particularly appealing for countries that applied before tariff levels dropped globally, at the time when the core economies were expanding quickly, prior to the surge of the Far Eastern and South American markets, and where countries for political reasons were seeking ways to replace their old trading links. With shifting trade patterns and new dominant and exploitable markets, the economic appeal for the EU is not, however, what it was.

There is also in play the sovereignty paradox, with countries surrendering aspects of self-government in order to protect against other external influences, whether geographic (such as having Russia as a neighbour) or strategic (such as allowing protectionism in key industries). The expansion of NATO and ongoing WTO agreements have affected these needs, however, while the democratic costs have come under question.

Overall, as interests and priorities have changed, and as the shape of the EU itself has metamorphosed, the urgency of membership across the Union is no longer the same. A question we will consider throughout the book is whether value still remains for existing members.

PRT

TWO

How Brussels Works

MAY CONTAIN TRACES OF
POLITICIANS, PUBLIC MONEY
AND STRANGE SCULPTURES

PART

TWO

New Artists' Works

Once you are in, you're in. Regardless of the motives that drew them into the EU in the first place, the diplomats and politicians of the member states now have to confront the realities of common policies, complex treaties and a bewildering mass of offices. We've seen what countries wanted from membership, but to understand if those objectives are fully met we now have to turn to how the EU operates. Let's begin with the main institutions.

There is the **Council of Ministers**, which brings together the member states to argue about proposals based on national governmental lines.

There is the **Commission**, which is a civil service intended to propose legislation and to ensure that what has been agreed is implemented. It is ostensibly impartial, though is by definition a centralising force with inherent interests at stake.

There is the **European Parliament**, which brings together representatives of the political parties and typically acts as an amending force, though in practice the scale of the legislation prevents significant review.

There is also the **European Court of Justice (ECJ)**, which exists to provide legal interpretations in areas of dispute over treaty law, or the resulting EU law made on its basis.

Increasingly, the **European Central Bank (ECB)** is assuming a role and importance on a par with these. Like the Commission, this too is supposedly an independent body, though in practical terms inevitably leans towards the interests of the core economies.

In addition to these five main institutions, there are a very large number of tier two and tier three bodies; we'll turn to these sometimes surprising creatures later.

National Parliaments fall well down the food chain. Some have reserved for themselves the right to sign off on agreements made by their government, but most have little more power than as a debating chamber before applying a rubber stamp. A 'red card' procedure can pause legislation if a sufficient number of them object as a group, but the preconditions for this to happen make such a showdown extremely unlikely, and it is improbable such universally controversial legislation would be agreed in the first place.

Some shorthand explained

BRUSSELS

★ A Belgian city, known locally as Bruxelles or Brussel depending on whether you are Walloon or Flemish. Unless you are physically on a plane to work, or looking for a local school for your children, this meaning is not typically meant within the EU.

★ Shorthand for the EU as a whole, particularly though not exclusively for critics of the process who have long tried to link the dream pushed by European integrationists with the practical realities of a capital city of a small, slightly dull and highly dysfunctional country.

★ A misnomer. The European Parliament has a second seat in Strasbourg; the Commission has offices in Luxembourg; and the ECB is based in Frankfurt.

★ A way to tell a tale of two cities, since Brussels neatly distinguishes between the EU capital on one hand and the national capital on the other.

★ A way to neatly mark out the EU context when discussing European co-operation, since the Council of Europe seat is Strasbourg.

EUROPE

★ A continent on a map.

★ A sloppy way of saying the EU. Not all of Europe is in the EU, and parts of it indeed are in separate European groupings, most notably EFTA. Some parts, the overseas territories, can even be on different continents.

★ A way of confusing the EU with the Council of Europe, which due to a considerably larger membership has a much stronger claim to the title.

★ For Eurosceptics, a distant aspirant empire, of which member states will only be provinces or satrapies; the pro-European meaning is one of unity, harmony and integrity on the world stage. Readers can take their pick.

THE EU

★ The founding Rome Treaty established the European Economic Community or EEC.

★ The Single European Act of 1986 turned this into the European Community or EC.

★ The Maastricht Treaty created two parallel treaty structures with a Treaty on European Union (TEU) running alongside the Treaty on the European Community (TEC). The EU aspect added new elements on international affairs and home affairs, and as these at the outset were basically intergovernmental it was felt it would be better to keep them apart from the economics as three 'pillars'.

★ Over the next decade, however, the TEU was essentially collapsed into the TEC (with all that this entailed for removing national vetoes), though the EU took over the name of the whole.

Given all these official terms, it is perhaps understandable that people still want to talk about Brussels and Europe.

The Council of Ministers

In a nutshell…

The Council is where national civil servants barter and national ministers sign off on agreements.

We begin with what the Council of Ministers isn't: it isn't the European Council. The European Council is the summit (typically numbering four a year) where heads of government meet with the head of the Commission to discuss the EU's general direction. It was first set up in 1974 as an informal forum and only later became, as it were, the tool for setting objectives. It acquired a formal status in 1992, but only in 2009 became one of the official institutions of the EU in its own right. In a sense, the European Council is the ship's bridge for what goes on in the Council of Ministers. Depending on your viewpoint, it is an opportunity for politicians to grandstand in front of the media or, alternatively, to set the agenda for the next three months, or steer a path through a particular crisis.

It may help to visualise there being two Councils of Ministers. One is the European civil service – the Council's General Secretariat – which runs in parallel to the Commission and whose job it is to implement what's been agreed, assist the current President's work (he also has a private office), and support the process of negotiations impartially. The other is the mass of delegations sent from national civil services to negotiate and barter deals between themselves.

The Council is broken down by subject matter, with relevant ministers meeting regularly but at different levels of frequency varying on the ministry. Much of the donkey work is done at the General Affairs Council typically attended by Europe Ministers. Countries take turns to chair meetings on six-month rotations.

The Council is mainly based in the Justus Lipsius building. It moved there approaching twenty years ago when the former building was proving too crowded. Ironically, it moved into a building that was itself out of date. Justus Lipsius has been estimated to have a total floor space of 215,000 square metres and fifteen miles of corridors. Even so, the move was originally based to cater for a pre-accession Council, with a move planned to a site where the adjoining land had unfortunately already been sold off.

The site is traditionally given a facelift by the current presidency adding artwork. Hungary placed a Rubik's cube bookcase and a chair that played Liszt. More controversially, a 'history carpet' was accused of displaying Hungarian territorial claims on their neighbours from Hapsburg days. Even more infamously, the Czechs included a major artwork resembling an Airfix kit, with the representation of Germany covered in autobahns resembling a swastika, Poland had monks lifting Iwo Jima-like a rainbow flag, France was on strike, and Bulgaria was a toilet.

A move from Justus Lipsius is planned in the near future, which will at least take staff away from the bugs (electronic devices, found in 2003) and the mice (furry, reportedly found near the waste bins). Other Council buildings currently include the Lex complex and a 1920s Art Deco construction.

Coreper (Committee of Permanent Representatives) is the Council's main engine. This is the assembly of the permanent representatives of the national governments, or delegated civil servants – in Britain's case, they come from the UK Representation (UKREP), occasionally with input from devolved government or from Whitehall ministries beyond the FCO. Coreper I looks at technical matters at a lower level, or individual policy areas, with Coreper II meetings taking a more strategic policy view, especially over big budget or sensitive matters. Over 150 committees and working groups are involved in supporting this work. Agriculture and some other competences are managed separately by Special Committees.

A AND B POINTS

A particularly contentious aspect of how the Council works takes the form of the A and B Points.

A Points are areas where national civil servants have agreed upon an item between themselves, while B Points require further work at ministerial meetings.

What this in practice means, however, is that A Points get rubber stamped without any significant democratic scrutiny. Given that civil servants are by nature of their job hard to move or fire (since that might affect their political independence), in a Brussels context this leads to a lack of accountability.

Figures are traditionally scarce, though it has been estimated by academics that 85% of decisions are concluded through Coreper or its delegate bodies, leaving only around 15% for ministers to agree between themselves. The precise figure may be open to question, though it is clear that with a high proportion of items of a highly technical nature involved, subsequently to be passed into UK national law through Statutory Instruments (SIs) with Parliament agreeing on the nod, perhaps this estimate is broadly accurate.

This little-understood aspect of the EU's democratic deficit may account for a large proportion of the negative publicity the EU currently earns, because when an SI is passed and carries unexpected consequences, the blame passes back up the food chain to 'distant dictatorial Brussels'.

A MATTER OF PERSPECTIVE

Non-Significant Actions – potentially the biggest misnomer in the EU, these were items for which no Council legal base was required.

Actions ponctuelles – projects or pilot actions of the European Commission, to acquire knowledge for proposed full-scale EU programmes and projects, for example to assess costs or pay for expert meetings. These typically featured as projects involving Non-Significant Actions.

This approach was challenged in the European Court of Justice over 1996-8 in a case brought by the UK, which found that the Commission had exceeded its authority. Several areas were suspended as a result. A number of other areas then had legal basis bolted on, sometimes controversially.

Actions autonomes de la Commission – the technically illegal projects thus funded. These included the following budget lines:

★ **B3-1020** Actions of social dialogue and preparatory measures for reinforcing co-operation

★ **B3-300** General information actions and communication on the European Union

★ **B3-301** Information Relays

★ **B3-302** Information programmes directed at third countries

★ **B3-304** Information action in universities

★ **B3-306** Prince (information programme for the European citizen) – Information actions for specific policies

★ **B3-4000** Industrial relations and social dialogue

★ **B3-4001** European unions institute

★ **B3-4002** Actions for formation and consultation in support of workers' organisations

- ★ **B3-4003** Information and consultation of business representatives

- ★ **B4-2000** Security inspections and inspector training

- ★ **B4-2020** Sampling and specific works

- ★ **B4-2021** Specific controls at large plutonium works

- ★ **B4-306** Public awareness and grant support

- ★ **B4-307** Nuclear safety and radiation protection

- ★ **B5-102** Consumer information

- ★ **B5-103** Actions intended to improve consumer health

- ★ **B7-610** Development training including third country posting attachments to the Commission

- ★ **B7-651** Coordination of development policy: evaluation, follow up and inspection

The sum total for these activities ran to 157.1 million ECUs in 1996. While a number have variously been incorporated into the treaty base since, they provide some insight into the Commission's past aspirations and approach.

€61.6 MILLION

Estimated cost to Cyprus of hosting its 2012 Presidency of the EU, involving:

15 Informal Ministerial Councils

180 lower level meetings

But excluding **3,500** working group meetings chaired in Brussels instead

---

Classification of documents with an EU caveat

TRÈS SECRET UE/EU TOP SECRET. This marking is applied to information and material the unauthorised disclosure of which could cause exceptionally grave prejudice to the essential interests of the European Union or one or more of the member states.

SECRET UE/EU SECRET. This marking is applied to information and material the unauthorised disclosure of which could seriously harm the essential interests of the European Union or one or more of the member states.

CONFIDENTIEL UE/EU CONFIDENTIAL. This marking is applied to information and material the unauthorised disclosure of which could harm the essential interests of the European Union or one or more of the member states.

RESTREINT UE/EU RESTRICTED. This marking is applied to information and material the unauthorised disclosure of which could be disadvantageous to the interests of the European Union or one or more of the member states.

MONEY TALKS

The Council's 2011 budget provides some insight into the scale and nature of the institution and how it functions:

★ €65,000 was spent on unstated entitlements in the office of Council President and €13,000 on social security cover

★ €900,000 was spent on the Presidency's travel and living expenses

★ €3.9 million went on the General Secretariat's mission expenses, with another €400,000 travel costs

★ Basic salaries amongst EU Council staff come to €208 million

★ An additional €3.8 million was available for various allowances, including overtime for chauffeurs. A separate €2.1 million went on overtime for office staff.

★ €55.4 million was spent on allowances relating to overseas residency, families, home country travel and the like

★ €9.2 million went on staff insurance policies, namely health and maintaining social security payments

★ €210,000 was used to re-weight employees' pay when they came from a country with a lower cost of living

★ €346,000 was spent on allowances for staff whose employment was terminated

★ €472,000 went as pensions to former Secretaries-General, i.e. head civil servants

★ €132,000 was spent as miscellaneous expenditure on recruitment

★ €1.6 million was spent on attending courses and seminars

★ €119,000 was spent on social events for staff

★ €66,000 went on welfare expenditure for staff and families

★ €432,000 was dedicated healthcare and medical expenditure

★ €1,115,000 was for restaurants and canteens

★ €1.8 million was for the Council crèche, and to pay for children attending the Early Childhood Centre and the Commission's own crèche and childhood facilities

★ Rent for the Council's premises in Brussels, Luxembourg, Geneva and New York historically runs to around €4 million

★ There is a €15 million budget to buy immovable property. €32.8 million was spent in 2009

★ €17 million has been set aside for cleaning and maintenance

★ There is an expected services bill of €4 million

★ €9 million is spent on security

★ €19 million is spent on external computer specialists and consultants – about four times the cost of new software

- €1 million has been set aside for new furniture

- The cost of the official cars comes to €788,000

- €33.7 million is the assessed cost for repaying the travel expenses of Council delegates

- The basic cost of interpretation runs at €94 million

- €2 million has been set aside for entertainment costs "incumbent upon the institution"

- €4.1 million goes on refreshments and meals served during internal meetings

- €1.26 million is the sum of the dedicated PR budget

- €971,000 is for office supplies

- €600,000 has been set aside for costs and damages for attempts to sue the Council. In 2009, the actual outlay was €829,500.

 A lot of very bright people work in the Foreign Office, but they do need watching otherwise they go off and do their own thing."
Jack Straw quoted in the *Chris Mullin Diaries*, 14 June 2003

The Commission

In a nutshell...

The Commission is the civil service of the EU. It drafts legislation and monitors countries to see if it is being implemented. Its loyalty is to the treaties.

The Commission's declared objective is to "promote the general interest of the European Union". Contention historically arises where its interpretation differs from that of member states, a position that has grown with its expanding role as the treaties have increasingly transferred powers to Brussels.

At the summit sits the College of Commissioners, which assumes political direction on a collegiate basis of shared responsibility. Commissioners are appointed on the basis of general competence and, while there has historically been a long fight to retain a national quota of a Commissioners per country, each appointee is supposed to be independent and takes an oath to that effect.

Directors-General and Heads of Service implement decisions made. The Commission may also hand over particular programmes to EU agencies, managed by a Director and with a Commission-appointed steering committee. In addition to an annual programme, the Commissioners set out a slightly Soviet-sounding five-year plan. The Commission works on a basis of around 230 distinct areas grouped into thirty policy areas. Interdisciplinary areas obviously bring together staff from disparate teams.

A TINY, TINY NUMBER

There are 24,000 staff in the European Commission. Supporters of the European Union point to comparative employment rates in urban councils – for instance, Birmingham employed a total workforce of some 19,000 staff before recent cutbacks.

This analogy is not, however, complete. In the first place, the Birmingham figure is made up of a significant number of front line staff such as street cleaners. These do exist in the Commission, but make up a smaller proportion.

Secondly, the European Commission operates as a top level administrative layer, sitting on top of existing civil service personnel. As such, it has been likened to the cream on a trifle and (with a purely scientific meaning though less generously) with a parasitical function. Without the lower levels, it would not be able to carry out its duties since it relies on national, regional and local government to enact its decisions and to enforce them.

A third objection sometimes raised relates to the effectiveness of this top tier bureaucracy. In the Commission's defence, it is sometimes stated that major universities employ thousands of staff these days too.

The comparison is not so great when you consider the backdrop to the current size of university administrations. As Benjamin Ginsberg at John Hopkins University has pointed out, even in the United States campuses saw costs tripling between 1975 to 2005, with staff to pupil ratios remaining broadly constant, while the number of administrators rose by 85% and the number of their staff by 240%.

A better example might be sought, but probably cannot be found, outside the modern era of great bureaucracies. The Indian Civil Service at its height of power comprised perhaps a thousand people running the entire Raj. The obituaries pages of broadsheets meanwhile are still occasionally replete with tales of isolated colonial officers in Sudan and elsewhere responsible for the fates of entire peoples. The comparison is not a solid one for this bureaucratic elite, nor is it a healthy one.

SOME STAFF STATS

★ For each age category from **21** to **45**, there are more women than men employed; from **46** to **65**, there are more men than women

★ **1,059** staff are on loan from national governments

★ There is a clear trend over time – three-quarters of **27-year-old** Commission staff are women, against only one-third of **61-year-olds**

★ Surprisingly, of the **33** top grade staff (known as 'AD 16') six are British, making them the highest represented. There are five Italians and four Germans

★ Across the top five grades, the British share is actually lower than the national share of Europe's population, with **458** out of **4,591** top grade employees (approximately **10%**) compared to around **13%** by population share

★ The discrepancy is even more pronounced at lower levels. The total of British fast stream managerial or 'AD' staff is **737** out of **12,731**, or **3%**. The total of 'AST' or 'support' staff is **412** out of **11,217**, or **2%** of the total

★ By comparison, Belgium, Germany, Spain, France and Italy all have more AD staff, meaning a greater proportion of people in policy-making roles from these countries. Germany and France have figures approaching double UK numbers (**1,347** and **1,337** staff)

★ Smaller countries comparatively do very well. Slovenia for instance has **160** AD staff; Malta **112**; Lithuania **193**; and Ireland **228**

★ The five largest locations for Commission employment are: DGT (Translation) **2,306** staff (**10%** of total); JRC (Joint Research Centre) **1,780** staff (**7%**); Development **1,213** staff (**5%**); Research and innovation **1,196** staff (**5%**); and Agriculture **965** staff (**4%**)

★ **489** staff work directly for the College of Commissioners as a sort of EU Cabinet Office

★ Reinforcing gender stereotypes on language ability, twice as many women as men work in the AD grades in interpretation and four times as many at the junior grades

★ **17,747** staff (three-quarters) work in Brussels; **3,407** (one-seventh) work in Luxembourg; **1,076** work in Italy; and the remainder are scattered with **609** also working outside the EU

COMMISSION STAFF BY NATIONALITY, 2011

Country	Staff	Proportion of total (%)
AT Austria	485	1.5
BE Belgium	6,026	18.3
BG Bulgaria	628	1.9
CY Cyprus	136	0.4
CZ Czech Republic	515	1.6
DE Germany	2,287	6.9
DK Denmark	456	1.4
ES Spain	2,284	6.9
EE Estonia	213	0.6
FI Finland	613	1.9
FR France	3,361	10.2
EL Greece	1,111	3.4
HU Hungary	711	2.2
IE Ireland	521	1.6
IT Italy	3,662	11.1
LV Latvia	236	0.7
LT Lithuania	361	1.1
LU Luxembourg	216	0.7
MT Malta	152	0.5
NL Netherlands	734	2.2
PL Poland	1443	4.4
PT Portugal	896	2.7
RO Romania	989	3.0
SK Slovakia	403	1.2
SI Slovenia	258	0.8
SE Sweden	612	1.9
UK United Kingdom	1,322	4.0
Other	2318	7.0
Total	**32,949**	**100**

Personnel aside, the Commission's main home is in the Berlaymont, a 200,000 square metre site housing 3,000 staff, though as it is broken down into a large number of Directorates-General and sub units it has scores of other buildings, of which the Charlemagne building is one of the largest. The building diaspora proved useful twenty years ago when Berlaymont was shut down during an asbestos scare. However, the clean up turned into something of a Belgian national scandal. With refurbishment only agreed after a major crisis with the unions, who were understandably concerned with the nonchalant attitude of their superiors, an agreement was reached to strip out the offending substance and in the process attempt to make the building generally more inhabitable. But the work ran years behind schedule and costs overran reportedly by a factor of at least seven.

HOW DOES THIS SPENDING TRANSLATE INTO OFFICE REALITIES?

The 2011 budget here gives us some pointers.

★ Commission pay and primary allowances across the board currently comes to €1,930,287,211 (or €1.9 billion) – an average of around €80,000 per person

★ Expenses and allowances relating to recruitment, transfers and departures amounts to €37.5 million

★ "Adjustment" allowances are currently running at €53.6 million

★ The current pensions bill for the Commission is running at €1.2 billion

★ Retired Commissioners are eligible for €2.6 million of transitional or family allowances

★ Retired Commissioners currently receive a total of €4.7 million in pensions for themselves or their surviving partner. Another €455,000 has been set aside for weighting on cost of living or exchange rate grounds

★ €7.9 million is in a special budget line for people who have been retired or actively dismissed

★ Conference and meeting costs are projected to run at €30 million, with another €13.4 million for committee meetings

★ €9.4 million has been earmarked for studies and consultations

★ The furniture and office equipment budget is €88.6 million

★ €9 million is spent conducting surveys on the impact of the euro and in continuing surveys that were begun in the early 1960s

★ The Commission's budget is so large, in 2009 its current accounts made a total of €43.3 million in interest. Another €62.4 million was raised in interest through pre-financing

★ Late payments into the Commission's accounts trigger interest payments. In 2009, these came to €76.4 million

★ There is a special Commission account on such fines, with a special budget line associated with it, and with interest to be paid for the late payment of the fines themselves

★ In 2009, the Commission levied €724.8 million on member states in fines

★ It costs €12.1 million to publish the *Official Journal*, the publication in which EU laws are binding once printed

★ The Office for the Administration and Payment of Individual Entitlements itself costs €34.7 million to run

★ The Office for Infrastructure and Logistics in Brussels costs €68 million

★ Rent and building for the Commission within the EU costs €206.7 million, and €78.6 million on utility bills and maintenance just in Brussels. €5.9 million is spent on removals, storage, deliveries and "the provision of protocol restaurant services" in the city

★ Luxembourg rent comes to €41.1 million

★ €36.9 million is spent on guarding Commission buildings in these two cities

★ €6.3 million is spent on paying for check ups and medical centres

★ €8 million is dedicated to "interinstitutional co-operation in the social sphere", including an intranet site; a weekly magazine; promotion campaigns; part-time staff for child minding centres, holiday centres and open-air centres; support for the recreation centre, staff clubs, sports centres, courses in languages and the arts; and purchasing medals for staff who have served 20 years, or who are retiring

★ €400,000 is reserved for staff who may be taking a pay cut due to their being on attachment to a national civil service or an international institution

★ €150,000 has been put apart as damages arising from civil claims

★ €8.6 million has been assigned for the central admin of the European Schools, the private schools for EU staff. There are fifteen such schools across the EU, costing €155 million in 2011

★ The 2011 budget has a commitment for €54 million for the current EU statistical programme. This book aspires to not let these particular resources go entirely to waste!

PRECONDITIONS OF ENTRY INTO THE EU CIVIL SERVICES

An official may be appointed only on condition that:

★ (a) he is a national of one of the member states of the Communities, unless an exception is authorised by the appointing authority, and enjoys his full rights as a citizen;

★ (b) he has fulfilled any obligations imposed on him by the laws concerning military service;

★ (c) he produces the appropriate character references as to his suitability for the performance of his duties;

★ (d) he has, subject to Article 29(2), passed a competition based on either qualifications or tests, or both qualifications and tests, as provided for in Annex III;

★ (e) he is physically fit to perform his duties; and

★ (f) he produces evidence of a thorough knowledge of one of the languages of the Communities and of a satisfactory knowledge of another language of the Communities to the extent necessary for the performance of his duties.

Article 28, Staff Regulations

HOW TO BECOME A 'EUROCRAT'

A new process was begun in 2010

★ Ensure you fulfil the qualifying criteria (see above)

★ Complete an online form and return it to the personnel office (EPSO) to register an interest in the Concours

★ Take a computer-based admission test, contents and timing to vary on whether you want to be an administrator, linguist, assistant or specialist. The EU-knowledge part of this has now been dropped in favour of assessing analytical skills

★ Attend an assessment centre for another half or full day of tests, much of which is in your second language

★ Feedback is provided

★ Successful applicants are put on a *reserve list* database

★ The list is reviewed by EU institutions looking to fill posts

★ EU institutions approach people on the list

★ An interview takes place

★ You get the job – on probation

Skill sets looked for by recruiters

★ Analysis and problem solving

★ Communicating

★ Delivering quality and results

★ Learning and development

★ Prioritising and organising

★ Resilience

★ Working with others

★ Leadership

Example of a test question (as offered to applicants)

From the multiple choice answers to each question on a work-related scenario, you must make TWO choices – the most effective action AND the least effective action.

Each question can score between 0-2 points.

You have recently been appointed to a position in a new project team. Although you are experienced in the technical aspects of the job, there are aspects of the work that you need to understand. Your job will eventually require internal liaison and collaboration with other project teams. Although your manager has proposed an induction and training period for you, many of the issues you are responsible for require urgent attention.

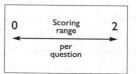

0	Scoring range	2
	per question	

a. Immediately arrange meetings with those individuals you feel you will need to work with. **(Most effective)**

b. Quickly try to establish how your objectives will relate to your project manager's objectives. (Neutral)

c. In the initial stages, make sure that you are doing your job as you understood it from the job description. **(Least effective)**

d. Spend time building your understanding of the team's objectives for the future. (Neutral)

1	⬤	◯	0
0.5	◯	◯	0.5
0	◯	◯	1
0.5	◯	⬤	0.5

The European Parliament

In a nutshell...

MEPs modify legislation and, theoretically, hold the Commission to account.

The European Parliament is the establishment that has gradually morphed into what identifies itself as the democratic element of the European Union. Previously the European Assembly and made up of parliamentarians assigned from national parliaments, it styled itself the European Parliament for several years before the name was formally – and legally – recognised in the treaties themselves. There are presently 754 Members of the European Parliament, or MEPs – 18 of these have been 'ghost MEPs' waiting for changes in numbers to enter into force.

Direct suffrage came in 1979. The method of election was left to national preference, resulting in the United Kingdom retaining direct suffrage under First Past the Post until 1999. A list system has operated since then, resulting in the election of candidates based on the party's vote but selected individually on their ranking on a party slate. Critics claim that this creates a heightened level of distance between candidates and their electorate in these new mega-constituencies, each of which has now been given several individuals as their MEP. Worse, there is also the danger of increased party patronage in how candidates are selected or appointed, since prioritisation on the list can be done on the Party leadership's terms, for instance by requiring alternating gender on candidate lists.

The Chair of the European Parliament is the President, elected to serve half of the five year set Parliamentary term.

Parliament's timetable is organised through the Conference of Presidents, which brings together the President and the chairman of each of the political groups, plus a representative of the independents who can't vote. The rest take decisions based on consensus or by vote, with votes weighted by the number of MEP delegates represent. In practical terms, this means that where the Centre Left and Centre Right have reached an agreement, the deal was stitched up. With an increased workload, the mathematics has become slightly more complicated in recent years.

SECOND TUESDAY IN MAY

The annual meeting schedule for the Parliamentary Assembly of the ECSC.

In the event, owing to the treaty ratification process passing this date, the very first meeting took place over 10-13 September 1952. At these meetings, of 38 Christian Democrats, 24 Socialists, 11 Liberals and 5 Independents only four of these were Gaullists, i.e. clearly opposed to deep European political integration. Perhaps an early pointer to the phenomenon of European-level politicians being more integrationist than their voters?

Number of full or part days marked out for meetings or plenaries on the European Parliament calendar for 2011

There are 14 Vice-Presidents who are also elected, and there are five Quaestors who are responsible for the administration and financial management. The Presidents and Vice-Presidents run the Bureau, which the Quaestors attend as advisors. The Bureau is the main administrative body of the EP and appoints the Secretary-General, its chief bureaucrat.

Parliament's political functions are carried out in no small part through its 20 standing committees, each of which has a Chairman and four Vice-Chairmen, plus its own dedicated secretariat. Special, temporary, committees can also be formed. In a manner not dissimilar to the Commons, the Committee Chairmen jointly hold regular meetings to discuss matters of common interest, particularly with reference to which committees should be assigned which legislative items.

An ongoing area of controversy is over the persistent requirement that MEPs (literally) up trunks and move from Brussels on average around once a month to hold their plenary sessions in Strasbourg. This is almost universally regarded as an expensive extravagance, except by the French in whose territories lie the restaurants and hotels used by the visiting staff. It is a measure of the change in the times that the old French reasoning, that Alsace typifies the need for a new Europe of reconciliation, no longer holds the water it used to.

THE EUROPEAN PARLIAMENT: A FACTORY OF PRESS RELEASES

"To keep silent is the most useful service that an indifferent spokesman can render to the Commonwealth.

"Constituents, however, do not think so."

Alexis de Tocqueville, *Democracy in America*

As with the other main institutions, let's review some of the big spending areas.

★ MEP salaries cost €66.8 million

★ Their travel expenses come to €84.8 million

★ Costs from MEPs carrying out their duties come to €38.3 million

★ The President has an allowance of €179,000 for subsistence and representation

★ MEPs have a sickness and accident insurance budget of €3.5 million

★ €380,000 has been set aside to assist seriously-disabled MEPs

★ €1.5 million has been put aside for MEPs retiring this year, despite this not being an election year

★ €9.4 million has been set aside to cover the arrival of 18 new MEPs that followed the signing of the Treaty of Lisbon

★ €555.8 million is for pay and allowances for the Parliament's staff. This includes insurance premiums to cover the EP's sports centres in Brussels and Strasbourg. It also covers the recruitment of temporary staff with disabilities in order in accordance with new recruitment targets

★ €5 million is for staff joining, transferring or leaving, including compensation for a probationary official "because his work is obviously inadequate". €1.9 million is elsewhere on the books for those retired compulsorily

★ €60 million for conference interpretation

★ €650,000 for social welfare

★ €310,000 for social contacts

★ €1.3 million for its medical service

★ €2.6 million subsidises restaurants and canteens

★ €5.35 million supports the Early Childhood Centre and approved nurseries

★ Rent and lease payments cost €46.5 million

★ In late 2011, €38 million was set aside for the purchase of another three buildings for the EP from unspent budget, requiring €110 million more in restoration

- ★ Maintenance and cleaning is €44.7 million

- ★ The energy bill is €19 million, which includes carbon offsets after a controversial review of power use

- ★ Security costs €37.6 million

- ★ €6.5 million covers the EP's vehicle fleet, including chauffeur-driven cars and less-well-known bicycle collection

- ★ €1.3 million is reserved for being sued

- ★ €29.8 million is set aside for cost (and carbon offset) of staff having to move between the three European Parliament sites in Brussels, Strasbourg and Luxembourg

- ★ €2 million is available for official entertainment, such as around the presentation of medals for 15 and 25 years' service

- ★ €858,000 is for WTO delegations; €451,000 for ACP meetings; €80,000 is for EU-Latin American Parliamentary meetings (EuroLat); €216,000 is for the Parliamentary Assembly of the Union for the Mediterranean; €520,000 is for bilaterals with national parliaments globally; €700,000 is for bilaterals with national parliaments

- ★ The in-house travel service costs €2.1 million just to operate

- ★ €11.6 million is being spent on getting expert advice on archive retention

- ★ €31.7 million supports official visits to the EP

- ★ €2.5 million traditionally supports a peace prize, a European cinema prize and others

- ★ €22.6 million goes on a dedicated TV channel and broader audiovisual support

- ★ €1.2 million supports the EP's Information Offices for it to circulate its publications

- ★ €200,000 funds meetings of the association of former MEPs

- ★ €140,000 is for the European Parliamentary Association, which is a serving MEPs club. It organises conferences, debates, dinners, concerts, excursions, and sports-bar-style gatherings. A key motivator is to promote European identity amongst its membership. Its HQ is in a late Victorian building in Strasbourg

- There are 2,479 AD (high flyer) EP staff and another 2,930 AST (secretarial) staff, making a total of 5410 staff in the EP. That means for every MEP, there are around seven support staff within the institution. It is also an increase of around 190 on the previous year. However, that figure excludes the politically-engaged personnel, of which there are another 1,004 centrally on the books for the political groups, plus MEPs' own staff

- €186.6 million is spent paying for the MEPs' own staff

L'ART NOUVEAU

The EP has its own dedicated art collection. The author possesses the one known surviving copy of its illustrated catalogue, covering works collected between 1980 (when it was begun) and 1994.

Here are some tasters of the pieces in the catalogue:

Personaggio. A man with a hat covering, or perhaps slapping, his face

Passagio di Buci. Psychedelic landscape

Blackmagic. Naked woman sits by an upturned vase of flowers, as a lightning bolt splits a neighbouring dog asunder

Untitled. Small heart with six dots

Sans titre. Giant sculpture, possibly of a pretzel

Skin with elegantly written text on leprosy. Text appears to be medical instructions for treatment

Il dolore (la ballerina). Generously endowed nude female at leaning crucifixion

Self portrait. Two hands holding a brain

Rural electrification, Glencullen. Countryside with electricity pole

Dark Green painting. Uniform broken white lines on green background

Union 2. Blurry sperm

Le prophète. Sculpture of a walnut on a pedestal in a hand shake

Untitled (Swarm of flies/Hole in ground). A post hole; no flies visible

The Convert. Man up tree with a saw

Expert tease. Man on stage hidden by spotlight beam

Parmi les fleurs, ma préférée. Attractive redhead in transparent shirt amongst lilies

Blue exercise. Andy Warhol style image of a lady's intimates

Oz prazeres da Alcamé. Six shapes seemingly felt tipped on brown paper bags

A group portrait of British Members. Huge wall depiction of all British MEPs from 1994, including Geoff Hoon

Medicijnkastje. Wall cupboard

The EP's art collection reportedly contained 363 purchased paintings and sculptures by 2010, including 59 bought specially in the wake of the latest wave of accessions. The budget for the Maltese works alone ran at €14,625. A review of all stock including gifted items now suggests a figure of around 550 pieces held.

The collection is managed by one of the Quaestors (there is no curator). In 2012 it underwent a six-week conservation review by outside consultants, part of a broader audit process understood to have cost €120,000.

The figures that began to emerge in early 2012 suggested that the €4.2 million insurance estimate for the collection was an undervaluation. The more valuable pieces have been taken off the walls. This is, after all, a building where the parliament's bank has been held up by robbers and an MEP used to travel the corridors on a bicycle.

The process for buying art for the collection:

★ Works are pre-selected by the European Parliament office in the country in question, assisted by an art enthusiast

★ If the purchase is to commemorate an EU accession, the budget runs at around €3,000 per MEP in that country

- ★ An artistic committee comprising one quaestor and two EP vice-presidents submits the proposed art to the College of Quaestors
- ★ The Quaestors make a recommendation to the President of Parliament
- ★ The President decides

The inner workings of the EP have come under frequent criticism, not just in terms of occasional dispute over partiality from the Chair (the institution is overwhelmingly integrationist), but more particularly through its funding. As recently as November 2011, and despite changes to the system, the Court of Auditors found that payments to visitors could still be made that were higher than the actual cost of group travel; that big cash payments up to €55,236 were being regularly made in bloc transactions that might encourage fraudulent claims; and that €2.36 million was overpaid to political groups.

It seems likely that funding will continue to remain under the public spotlight. This is particularly the case with respect to prestige spending. Public money has for some time been used to support EP archives, with €400,000 have been spent to date on cataloguing eleven former MEPs' archives. Former MEP President Simone Veil's documents also form part of this archive, ranging from a polite letter from Margaret Thatcher to a politically unwise condolence telegram sent from Veil on the death of Tito. As we shall see later, what was once a controversial Commission flaw in spending public money on selling the EU in vanity PR projects has now drawn in the EP as well.

WINNERS OF THE 2010 EUROPEAN PARLIAMENT'S CITIZENS' PRIZE

- ★ Jugendhilfsorganisation Schüler Helfen Leben
- ★ Międzynarodowy Festiwal Filmów Młodego Widza Ale Kino!
- ★ Ing. Wolfgang NEUMANN
- ★ Union européenne des étudiants juifs
- ★ Csaba BÖJTE

- ★ Lothar CZOSSEK

- ★ Fate VELAJ

- ★ Elżbieta LECH-GOTTHARD

- ★ Carlo PETRINI

- ★ Inicjatywa Wolna Białoruś
- ★ Fundacja Świętego Mikołaja

- ★ Open Society Foundations

- ★ Stowarzyszenie „Jeden Świat"

- ★ Europ'age Saar-Lor-Lux e.V

- ★ Sermig-Servizio Missionario Giovani

- ★ Europees Grenslanden Vrouwenvoetbal Toernooi

- ★ Stowarzyszenie Lednica 2000EN C 115/2 Official Journal of the European Union 13.4.2011

- ★ Chris DELICATA

- ★ Enrico PIERI

- ★ Jacques GROFFEN

- ★ Beneluxliga handbal

- ★ ΙΝΣΤΙΤΟΥΤΟ ΟΔΙΚΗΣ ΑΣΦΑΛΕΙΑΣ «ΠΑΝΟΣ ΜΥΛΩΝΑΣ»

- ★ Smaranda ENACHE

- ★ EYV 2011 Alliance

- ★ Fondazione Banco Alimentare

- ★ Polska Fundacja im. Roberta Schumana

- ★ Zsuzsa FERGE

- ★ Hans BIENFAIT

- ★ Marek SOŁTYS

NOT THE TOUGHEST...

SANCTIONS AVAILABLE AGAINST REGISTERED LOBBYIST PASSHOLDERS WHO BREACH THE CODE OF ETHICS

Type of non-compliance 1: Unintentional non-compliance, immediately corrected

★ Measure: Written notification acknowledging the facts and their correction

★ Mention of measure in the register: No

★ EP access badge withdrawn: No

Type of non-compliance 2: Deliberate non-compliance with the code, necessitating a change of behaviour or rectification of information in the register within the deadline laid down

★ Measure: Temporary suspension for up to six months or until such time as the corrective action requested is completed within the deadline set

★ Mention of measure in the register: Yes, during the suspension period

★ EP access badge withdrawn: No

Type of non-compliance 3: Persistent non-compliance with the code (no change of behaviour, failure to correct information within the deadline laid down)

★ Measure: Removal from the register for one year

★ Mention of measure in the register: Yes

★ EP access badge withdrawn: Yes

Type of non-compliance 4: Serious, deliberate non-compliance with the code

★ Measure: Removal from the register for two years

★ Mention of measure in the register: Yes

★ EP access badge withdrawn: Yes

EXAMPLES OF BREACHES

★ Failure to declare interests

★ Attempted blackmail or inducement

★ Misrepresenting their role/influence within the EU

★ Selling documents obtained

★ Encouraging employees to break the rules or contravene standards of behaviour

★ Pushing employees who used to work within the EU to breach confidentialities

How do these institutions fit together in reaching decisions and making laws?

In a nutshell...

The Commission proposes, the Council barters and consents, MEPs try to amend.

The way EU laws are made has changed considerably over the past six decades and indeed several different systems have been used simultaneously in the past allowing different rights to different parties at different times. A review of the history of, for instance, the co-decision process falls outside the scope of this book (thankfully, since the official summary of that process as it currently stands runs at 52 pages alone, with a page-sized flow chart – and that only relates to one phase of the law-making process). [An insomniac reader can find out more by reading *How EU Laws are Made*, by this author, published on the Bruges Group website.]

At the risk of over-simplifying, we can say that the Commission is responsible for drafting the proposals; national civil servants then negotiate changes on behalf of national governments at Council level; the European Parliament then puts in its own amendments based on party politics; the Council and EP then deal over those changes; the resulting document gets printed in the *Official Journal* and becomes European law; national legislatures are then expected to pass that into domestic law; and the Commission ensures that the EU law is both enacted and enforced.

A key aspect in recent years has been the increased role of MEPs, whose former advisory position has expanded in many areas to something akin to equality with the Council and has led to the establishment of a special conciliation committee. 27 MEPs and three Vice-Presidents are part of this grouping, negotiating directly with national civil servants and Commission delegates.

A direct level of input from people carrying a democratic mandate is seen by some as a positive aspect to the process. This is not universally felt. Some understandably question the mega-mandate that MEPs on the committee carry, both as being elected on the list system earlier referenced, and then as only 5% of the whole EP. More cuttingly, critics point to the voting process in the European Parliament itself.

Moreover, the EP is divided into large voting blocs, voting on huge numbers of amendments put forward back to back, with no individual debate but limited allocated and general time for set speeches running to perhaps a minute a shot. The EP is a hemisphere rather than a confrontational parliament, which results in contributions that are predictable, staid, and typically read out without passion or insight. MEPs do not, generally, make great speeches, because the Chamber is not designed as the place for them. When they do, they tend to be on controversial subjects that set the place alight as much for the outraged reaction of the majority and the President as for anything actually said.

TAKING THE COMMISSION'S MATHS ON TRUST

NATIONAL IMPACT ASSESSMENTS (IAS) ON COMMISSION PROPOSALS: INTERNATIONAL 'GOOD PRACTICE' AS VIEWED BY THE COURT OF AUDITORS (2010)

"The United Kingdom carries out national IAs on significant Commission initiatives to support the negotiating position of its Permanent Representation. It carries out its own IA, generally using data related to the United Kingdom, and thereby challenges the analysis provided in the Commission's IA. In Germany, the Bundestag has introduced a requirement to assess the implications of proposed EU legislation, but in actual fact this has not yet been implemented. In Poland, the authorities also have the mandate to prepare a national IA in the event of a significant legislative proposal, but this has not yet resulted in a formal IA."

The auditors noted an occasional tendency in the Commission to proceed with projects before the impact assessment had been made. Meanwhile, a Council working group found one-third of IAs lacked a summary, were not available in the relevant language or used excessive jargon, while half had issues relating to their length.

HOW DOES PARTY POLITICS FIT IN?

In a nutshell...

Party Politics is a significant permanent factor in the European Parliament, but also sets the agenda for the Council and therefore for the Commission which is tasked to implement policy.

Since MEPs are elected on the basis of their political allegiance, it should come as absolutely no surprise that party politics is a central element of the EP. However, parties there do not stay as isolated elements, but group together based on ideology. For some years, this has meant the existence of two main groups and several smaller ones in orbit.

On the Centre Right (although it sees itself as simply Centre) is the European Peoples Party, or EPP, bringing together the Christian Democrat parties. On the Centre Left is the Party of European Socialists, or PES. There is also a Liberal grouping, a Green grouping, a Marxist-Green grouping, at least two EU-critical groupings at any one moment in time and the Non-aligned members who come together just on administrative grounds. Attempts to form an anti-immigrant grouping have failed to reach the required threshold of supporters, partly because the threshold was set to exclude them.

Some figures may help explain how seriously these groups are taken as a means to stimulate a common European identity:

★ €54.8 million is set aside for the groups' political and information activities

★ €17.4 million is granted to finance them

★ €11.4 million funds their think tanks

★ Funds are based on share of vote. Since MEPs in Brussels are predominantly in favour of having more powers at Brussels, these are the campaigns and the political think tanks that get the most money

DRAWING A MAP OF POLITICAL AFFILIATION

Visualise a line on which MEP groups sit. If we imagine that this chart has a political axis running right and left and representing their political radicalism, the three largest of these groups (EPP, PES and Liberals) are clustered very closely in the middle.

However, there is another dimension at play. On that same chart we can put another axis running up and down. This is the integrationist axis, indicating where the groups stand on European integration. On this axis the same big groups hover closely together on the more radically pro-EU level. But, in addition, there have traditionally been at least two separate groups standing apart from this political cluster, along with the Marxist-Greens who are often quite critical of what they view as corporate wheeler-dealing. These define themselves more along the grounds of their position on what Brussels should be doing and distinguish themselves more along the vertical sovereignty axis. It is often here that the real political divide, and debate, takes place.

The Conservative MEPs have long been at odds with their MEP colleagues in the EPP. Despite having somehow managed to despatch their more neo-Heathite elements to Brussels, by the late 1990s surveys were showing Conservative voting patterns diverging from EPP lines by one vote in three. This divergence could only grow as, unlike MEPs in Labour, representatives increasingly came to represent the more EU-critical opinions of their grass roots. After a long campaign by people aware of the disparities at play, the Conservative MEPs finally split with the EPP and formed a distinct Eurosceptical group along with other centre right parties that were not at home with the particulars of the Christian Democrat political tradition.

What that means is that MEP politics is not simply a question of Right and Left; given the amount of coffee morning backdoor deal-making that used to go on between the EPP and PES (and still does to some extent), that division was often notional. The existence of distinct Eurocritical groups increasingly means arguing not just about the level of decibels on a lawnmower but whether a law needs to be made about it in the first place.

The Eurocritical parties, however, remain a minority in a body that is institutionally integrationist. The increasing role of the European Parliament does not, taken as a whole, lend itself in support of countries who seek to develop or maintain loose ties based on motives of free trade and friendship rather than the drive towards union. This is another factor in any assessment of what countries get out of the EU – regardless of whether the Right or the Left predominate after elections, MEPs are not a brake to a bigger Europe.

In the Council, the party politics is often less on show. Ministers obviously come from parties and represent governments that have been formed after an election. Coalitions can often complicate matters by bending or breaking manifesto commitments. But we can make two general observations here.

In the first instance, the EU's agendas can be determined by the colour of governments and not simply by basic national perspectives. An example is the emphasis on the development of the Single Market when Thatcher and Kohl were in power at a time when the Centre Right was doing relatively well across the Community.

The second point relates directly to that example, because that policy drive happened despite Mitterand being President in France. While he saw that programme as a thing of London and Berlin, and he himself was a Socialist and a French Socialist to boot, he also saw it as a mechanism to push for more of a social programme in its wake, and a mechanism for closer co-operation with Germany on monetary policy. In sum, ideological political forces do push policy, and direct the Commission's energies and priorities as a result. New Labour's interest in Social Policy generated policy movement at Brussels that would have been impossible a decade before. But the politics of Right and Left slot into a bigger mosaic of the politics of European integration. It is an aspect that tends to get overlooked by political leaders when they explain which vetoes they have surrendered in new European treaties.

How do these institutions defend national interests?

In a nutshell...

With the reduction in the ability of countries to deploy the national veto, delegates at the Council and at the European Parliament are obliged to try to form alliances from a very low voting starting point.

The days when a country could emulate de Gaulle and stymie measures by empty-chairing (i.e. not showing up) at the Council of Ministers are over. John Major's government had a hard time trying it over the BSE crisis and that was before several treaties ended more national vetoes. While it is difficult to compare one lost veto in terms of its importance and value compared with another, the numbers themselves are indicative of the trend.

THE COUNCIL
NUMBER OF NATIONAL VETOES REMOVED BY TREATY

Treaty of Rome plus related extensions	**38** articles
Single European Act	**12** articles
Maastricht	**30** articles
Amsterdam	**24** articles
Nice	**46** articles
European Constitution	**63** articles
	(**68** in the final Treaty of Lisbon)

On top of this, the treaties themselves have since been adapted to prevent any repeat attempts. In many areas, go-ahead states can set up their own action groups to circumvent obstructionism. The treaties ironically also now establish an inverse empty chair after a fashion, in that member states which are in breach of human rights principles can have their voting rights removed.

This shift is important when you consider the voting strength of governments under the Qualified Majority Voting (QMV) system itself.

COUNCIL VOTES HELD BY MEMBER STATES

France, Germany, Italy, United Kingdom	**29**
Poland, Spain	**27**
Romania	**14**
Netherlands	**13**
Belgium, Czech Republic, Greece, Hungary, Portugal	**12**
Austria, Bulgaria, Sweden	**10**
Denmark, Finland, Ireland, Lithuania, Slovakia	**7**
Cyprus, Estonia, Latvia, Luxembourg, Slovenia	**4**
Malta	**3**
Total	**345**

Currently, a qualified majority is reached if a majority of member states approve (in some instances a two-thirds majority) and if at least 255 votes are cast in favour of the proposal. A blocking minority in this instance would be 91. A new system is being phased in over 2014-2017 however. Decisions will need the support of 55% of member states (15 out of 27 EU countries) representing a minimum of 65% of the EU's population. However, on the other side a blocking minority must also comprise at least four member states, which means that highly contentious material opposed by three of the big countries could be forced through.

THE EUROPEAN PARLIAMENT

Clearly, no national vetoes apply at the European Parliament. Council voting strengths are weighted to weaken big state strengths to the benefit of the smaller states. The discrepancy also exists at the European Parliament, though Germany has been compensated with more MEPs since reunification.

NUMBER OF MEPS BY MEMBER STATES (PRE-CHANGES)

State	Number of MEPs
Germany	99
France, Italy, UK	72
Poland, Spain	50
Romania	33
Netherlands	25
Belgium, Czech Republic, Greece, Hungary, Portugal	22
Sweden	18
Austria, Bulgaria	17
Denmark, Finland, Slovakia	13
Ireland, Lithuania	12
Latvia	8
Slovenia	7
Cyprus, Estonia, Luxembourg	6
Malta	5
Total	**736**

(Note that the number of MEPs is in the process of a drawn-out transition that has seen 'ghost Members' and 'temporary Members', with Malta for instance ultimately gaining one seat and Germany losing three.)

Even were the MEPs of a major country such as the UK to drop all party partisanship and unite on an issue of perceived national interest, they would only muster less than 10% of the vote – far short of any majority – and blocking minorities do not exist in that institution.

THE COMMISSION

National mathematics works in a different way in the Commission. We referred earlier to significant discrepancies in that institution, with British nationals making up half the number of staff they should do if recruitment were based on the UK's national share of European population. While at the very top grade Britain is well represented, that advantage slips away rapidly as you review the nationalities holding key posts in sensitive Directorates-General (DGs).

British personnel are proportionately considerably underrepresented in Economic affairs (18/543 staff, 3.3%); Competition (25/743, 3.4%); Employment (17/577, 2.9%); and Budget (13/410, 3.1%). Administrative sectors are considerably undermanned, with no staff at all in infrastructure work in Luxembourg. Far more serious is the level of UK manning in big-spending Agriculture (20/965, 2.1%), and Taxation and Customs (11/437, 0.9%).

This compares with an average of 4.8% to the UK as a whole, which is itself less than half pro rata what the UK representation should be. The UK does better at media work, probably due to the staff being native English speakers.

Belgium does best, which is perhaps not so surprising given it is the leading host nation – its nationals make up just short of one staffer in five. France supplies 9.9%, Germany 8.3% and Italy 10.1%.

Commission staff are supposed to leave national interests at the door. Even if they do – and anecdotally there are masses of examples to indicate that they don't – officials come from traditions and, as with any human being, come with preconceptions.

Belgian domination apart, the straight fact that there are clusters of national staff in certain parts of the Commission points clearly to national interests and priorities being fostered. Germany has a large presence in the Secretariat-General supporting the College of Commissioners. France is visible in Enterprise and Industry. Germany, France and Poland have numbers in Competition. Spain, Italy and France are in Agriculture in force. France, Italy and Germany have numbers in research areas. Spain is strong in fisheries and in regional aid. France, Spain and Italy have a significant showing amongst staff in international development.

These trends indicate why policies may emerge that tend to favour some countries over others (whether intentionally, or via inherent starting viewpoints). They also suggest continuing areas of gain for these countries that we may care to factor in later on, when considering why these countries still see positives emerging from EU membership.

So, with respect to the Council, countries that share common interest with a large number of member states in areas of economic debate, coupled with a strong diplomatic service, have considerable potential. This, as well as vested self-interest, is why the EU system appeals to the FCO. However, the institutions taken as a whole, both in terms of their composition as well as in the way they operate, more broadly serve the purpose of the integrationists. The reality of where power increasingly lies, meanwhile, has not been lost to the world community. The list of approved third-party diplomats to the EU currently runs to 244 pages.

The European Court of Justice (ECJ)

In a nutshell...

The ECJ is the guardian of the EU treaties and laws and arbiter of its institutions.

The ECJ (not to be confused with the European Court of Human Rights, or ECHR – a Council of Europe institution) is made up of one judge per EU country and eight Advocates-General. Its role is to review the legality of the acts of the EU institutions, ensure member states follow treaty obligations and interpret EU law when national courts refer it to them for clarification. Of the 619 new cases put before it in 2010, one in ten related to taxation, another tenth to the environment, with other significant proportions in areas relating to the Area of Freedom Security and Justice, Single Market freedoms, social policy and areas involving copyright. One in a hundred had a declared relevance to fighting fraud. The top six sinning states by far for new cases brought against it for breach of EU law are Greece, Italy, Spain, Portugal, Luxembourg (surprisingly) and Belgium, each averaging 15-20 cases a year over the past half decade (Britain averages around 3 or 4, about a third of France's).

A special tribunal sits apart to rule on disputes involving the EU civil service.

THE ECJ AT WORK

Up until 2010, the Court had been involved in 8601 "Direct Actions" (against institutions or member states), had been asked to supply 7005 Preliminary Rulings and provided 1118 appeals.

British courts had requested input on 505 occasions to judge the compatibility of their views with Community law – this number of requests is second only to the member states that had been in the Club since the beginning.

40 of these requests for review came from the House of Lords, 64 from the Court of Appeal and the balance came from other lower courts or tribunals,

demonstrating the degree of influence that EU law now has in the domestic legal system. This is not so controversial when it is a matter of ensuring that one member state is not skewing the playing field in favour of its own businesses against fair competition; it becomes more contentious when Parliament's version of an EU law is being challenged.

The Court has increasingly been seen as much as a supporter of political integration as an agent for fair play in the marketplace. Infamously, in 2000, it used blasphemy precedent to determine whether a critic of the Commission could be legally fired for his (anti-EU) views he expressed.

SOME BUDGETARY BACKGROUND PROVIDES INSIGHT INTO THE SCALE OF THE INSTITUTION

★ Salaries and basic allowances for 2011 come to €22 million for the judges

★ Judges' pension costs come to €6.1 million

★ €284,000 is set aside for judges' 'missions'

★ €300,000 is assigned for language and similar forms of training for them

★ Salaries and allowances for their support staff run at €201 million – there are 1,954 staff

★ There is a further €731,000 set aside for overtime

★ €201,000 is budgeted for social contacts, such as clubs and sports

★ €75,000 supports a restaurant and cafeteria

★ €2.15 million helps fund the Early Childhood Centre and study centre in Luxembourg, where the Court is based

★ €1.5 million is spent on official vehicles

★ €209,000 is for representation and entertainment expenses

★ Loyal co-operation: the principle whereby national governments should do their utmost to turn EU legislation into the appropriate national law, rather than deliberately engineer loopholes that then get challenged by the ECJ

★ £514,111: amount the UK government spent at the ECJ in 2009/9 in legal fees

The European Central Bank (ECB)

In a nutshell...

 The ECB is the central hub of the national central banks of the eurozone.

The ECB is the standing core of the eurozone system. Its governing council comprises the seventeen national central bank governors, plus six ECB members, whose main task is to keep inflation under a rate of 2% and therefore keep price rises under control. It also tries to support the growth of the EU economies in the process.

SOME FACTS TO PUT FLESH ON THE ABSTRACTS

★ As at 2010, the ECB employed 1,607 staff. On average, 235 staff telework each month

★ Staff costs ran at €167.7 million

★ ECB employees come from all member states and not just the eurozone

★ The President has an official residence, owned by the ECB

★ The President's salary in 2010 was €367,863. Together, the Executive Board's salary ran to €1.7 million.

★ An extra €660,000 went into the board's medical and accident insurance schemes, with another €35,000 continuing to be paid into schemes for past members

★ Academic sponsorships of up to €100,000 per year for up to three years are available for work on themes of interest to the bank

★ At the end of 2010, there were 14.2 billion euro banknotes in circulation, with a face value of €839.7 billion – an increased circulation on the previous year of 600 million notes (worth €33.4 billion)

- An estimated 20% to 25% of euro notes in circulation in value terms are used outside of the eurozone itself

- In 2010, euro coinage in circulation increased by 6.2%, to 92.9 billion coins

- The value of those coins ran at €22.3 billion

- 61% of euro coins are one, two and five cent pieces

- It was only in 2011 that the legislation relating to euro coins was changed to recognise the fact that the technical specifications of euro coins were significantly different from the actual size of the coins which had been in circulation for the previous decade. In some cases the thicknesses of the actual coins were 20% out

- In 2010 national central banks handed out 33.6 billion new notes in exchange for 33.1 billion old ones. Higher value notes tend to get hoarded – €500 notes are seen in banks thirteen times less frequently than €10 notes

- The euro notes are backed up. The ECB for instance held 16,122,143 ounces of gold in 2010 – whose value rose over the course of the year

- €752,000 counterfeit banknotes were received by the bank in 2010, 43% being €50 and 40% €20 notes

- The ECB in 2011 issued a decision setting out the environmental and health and safety legal framework for the production of euro banknotes, running to seven pages. Manufacturers now need ECB accreditation for both

- Someone in the Commission has been watching *The Italian Job*. The first regulations covering transport of euro banknotes were agreed in November 2011. These allowed armoured vehicles and bullet proof vests. To discourage poorly planned bank jobs, vehicles carrying just coins would have huge pictograms painted on the side explaining this. Weapons could be carried by guards, though these would be stashed with control-centre locking for countries where arms were forbidden.

- In 2010, the ECB organised 15 training/briefing visits for journalists and hosted 13,000 visitors

- Non-eurozone countries have an assigned share of capital to subscribe; if they remain out, a portion of this is still paid up. In the UK's case, that would be 14.5% of the total or €1.56 billion. As at 2010, the UK was contributing €58,580,454

★ Work has begun on new ECB buildings; an entrance building, a remodelled Grossmarkthalle and a spiralled tower. The Grossmarkthalle is a listed fruit and veg building from the 1920s. Around 4,000 tonnes of steel was needed to reinforce the tower.

SOME COMMEMORATIVE €2 COINS

2011

200th anniversary of the Bank of Finland; the wedding of Prince Albert and Charlene Wittstock; 30th anniversary of the Day of Music; the 500th anniversary of the publication of *Laus Stultitiae* by Erasmus; 50th anniversary of the appointment by the Grand-Duchess Charlotte of her son Jean as *lieutenant-représentant*; 20th anniversary of the formation of the Visegrad Group; Court of the Lions, Granada – UNESCO World Heritage series; 100th anniversary of the birth of partisan Franc Rozman-Stane; Federal state of North Rhine-Westphalia; first election of Maltese representatives in 1849; 100th anniversary of International Women's Day; 500th anniversary of Fernão Mendes Pinto's birth; 500th anniversary of the birth of Giorgio Vasari; The 150th anniversary of the unification of Italy; The Special Olympics World Summer Games – Athens 2011

2010

Córdoba's historic centre – UNESCO World Heritage series; coat of arms of the Grand Duke of Luxembourg; 200th anniversary of the Botanical Garden in Ljubljana; Federal state of Bremen; 70th anniversary of the Appeal by de Gaulle of June 18; 200th anniversary of the Count of Cavour's birth; 100th anniversary of the Portuguese Republic; Belgian Presidency of the Council of the European Union in 2010; 2,500th anniversary of the Battle of Marathon; 500th anniversary of the death of Sandro Botticelli; Year for Priests; Currency Decree of 1860 granting Finland the right to issue banknotes and coins

200th anniversary of Finnish autonomy and Porvoo Diet; 200th anniversary of Louis Braille's birth; International Year of Astronomy; 20th anniversary of 17 November 1989; 2nd Lusophone Games; Federal state of Saarland; European Year of Creativity and Innovation; 10th anniversary of Economic and Monetary Union; Grand-Duke Henri and Grand-Duchess Charlotte

The ten guiding principles of the European project

In a nutshell...

We can identify ten rules that define how the EU works. It requires constancy of integration, trust in the elite and deal making.

1. A EUROPE OF PRESIDENCIES

There is a permanent President of the European Council (as at early 2012 this is Herman van Rompuy) and a rotating President of the Council of the European Union; there is a President of the European Parliament; there is a President of the European Commission (Barroso in early 2012); there is a President of the European Court of Justice; there is a President of the Euro Group and probably a President for the new eurozone working group; there is a President of the European Economic and Social Committee, and a President of the Committee of the Regions; there is a President of the Court of Auditors and a President for the ECB.

2. DITCHING THE ACQUIS MEANS DEFEAT

The *acquis communautaire* is the sum of all the legislation in force. Even deliberate attempts by Commissioners to cut back on it have only weeded out

the odd document relating to East Germany. Best estimates suggest the acquis now runs at 110,000 pages.

3. BY CONSENSUS AND BY CONVENTIONS

Votes indicate dissent and disagreement, and encourage grandstanding to electorates: it is better to reach an understanding. Conventions are a useful tool to legitimise this, bringing together unelected delegates to provide a veneer of accountability.

4. QMV IS THE GOAL

Power accumulated should not be returned. By removing national vetoes more widely, a Europe of Compromises is born.

5. POPULAR MEANS POPULISM

Appeals over the heads of the Brussels nomenklatura direct to the people are a form of devilish demagoguery. Eurosceptic appeals by politicians evoke the spirit of the 1930s.

6. EVER-CLOSER UNION IS THE GOAL

The long-term aim is a country called Europe and this is the great yardstick for the ideologues. Stoppages can be circumvented over time. [For instance, attempts to make North Sea oil and gas an EU competence were defeated repeatedly in the 1990s and featured as a surprise power grab attempt at the end of the EU Constitution. A different approach followed. In January 2012 an EU Offshore Oil and Gas Authorities Group was set up. Since there is no treaty base, Health and Safety was used. A similar example was in the Commission/Council using Health and Safety to get round the UK opt out from the Social Chapter with respect to the Working Time Directive.]

7. EUROPE NEEDS A NATIONAL IDENTITY

From passports to anthems and flags, the EU needs to acquire the trappings of a sovereign state.

8. COMITOLOGY IS THE MAGIC INGREDIENT

The key decisions should be made in committees and in secret, before journalists and politicians have a chance to interfere.

9. ALL MUST HAVE PRIZES

The rewards should be shared out equitably across its member states, even if it means duplication of effort. Only trusted integrationists can be let loose to run things.

10. BRUSSELS TALKING TO BRUSSELS

There is nothing wrong with the EU subsidising pro-EU groups to offer it advice and justify its activism.

★ ★ ★ ★ ★ ★ ★ ★ ★ ★ ★ ★

SYMBOLS OF NATION STATE IDENTITY POSSESSED BY THE EU

Passport; national identity; anthem; flag; taxes; police college; Supreme Court, and Court of First Instance; regional aid; universities; diplomats; Declaration of Human Rights (Charter); propaganda agency; Central Bank; diplomatic immunity; national holiday; R&D agency; patents office; patron saints (pending post-canonisation process of the Founding Fathers); designated army, navy and air force; police agency (Europol); external borders; president; military HQ; auditors; fraud agency; Cabinet; capital city (shared); development aid; press training college; passport-free internal travel area; buildings with armed security (sniper rifles and SMGs); fisheries waters; agriculture policy; budget; Parliament; intelligence system (Schengen et al); independent civil service; Foreign Minister; currency; nuclear agency; constitution (presently, the Treaties); ombudsman; libraries; embassies; viceroys; Zollverein; Oath of Allegiance; museum; classified document caveats; TV station; supremacy of Community law; UN presence

WHAT ARE THE WORKING GROUPS?

The Commission has an online database of (most of) the expert groups formed for consultation purposes. You can find the list at:

ec.europa.eu/transparency/regexpert/search.cfm?page=search&resetValues=1

Some groups currently on the register

★ Groupe d'experts information et communication dans le domaine agricole (**E01858**)

★ Classification of Beef carcasses (**E00128**)

★ European Group on Ethics in Science and New Technologies (High Level) (**E01566**)

★ Ad Hoc Expert Group for Forest Law Enforcement, Governance and Trade (**E01677**)

★ European Tropical Forest Advisers Group (**E01586**)

★ Member States' Expert Group on Water (**E01610**)

★ Member States' Gender Experts (**E01607**)

★ Mint Directors Working Group (**E00262**)

★ European Heritage Label (**E02229**)

★ National Bankruptcy Coordinators (**E02286**)

★ Climate Broadcasters Network Europe – Core Group (**E01985**)

★ Counterfeit Coin Experts Group (**E00658**)

★ Groupe d'experts "Eaux minérales Naturelles" (**E01502**)

★ Cinema Expert Group (**E01372**)

- Contact Network of Spam Enforcement Authorities (CNSA) (**E01382**)
- Internet of Things Expert Group (**E02514**)
- Group of Experts on Banking Issues (**E02412**)
- Technical Advisory Group on the integration of maritime surveillance (TAG) (**E02518**)
- High Level Group on gender mainstreaming (**E01240**)
- Network of national gender equality bodies (**X01883**)
- Weight and dimensions of certain road vehicles (**E01068**)
- Informal expert group on simplification (**E02257**)
- The World and Europe up to 2050: EU policies and research priorities (**E02398**)
- High Level National Expert Group on Better Regulation (**E01537**)
- Pool of Trainers for eForms in Direct Taxation (**E02575**)
- Linguistic Network of Excellence for Institutional Romanian (**E02521**)
- Slovak Terminology Network (**E02056**)
- Expert group dialogue on the use of sex as an actuarial factor (Directive 2004/113) (**E02273**)

10

Number of slots made available on the Stakeholder Dialogue Group in the Areas of Public Health and Consumer Protection, in 2009

36

Number of days people had to submit the paperwork – provided they first spotted the notice in the *Official Journal*

56

Number of applications received from across Europe

The pool of campaign groups and bodies lobbying and providing advice to the Commission is also now a matter of public record:
europa.eu/transparency-register

The list includes:

★ Academy Of Universal Global Peace
★ Action for Teens
★ Association Générale des Producteurs de Blé et autres cereals
★ Association of European Storage Battery Manufacturers
★ Association Royale belge des industries du biscuit, du chocolat, de la confiserie et de la praline
★ Buglife – The Invertebrate Conservation Trust
★ Central Bedfordshire Canine Trust
★ Conseil Européen des Podologues
★ Energy Efficient Buildings Association
★ Estonian Monarchist League
★ Euroclio, the European Association of History Educators
★ Eurogypsum
★ Europa Esperanto-Unio
★ EUROPARC Federation
★ European Association for the Study of the Liver
★ European Barge Union
★ European Composer and Songwriter Alliance
★ European Dignity Watch
★ European Federation of Older Students at Universities
★ European Federation of Road Traffic Victims
★ European Fire Sprinkler Network
★ European Fishing Tackle Trade Association
★ European Flavour Association
★ European Geothermal Energy Council
★ European Heating Oil Association
★ European Ice Cream Association
★ European Intelligent Cash Protection Association
★ European Lamp Companies Federation

- ★ European Large Families Confederation
- ★ European Lift Components Association
- ★ European Lobbying of Grape musts and Juices Producers
- ★ European Network for Smoking and Tobacco Prevention
- ★ European Organisation of the Sawmill Industry
- ★ European Pet Network
- ★ European Plastic Window Association
- ★ European Portable Battery Association
- ★ European Smokeless Tobacco Council
- ★ European Snacks Association
- ★ European Squirrel Initiative
- ★ European Union of the Potato Trade
- ★ European Wax Federation
- ★ European Women's Lobby
- ★ Europe Jazz Network
- ★ Fédération Française des Tuiles et Briques
- ★ Federation of Western Thrace Turks in Europe
- ★ Friends of the Supergrid
- ★ FRUCOM – European Federation of the Trade in Dried Fruit, Edible Nuts, Processed Fruit & Vegetables, Processed Fishery Products, Spices and Honey
- ★ International Federation of Actors
- ★ International Geo-plutonic Energy Association
- ★ International Margarine Association of the Countries of Europe
- ★ International Rainwater Harvesting Alliance
- ★ Movement for Rural Emancipation
- ★ Ornamental Fish International
- ★ Ordre Maçonnique International "Delphi"
- ★ Patagonia Bioenergia
- ★ Quaker Council for European Affairs
- ★ Reindeer Herder´s Association
- ★ Shark Alliance (EU)
- ★ Union of European Federalists
- ★ United European Tattoo Artists
- ★ United Nations Of Indians

* Women in Europe for a Common Future
* World Apple and Pear Association
* World Association of Zoos and Aquariums
* World Uyghur Congress
* Young European Federalists
* Numerous universities
* Three Oxfams
* At least eight organisations claiming to represent the Order of the Knights Templar

Actual weight of influence will naturally vary from group to group.

The lobbyists are also jointly represented by their lobby group, the Association of Accredited Lobbyists to the European Union, which lobbies for their lobbying interests

THE EUROPEAN CANDLE ASSOCIATION

The ECA is one of the lobbying groups cited on the list.

In 1845, celebrated free market economist Frédéric Bastiat penned a short letter from a spoof lobby group representing the Makers of Candles, Tapers, Lanterns, Sticks, Street Lamps, Snuffers, and Extinguishers, and from Producers of Tallow, Oil, Resin, Alcohol, and Generally of Everything Connected with Lighting.

The fake petition called for all houses to have their windows covered to stop unfair competition from the sun, and thus to boost trade from the candle industry and its supply industries. The consumer could go hang.

The example was used to show how barrier tariffs on competitive imports were equally illogical on protectionist grounds. Blocking imports of oranges because they were cheaper to grow in a sunnier clime than France would be as nonsensical as blocking steel or textiles which happen to be cheaper for other practical reasons.

In 2008, the EU imposed tariffs of 66% on Chinese candles.

GREAT EUROPEAN MISTAKES OF OUR TIME

Number One – The Commission opinion on Greek entry into the eurozone

> *The 1999 update of the Greek convergence programme restates the economic strategy with a view to the smooth entry for Greece into the euro-zone in 2001. The programme projects the government balance to turn into a surplus of 0.2% of GDP in 2002, while the level of the government debt should fall to below 100% of GDP in 2001. However, the cyclically adjusted budgetary balance suggests that medium-term budgetary adjustment will primarily proceed from the rapid reduction in interest payments, i.e. no additional discretionary adjustment is provided.*
>
> *"This points to the need to tackle structural challenges if the debt ratio is to decline at a faster pace. Firstly, the size of the public sector needs to be addressed, as reflected in the still high primary expenditure ratio which has not yet started to decline. Current primary expenditure is characterized by rather inflexible wages and grants, despite some progress made in improving their control with the implementation of laws adopted since 1997."*

European Economy; Public Finances in EMU 2000

Greece was accepted into the eurozone in 2000 on the basis of the Commission's audits. But in the absence of meaningful enduring reforms, a nigh-bankrupt Greek economy first plunged the eurozone into crisis in 2010.

GREAT EUROPEAN MISTAKES OF OUR TIME

Number Two – Estonian informed opinion on the need to join the eurozone

> *In the long term eurozone membership will create stability and inject trust in Estonia's economic environment. By gaining entry into the eurozone, approximately at the same time as OECD membership, Estonia will give a clear message – we have a strong economy worth investing in."*

Estonian Prime Minister Andrus Ansip, December 2009

Estonia joined the eurozone a year later, on midnight of New Year's Eve 2010 – during the Irish eurozone crisis and only months before the evidently looming Greek and Italian ones. The jury is still out on the long term, but in the short term practically the PM's first eurozone act was to agree to help bankroll other countries' bailouts.

GREAT EUROPEAN MISTAKES OF OUR TIME
Number Three – "This country will face disaster if it says No"

The referendum on 28 November is about saying yes or no to 100,000 jobs."

Svein Aaser, President of the Norwegian CBI, and a backer of accession

A Statistics Norway survey showed that after the referendum, employment rose by 11,000 from third quarter 1994 to third quarter 1995. As at 30 October 2011, Norway had one of the lowest unemployment rates in Europe at 3.3%.

If Norway votes no, the border with Sweden will be our border to the EU. The price could be higher interest rates, the most expensive food in Europe and fewer jobs."

One-page advert from the Yes Campaign in the newspaper *Arbeiderbladet*, also on 28 November

Three days after the referendum, *Dagens Næringsliv* (a daily business newspaper) reported this picture:

The value of the Norwegian kroner has strengthened, the interest rate is falling and the stock exchange is sky rocketing. Most foreign interest rates rose yesterday but the Norwegian rate fell."

Source: Nei til EU

A recurring feature of the European debate is the appearance of businessmen with large interests at stake before the Commission, trying to gain influence by supporting integration and threatening disaster as the alternative. To the credit of the Commission officials dealing with Trade rather than PR, once the referendum is over, favours do not appear to be automatically returned.

GREAT EUROPEAN MISTAKES OF OUR TIME

Number Four – The urgent case for Britain joining the euro

> *If the decision is put off again, the international investment community will conclude – probably rightly – that New Labour hasn't simply got the bottle to face down the eurosceptics and that will have serious economic and political consequences."*
>
> John Monks, TUC Secretary General, December 2001

A number of trades union and business leaders shared platforms for many years, warning that if Britain did not join the euro it would be disastrous for the economy. Those threats did not materialise.

The CBI has an unhappy record of wrongheadedness, from its predecessor's role in appeasement, to its non-confrontational stance on the trades union in the 1970s.

Attempts today to track down quotes from former CBI leaders endorsing the euro run into an archive gap on the main CBI website, or trigger the response "An unexpected error occurs". The devastating 2011 paper by Peter Oborne and Frances Weaver, 'Guilty Men', revisiting such lost quotes therefore acts as a useful reminder of the occasional folly of lobbyists with interests at play.

GREAT EUROPEAN MISTAKES OF OUR TIME

Number Five – "No threat to British sovereignty or interests "

> *The commitment represents the voluntary undertaking of a sovereign state to observe policies which it has helped to form. There is no question of any erosion of essential national sovereignty; what is proposed is a sharing and an enlargement of individual national sovereignties in the general interest."*
>
> Government White Paper on EEC accession, 1971

Assurances such as these pepper the accession debates in the UK and elsewhere. Privately, however, ministers and FCO staff were meanwhile noting that national sovereignty in the middle to long term was inevitably to be lost in a wider area, and such items as a common currency were on the cards.

By hiding behind fuzzy definitions of what makes up *essential* losses of sovereignty, pro-EEC governments won the debate in the 1970s but have lost public trust and sympathy today.

GREAT EUROPEAN MISTAKES OF OUR TIME
Number Six – Eurostat reveals the true, hidden state of the Greek economy

> *Recently, the Greek budgetary statistics have undergone a very large revision. The government deficit for 2003, which was initially reported at 1.7% of GDP, stood at 4.6% of GDP after the September 2004 notification. The deficits notified to the Commission for 2000, 2001 and 2002 were also revised upwards by more than two percentage points of GDP. Such substantial increases resulted from earlier actions undertaken by Eurostat as well as initiative taken by the incoming Greek government in spring 2004 to launch a thorough fiscal audit."*

Report by Eurostat on the revision of the
Greek government deficit and debt figures, 2004

Eurostat's Report confirmed officially what was already privately acknowledged: eurozone entry criteria had been massaged to make debtor states politically acceptable. In Greece's case, a large portion of this was hidden debt arising from classified military expenditure. But as Eurostat observed, "Data revisions of such a scale have given rise to questions about the reliability of the Greek statistics on public finances." The markets would inevitably catch up.

P(A)RT THREE

Policies and their Masters

MAY CONTAIN TRACES OF COMMISSIONERS, MONETARY UNION AND COPYRIGHTED CABBAGE

Who does what within the Commission?

In a nutshell...

The Commission plays the part of the legislative motor. This is broken down by Directorates-General (DGs), headed by a Commissioner, which mimic government departments. These may vary over time and depending on how many Commissioners need to be accommodated (one per country, historically).

IN 2012 THE DGS ARE AS FOLLOWS:

(THIS LIST ACTS AS A KEY TO THE ABBREVIATIONS IN THE CHAPTER.)

★ Agriculture and Rural Development (AGRI)

★ Budget (BUDG)

★ Climate Action (CLIMA)

★ Communication (COMM)

★ Competition (COMP)

★ Economic and Financial Affairs (ECFIN)

★ Education and Culture (EAC)

★ Employment, Social Affairs and Inclusion (EMPL)

★ Energy (ENER)

★ Enlargement (ELARG)

★ Enterprise and Industry (ENTR)

★ Environment (ENV)

★ EuropeAid Development and Cooperation (DEVCO)

★ Eurostat (ESTAT)

★ Health and Consumers (SANCO)

- ★ Home Affairs (HOME)
- ★ Humanitarian Aid (ECHO)
- ★ Human Resources and Security (HR)
- ★ Informatics (DIGIT)
- ★ Information Society and Media (INFSO)
- ★ Internal Market and Services (MARKT)
- ★ Interpretation (SCIC)
- ★ Joint Research Centre (JRC)
- ★ Justice (JUST)
- ★ Maritime Affairs and Fisheries (MARE)
- ★ Mobility and Transport (MOVE)
- ★ Regional Policy (REGIO)
- ★ Research and Innovation (RTD)
- ★ Secretariat-General (SG)
- ★ Taxation and Customs Union (TAXUD)
- ★ Trade (TRADE)
- ★ Translation (DGT)

The External Action Service is a hybrid of the Commission and the Council.

DG AGRI

TASKS OF DG AGRI

- ★ Promote a viable and competitive agricultural sector which respects high environmental and production standards, ensuring at the same time a fair standard of living for the agricultural community
- ★ Contribute to sustainable development of rural areas
- ★ Promote the European agricultural sector in world trade

18%

Amount of CAP payments not judged to be cross-compliant to these various objectives

18%

Percentage of staff unaware of the unit's objectives set out in the management plan, with 30% stating they were partially aware

DG AGRI has a staff of around 1,000 operating in 13 Directorates

The DG spends money on programmes designed to explain the Common Agricultural Policy.

Programmes backed in 2010 included:

★ Committee of Professional Agricultural Organisations in the European Union (Belgium): The Common Agricultural Policy post-2013: a fair and stable income for farmers (€94,140.55)

★ Strategma Agency (Bulgaria): CAP for youths (€83,513,40)

★ Passion céréales, une culture à partager (France): Realisation and diffusion of a teaching tool for French colleges and schools in order to explain and inform about CAP (€97,750)

★ Chambre d'agriculture des Pyrénées Orientales (France): Fruits, vegetables and young people: how to explain the CAP to children? (€32,975)

★ There were 35 grants awarded in 2010, for €2.7 million

-2%

Change in level of public awareness about the existence of the CAP between 2007 and 2009 (down to 41% of the public who had heard of it)

6%

Share of population of EU countries today employed in agriculture, hunting and fishing

60%

Share of population living in what are classed as rural areas

90%

Amount of territory judged to be rural

STRATEGIC MESSAGES FROM THE COMMISSION'S CAP INFORMATION CAMPAIGN

★ *The CAP needs a reform to help the agricultural sector and to make the CAP more efficient, effective, simple, and more equitable.*

★ *All citizens will benefit from food security, better environment and actions to fight climate change.*

★ *Farmers and rural areas will benefit*

★ *The CAP is a common policy and should continue to be funded from the EU budget.*

★ *The CAP is ensuring a level playing field*

★ *DG AGRI ambassadors are called upon to give presentations in various conferences, events and to visit schools and universities, raising awareness and understanding on agricultural and CAP related issues.*

AUTHORISED SLOGANS FOR THE CAP INFORMATION BUDGET

Agriculture, the taste of life

The CAP: looking ahead

The CAP: a policy that affects us all

The CAP: at the heart of our lives

The CAP: preserving our rural communities

The CAP: preserving our environment and biodiversity

The CAP: promoting growth and jobs in rural areas

The CAP: for sustainable development

Know your food, know where it comes from

EU food: quality products

€20,000-€300,000

Grant available per scheme

9%

Average household's spending on food in Luxembourg

44%

Average household's spending on food in Romania

BUTTER MOUNTAINS

The infamous food mountains and wine lakes have not disappeared entirely. Foothills and lagoons still remain. In 2010, these stood at:

Cereals	**4.53** million tonnes (MT)
Alcohol	**62,103** hectolitres (HL)
Butter	**1,544** tonnes
Skimmed milk powder	**194,806** tonnes
Sugar	**9** tonnes (down from **317,853** tonnes held two years before)

175,000

Number of hectares of vineyard to receive subsidies to be grubbed up over three years from 2008. The budget is three-quarters of a billion euro.

VOLUME OF INTRA-EU AGRI-TRADE IN 2010

Wheat	**28.4** MT
Maize	**14** MT
Wine	**14** million HT
Butter	**729,000** tonnes
Pigmeat	**7.9** MT

€96 MILLION

EU grants spent on supporting publicity for national wines in 2010

450,000 TONNES

Amount of EU food mountain intervention stock handed out for free in member states in 2009. The UK no longer participates in this scheme on cost effectiveness grounds (the scheme receives €500 million centrally)

18.8 MILLION

Number of schoolchildren who received 'whole milk equivalent'

€90 MILLION

Amount provided under the school fruit programme. The UK withdrew from this scheme in 2009/2010

PARMA HAM MUST BE SLICED IN PARMA, FETA CHEESE MUST BE GREEK

Top six countries for copyrighting food carrying a place name

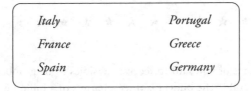

Italy	Portugal
France	Greece
Spain	Germany

Italy by 2010 had three times as many as Germany, and six times as many as seventh in the list, the UK. Colombia and China have also begun to register place name foodstuffs.

24

Number of countries where fewer than 10% of consumers identified the scheme's logo when asked

LESS THAN HALF

Proportion of those who then knew what it meant

€29.7 MILLION

Amount spent on advertising the scheme in 2010

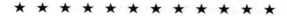

A BEGINNER'S GUIDE TO CABBAGE

Parts of the justifying text of EU-registered FILDERKRAUT/ FILDERSPITZKRAUT

Both in the trade and in common language, *Filderkraut* means a pointed white cabbage grown in the Filder area. Colloquially, Filderkraut is also referred to as *Filderspitzkraut*. Filderkraut/Filderspitzkraut (Brassica oleracea var. capitata for. alba subv. Conica) is a very tasty sub-variety of white cabbage with a characteristic point which has become a rarity. It belongs to the Brassicaceae family and has fewer and finer leaf ribs than the round cabbage.

The shape of the pointed cabbage varies with the particular holding on which Filderkraut/Filderspitzkraut is propagated. However, the striking feature they all share is their pointed head. The shapes range from what looks like a round cabbage with a point stuck on top to large, very pronounced conical tips. The shape and thus, in part, the different stalk and head structure, depend on the individual holding. The heads can be up to 50cm in size and often weigh over 8kg.

Filderkraut/Filderspitzkraut has a centuries-old tradition and cabbage growing in the Filder area has a long history. As early as 500 years ago monks at the monastery in Denkendorf were growing pointed cabbage, which would eventually become a speciality of the Filder plateau. The earliest documentary reference to cabbage growing in the Filder area dates back to 1501 in a store ledger at Salem monastery (quoted from the Leinfelden-Echterdingen town archives, 1995: Das Filderkraut. Stadt Filderstadt und Leinfelden-Echterdingen). The earliest written reference to Filderkraut/Filderspitzkraut is by the Bernhausen parish priest Bischoff in a document from 1772, writing about cabbage growing in the Filder area: "The white, pointed cabbage is the only (cabbage) grown here" (quoted from Grabinger 1974: *Bernhausen, Ortsgeschichte Bernhausen*, p. 200). [etc. etc.]

A BEGINNER'S GUIDE TO SCALLOPS

Parts of the justifying text of EU-registered ISLE OF MAN QUEENIES

The queen scallop (*Aequipecten opercularis*) is a medium-sized species of scallop, an edible marine bivalve mollusc of the family Pectinidae. The shell can vary in colour including yellow, orange, red, brown and purple and grows to a maximum of 90mm in diameter. There are some 19-22 broad radiating ribs on both halves, with numerous concentric growth rings running across the shell. The meat or main body of the Queenie is far smaller than a king scallop; it is a circular muscle, cylindrical in shape, 20mm in diameter and 15 mm in height. The meat is opaque/cream in colour; a two-part orange/white, crescent shaped roe is attached to the body. The Queenie can be served with the roe left intact or removed.

Isle of Man Queenies can only be caught during the Queenie season which traditionally starts on 1 June. This is entirely due to the physiology of the animal, and the unusual way in which it is caught. Most species of scallop are harvested by means of some sort of dredge, which scrapes the scallop from the seabed floor. Unusually, Isle of Man Queenies are taken by means of a light otter trawl. This relies on the escape response of the Queenie to stimulation – they flap up into the net when disturbed by a light chain towed slightly ahead of the net. The escape response is very slow at low water temperatures, meaning that the trawl fishery is only viable between June and December, when water temperatures are at their highest. In years with a very cold spring, water temperatures may not have risen sufficiently until the middle of June.

This unique method of taking Queenies means that, unlike dredged scallops, no grit is forced inside the shell during capture. This leads to a much higher quality meat compared to dredge caught Queenies, higher meat yields, and also ensures that undersized Queenies returned to the seabed have extremely high survival rates, unlike dredge caught scallops, where discard mortality can be very high. [etc. etc.]

Pigs are animals that are naturally endowed with a snout allowing them to root around in the soil."

From the justifications for recognising porc d'Auvergne
as a designated regional foodstuff

49,000%

Increase in Spanish flax growing in Spain over five years after the introduction of subsidies. Much of the flax proved to be substandard and was destroyed before investigated. The scheme cost €75 million and some beneficiaries were later alleged to be working in the office of a Spanish agriculture minister (and future Commission Vice President).

Source: Marta Andreasen

ITEMS DEEMED BY THE COMMISSION IN BREACH OF ADVERTISING STANDARDS, AS RULED ON THE SAME DAY AS THE 'WATER REHYDRATION STORY'

★ **Water:** Regular consumption of significant amounts of water can reduce the risk of development of dehydration and of concomitant decrease of performance

★ **Calcium-containing fruit juices**: Reduced risk for dental erosion

★ **Daily consumption of live Lactobacillus casei strain Shirota as present in a fermented milk product**: helps maintain the upper respiratory tract defences by helping to support immune functions

★ **Lactobacillus plantarum**: Regular consumption of 50g/day Sudamejuust (heart cheese) of x brand helps to maintain the cardio-vascular system/heart health through reduction of blood pressure/symbol of heart

€250,000

Grant available for a study on consumer acceptance in the EU and in third countries of pig meat and meat products from male pigs not surgically castrated.

This is from part of a 2011 grant line worth €1.33 million, including €30,000 for a website on EU work in the field.

COSTING THE COMMON AGRICULTURAL POLICY (CAP) TO BRITAIN

In a nutshell...

The UK does not do as well as other countries from the CAP, which therefore means that UK money goes to support non-UK farmers as well as higher food prices due to protectionism.

AN AUDIT OF THE COST OF THE CAP TO THE UK WAS UNDERTAKEN BY THE TAXPAYERS' ALLIANCE IN 2010 (MORE DETAILS CAN BE FOUND WITHIN THE PAPER ON THE TPA WEBSITE)

TABLE 1.1: THE COST OF THE CAP

Item	Cost
Increased food prices in the UK	£5,300 million
UK share of CAP budget	£4,700 million
Increased social welfare costs from compensating for higher food bills in welfare	£317 million
Regulatory burdens	£264 million
Duplication of food safety agencies	£5 million
Subtotal	£10,600 million
Less double counting of agriculture and sugar levies in EU budgetary contributions and higher prices at the till	-£336 million
Total	**£10,300 million**
Cost per UK household in 2010	**£398**

£34 BILLION

UK government estimate in 2006 of the cost to EU consumers of higher food prices under the CAP

Since the UK entered into the tariff zone of the EEC, access was increasingly blocked to traditional and cheaper Commonwealth imports. Between 1970 and 2004, food prices increased by the following factors:

Cheddar cheese	x	13.9
Imported lamb loin	x	12.8
Unsliced white loaf	x	10.3
Back bacon	x	9.9
Imported butter	x	9.1
Granulated sugar	x	8.9
Carrots	x	7.8
Pork sausages	x	7.7
Granulated coffee	x	7.7
Pasteurised milk	x	7.4

£4.7 BILLION

UK share of CAP budget in 2008

NUMBER OF FARMS BY EU STATE (2005)

Germany – **390,000**

Spain – **1,079,000**

France – **567,000**

Ireland – **133,000**

Italy – **1,729,000**

Poland – **2,477,000**

UK – **287,000**

EU total – **9,688,000**

AVERAGE USED HECTARES BY FARM (2005)

Germany – **43.5ha**

Spain – **23ha**

France – **48.6ha**

Ireland – **31.8ha**

Italy – **7.4ha**

Poland – **6ha**

UK – **55.4ha**

EU average – **16ha**

AGRICULTURE AS A SHARE OF GDP

Germany – **0.6%**

Spain – **2.3%**

France – **1.4%**

Ireland – **0.9%**

Italy – **1.7%**

Poland – **2.4%**

UK – **0.4%**

EU average – **1.2%**

2.9%: THE GRAIN BARONS

Number of cases where CAP grants exceeded €100,000 in the UK on 2006 stats. The comparative figure for Poland was 0.01%.

SOME UNEXPECTED EXAMPLES OF BRITISH CAP GRANT RECIPIENTS, 2002-2007

Grant, £	Recipient
£750,000	Vetspeed Ltd T/A Cambridge Pet Crematorium
£332,000	National Starch and Chemical Ltd
£290,000	HM Prison Service (outer London)
£223,000	Defence Science and Technology Labs
£112,000	London Borough of Tower Hamlets
£88,000	Imperial London Hotels
£82,000	British Wild Boar Association
£69,000	Cambridge Pet Crematorium
£60,000	Time Out Skiing
£42,000	Royal Agricultural College
£42,000	UK Coal Mining Ltd
£37,700	A steam engine museum
£28,000	British Gypsum
£27,000	British Telecom
£21,000	National Hedge Laying Society
£20,000	Royal School for Deaf Children
£18,600	Upchurch River Valley Golf Course
£17,500	Westminster City Council
£15,800	Anglian Water
£15,000	An archaeological site in the South West
£14,500	Jonjo O'Neill Racing

£10,000	Brian Perry Waste Paper
£9,300	Defence Estates
£6,800	British Worm Breeders
£5,600	National Museums of Scotland
£5,500	Glanlerry caravan site
£5,300	Eton College
£4,800	Salisbury Cathedral
£3,300	Oaksey Park Airfield
£2,300	Fire Services National Benevolent Fund
£1,500	Belfast International Airport
£600	Ulster American Folk Park
£600	National Society for Epilepsy
£283	Billinghay Tennis Club
£234	City of Derry Rugby Club

DG BUDG

TASKS OF DG BUDG

★ Liaise with MEPs and ministers over EU funding levels

★ Encourage sound management of Community funds

★ Account for spending, subject to audit

★ Collect its own resources (i.e. dedicated EU income) from member states

DG BUDGET HAS FIVE DIRECTORATES BASED IN BRUSSELS AND AROUND 420 PERSONNEL

EU regional funding alone is directed at around 280,000 projects a year

ONE-THIRD OF EU MEMBER STATES HAVE NATIONAL BUDGETS
SIGNIFICANTLY SMALLER THAN THE BUDGET OF THE EU:

Bulgaria	*Cyprus*
Estonia	*Latvia*
Lithuania	*Luxembourg*
Malta	*Slovakia*
Slovenia	

Additionally, three member states have budgets that are
nearly the same size:

Hungary	*Finland*
Ireland	

Between 2000 and 2010, the EU budget increased by 37%

SIX BIGGEST CURRENT EU SPENDING PACKAGES ON
TRANSPORT SYSTEM UPGRADES:

1   Railway from Berlin to Palermo   €971 million

2   Railway from Lyon to Ukraine   €838 million

3   SW Europe High Speed railway   €727 million

4   Railway from Paris to Bratislava   €531 million

5   Railway from Lyon to Antwerp   €451 million

6   Inland waterway Seine-Scheldt   €430 million

FIVE BIGGEST CURRENT ENERGY PACKAGES FROM EU MONEY

1	Installations at gas transmission facilities in Slovakia	€664 million
2	Upgrade of Baugarten gas hub	€425 million
3	Pipelines and compressors for Nabucco pipeline	€200 million
4	Increased interconnection between France and Spain	€176 million
5	Stations in Belgium and pipes for French Northern corridor	€175 million

COUNTRIES THAT RECEIVE OVER 1% OF THEIR GROSS NATIONAL INCOME FROM EU COHESION FUNDS

7%	Estonia
6%	Lithuania
5%	Latvia
4%	Poland, Hungary
3%	Portugal, Czech Republic, Slovakia
2%	Greece, Slovenia, Bulgaria, Malta

EU Cohesion policy spending over the current six-year cycle runs to €348 billion

	Billion €		Share of total budget (%)
	Committed	Paid	
1. Sustainable growth	64.5	53.3	45.5
2. Preservation and management of natural resources	58.7	56.4	41.3
of which direct aid, and market-related expenditure	42.9	42.8	30.2
of which rural development, environment and fisheries	15.7	13.5	11.1
3. Citizenship, freedom, security and justice	1.8	1.5	1.3
3a. Freedom, security and justice	1.1	0.8	0.8
3b. Citizenship	0.7	0.6	0.5
4. EU as a global player	8.8	7.2	6.2
5. Administration	8.2	8.2	5.7
of which for the Commission	3.3	3.3	2.3
Total	**141.9**	**126.5**	**100**

Source: Commission

THE 2011 BUDGET, IN MILLION EURO, AS PAID OUT BY MEMBER STATES

Note: these are the gross contributions and do NOT take into account receipts

	VAT own resource	GNI own resource	UK Rebate	NL and SE Rebate	Total 'national contributions'
BE	447.1	2,726.5	145.4	23.9	3,342.9
BG	50	262.4	14	2.3	328.7
CZ	198.4	1,054.3	56.2	9.3	1,318.1
DK	288	1,844.9	98.4	16.2	2,247.6
DE	1,617.9	19,221.1	182.2	168.7	21,189.9
EE	20.2	103.7	5.5	0.9	130.4
IE	199.4	1,002.3	53.5	8.8	1,264
EL	320.6	1,753.5	93.5	15.4	2,183.1
ES	1,194.1	7,938.4	423.5	69.7	9,625.7
FR	2,687.3	15,429.7	823.1	135.4	19,075.6
IT	1,865.2	11,912.3	635.5	104.6	14,517.6
CY	26.1	131.1	7	1.2	165.3
LV	20.3	129	6.9	1.1	157.2
LT	40.9	205.4	11	1.8	259
LU	43.8	220.2	11.7	1.9	277.6
HU	130.7	745.8	39.8	6.5	922.9
MT	8.7	43.5	2.3	0.4	54.9
NL	297.2	4,548.6	43.1	-625.1	4,263.7
AT	292.6	2,173.0	20.6	19.1	2,505.3
PL	552.5	2,776.5	148.1	24.4	3,501.5
PT	245	1,231.3	65.7	10.8	1,552.8
RO	145.3	965.1	51.5	8.5	1,170.3
SL	53.4	268.4	14.3	2.4	338.5
SK	79.8	518.7	27.7	4.6	630.7
FI	241.2	1,380.2	73.6	12.1	1,707.2
SE	153.8	2,642.6	25	-141.7	2,679.8
UK	2,567.4	13,313.3	-3,079.2	116.9	12,918.3
EU-27	13,786.8	94,541.9	0	0	108,328.7

Sugar levies(*)	123.4
Customs duties(*)	16,653.7
Other revenue	1,421.4
Total revenue	**126,527.2**

Source: Commission

DG CLIMA

★ Monitor member state compliance with climate change targets
★ Push the climate change agenda across the Commission and internationally

FEBRUARY 2010

Date of the establishment of this new DG

21%

Objective for reduction in greenhouse gas emissions by 2020 compared to 2005 quantities, under the Emissions Trading Scheme

75%

DG's current staffing levels at senior management

80 MILLION TONNES

Estimated emissions credits held by one steel magnate in 2009 that were surplus to actual requirement, since the quota was set too high. This could be sold on the market for £1 billion

€4.5 BILLION

Amount of indirect taxation to be raised by selling off 300 million EU-reserved credits in order to spend the revenue on carbon capture and renewable energy projects involving the new EU states

DG COMM

TASKS OF DG COMM

★ Keep the general public and the media up to date on EU activities

6 MILLION

The number of documents on the Commission's Europa website, the largest public website in the world

PRIORITY TARGET GROUPS FOR MESSAGING:

★ Journalists

★ National and local politicians

★ Civil society

★ Students and pupils

★ Teachers

EURONEWS, THE DEDICATED EU TV SERVICE

★ General budget: €6.5 million

★ 24/7 Polish service: €7 million

★ 24/7 Arabic service: €5.1 million

€6.3 MILLION

Budget spent on Euranet, a dedicated EU radio service

€3.1 MILLION

Budget for PressEurop, an online news clippings website on European matters

€24,946

Budget dedicated for any five to ten minute news report on the impact of EU policies on everyday life

WWW.EU4JOURNALISTS.EU

The EU's dedicated website intended to provided an intro for journalists, including key sections on what the EU has achieved

€10,000

Maximum value of prizes that can be offered to journalists and media personnel, in competitions reinforcing European identity and awareness

€8.3 MILLION

Budget available to support debates, events and conferences by DG COMM 'to enhance the European Union's profile'

STATED OBJECTIVES OF THE EUROPE FOR CITIZENS PROGRAMME

★ Give citizens the opportunity to interact and participate in constructing an ever-closer Europe, which is democratic and world-oriented, united in and enriched through its cultural diversity, thus developing citizenship of the European Union;

★ Develop a sense of European identity, based on common values, history and culture;

★ Foster a sense of ownership of the European Union among its citizens;

★ Enhance tolerance and mutual understanding between European citizens, respecting and promoting cultural and linguistic diversity, while contributing to intercultural dialogue

POSSIBLE PARTNERS FOR EUROPE FOR CITIZENS

★ Federations/associations of local authorities or other bodies with specific knowledge or experience of town twinning

★ Civil society organisations as described in the basic act

★ Non-governmental organisations

★ Survivors' associations

★ Entities managing remembrance

- ★ Museums
- ★ Local and regional authorities
- ★ Federations of general European interest
- ★ European public policy research organisations (think tanks)
- ★ Civil society organisations at European level, promoting active European citizenship
- ★ Platforms of pan-European organisations
- ★ Civil society organisations dedicated to Remembrance of the origins of the European integration

5 HOURS

Duration, including speeches and buffet, of the annual Golden Stars award to commemorate Active European Citizenship, and to 'help to increase their sense of belonging to the same community and their commitment to the European project.'

€28.4 MILLION

Amount available in 2011 to support Europe for Citizens programmes

€13 MILLION

Amount provided by the DG to support delegations' activities in member states in joint activities, particularly at schools

€0

Amount of this budget line dedicated to such activity in the UK today, after a series of negative media stories. Eight other states also do not receive such funds.

€500,000

Budget for school trips to the European Commission. Another €2.1 million supports arranging other visits

€20,000

Amount available for visitors to have meals with European Commissioners during their visit

★ Forum Jeunesse de l'Union Europeenne

★ European Movement

★ European Federal Movement, Rome

★ Fondation des Journalistes

★ Centre for European Policy Studies (CEPS)

★ Youth of European Nationalities

★ European Bureau for Conscientious Objection

★ European Union of Music Competitions for Youth

★ Yourope – The European Festival Organisation

★ World Federation of Democratic Youth

★ Youth of the European People's Party

★ Union des Jeunesses Musicales d'Europe

★ Europa Cantat

★ International Federation of Liberal and Radical Youth

★ Organizing Bureau of European School Student Unions

★ International Union of Socialist Youth

★ Jeunes Europeens Federalistes

★ Jeunesse Ouvriere Chretienne Internationale

BUYING GRATITUDE, SELLING A BRAND

€2.4 billion

Assessed amount of EU expenditure that carries with it direct PR 'brand value' for the EU

Source: Open Europe

AN EXAMPLE OF DELIBERATE INCIDENTAL PR

€500 MILLION

Budget for free food handouts for EU nationals (now in the process of big cuts)

THE LEGAL REQUIREMENT THAT GOES WITH THIS BENEVOLENCE:

The words 'European Union aid' accompanied by the emblem of the European Union shall be clearly marked on the packing of food distributed through the annual plans as well as at the distribution points.

For 2008 alone, the EU had a €206.6 million budget set aside specifically for 'Communication', run by the European Commission's Directorate-General for Communication.

This was three times the budget dedicated to tackling fraud, and two and a half times the size of the Commission's budget for negotiating international trade on behalf of 27 member states

151 PAGES

Length of the report 'The Hard Sell' by think tank Open Europe, looking into the PR machinery of the European Communities, which can be read online:

www.openeurope.org.uk/research /hardsell.pdf

HOW PR WORKS

Communication Matters Group. One representative per Directorate plus the Press Coordinator; meets regularly throughout the year for coordination.

Relations with the media are handled by the DG's **Press Coordinator**. A representative from the communication team of a DG meets with the Press Coordinator at regular intervals.

The **Jour Fixe Press** takes place once a week for information exchange and coordination of press/communication actions.

In the event of a crisis, either a communication crisis (false information on Commission initiative being spread) or a physical crisis, the **Commissioner's spokesperson** is the only contact for the media.

Individual DGs also liaise via the Press Coordinator with the **Commissioner's spokesperson** as well as with the **Cabinet's communication officer**.

There are also multilateral meetings with media managers from member states. For instance, the **European Communication Network on Taxation and Customs (ECNtc)** consists of one representative for taxation and one for customs from each Member State. Meetings are held twice a year.

KEY PRINCIPLES

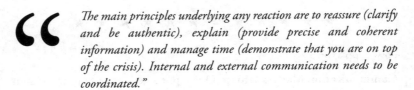

Rumours, false information or misrepresented facts on EU affairs have a tendency to spread at a breathtaking pace across media and countries.

They may in the process adversely affect the interests and reputation of the EU institution concerned."

The main principles underlying any reaction are to reassure (clarify and be authentic), explain (provide precise and coherent information) and manage time (demonstrate that you are on top of the crisis). Internal and external communication needs to be coordinated."

UK grant recipients of regional funds since 2007, fined for not flagging up the Brussels source of EU grants from the Regional Development Fund (ERDF)

Recipient	Misdemeanour	Fine
Doncaster Metropolitan Borough Council	Failure to appropriately advertise ERDF support during radio advert	€5,250
University of Northampton	Project did not have the required billboard up in time (eight-week period)	€56,477.70
Sandwell Metropolitan Borough Council	Failure to acknowledge ERDF Programme in text or display logos in job adverts	€5,046
The National Museum of Labour History	No logo on billboard	€7,223
North West Vision and Media	Marketing materials without logo	€12,005
Merseytravel	Insufficient publicity at project start	€13,600
The Merseyside Partnership	Use of incorrect logo	€5,492.50
Business Link	Job Advertisement without ERDF logo	€5,296.47

As a consequence of Article 7(2) EC Regulation 1828/2006, my Department is obliged to fly the flag of the European Union in front of its premises for one week every year, after Europe Day. There is no formal requirement to inform the European Commission, but I am informed that visible failure to comply would result in the European Commission imposing fines (described as 'financial corrections')."

Ministerial statement on EU flags on government buildings, 2011

DG COMP

★ Enforce EU competition rules, to make EU markets work better, by ensuring that all companies compete equally and fairly on their merits

TWO

Number of Hearing Officers employed on attachment to DG COMP to act as third-party arbiters with businesses

€3.06 BILLION

Fines levied in 2010, on 69 cartels

€1.1 TRILLION

Level of member states' state aid to the financial sector in 2009 – 9.3% of EU total GDP

€73.2 BILLION

Amount of approved traditional state aid in 2010

11%

Amount of illegal state aid still outstanding for repayment by June 2010

THREE FINDINGS OF A EUROPEAN COURT OF AUDITORS REVIEW IN LATE 2011 OF COMMISSION HANDLING OF STATE AID

★ *Insufficient commission checks to ensure member states are complying with their obligation to notify state aid.*

★ *The commission is not proactive enough in raising member states' awareness of their obligations to notify state aid.*

★ *The commission is hampered by a lack of reliable management information and by organisational problems.*

85%

Number of staff who could be contacted in the DG during a telephone cascade test within 1½ hours. 5% could still not be contacted after three hours

45%

Number of staff authorised and capable of working from home during any transport crisis

LISTS OF AUTHORISED POLICY MESSAGES AND LINES TO TAKE FROM DG COMP FOR 2010

1. **Way out of the crisis and financial stability**: *we are not out of the woods; recapitalization / rescuing goes with restructuring, irrespective of whether the institution is considered to be sound or distressed; a well-functioning single market is the key condition to reach a self-sustainable recovery; no sustainable growth without effective competition in the internal market.*

2. **Delivering for consumers, ensuring EU competitiveness**: *make sure that consumers can benefit from the effects of a healthy competition; making markets work better for consumers and businesses; finding a balance between protecting consumer welfare and creating the right conditions for business in Europe to grow to the scale needed to take on global competitors; compete on the basis of ideas, creativity, efficiencies and innovation to succeed globally.*

3. **Smart regulation: Effective deterrence, due process, transparency**: *the fight against cartels is one of the most important priorities; no sympathy for cartelists; deterrence is the primary objective of our enforcement; prevention is better than cure; strike the right balance between maintaining a deterrent level of fines and avoiding unwanted side effects, such as pushing companies out of business; our decision-making process must be open and respectful of the rights of defence of the parties*

POOR TIMING

October 2011

Date of the final report of the Hearing Officer looking at Standard & Poor's. The company had been under investigation by the Commission since 2009 on claims of charging unfair prices.

Standard & Poor's was also a key company determining the credit rating of eurozone states.

1961

Year that an ECJ ruling first defines the parameters of state aid (the *De Gezamenlijke Steenkolenmijnen in Limburg v Haute Autorité de la Communauté Européenne du Charbon et de l'Acier* case)

LENIENCY NOTICE

A form of Queen's Evidence for participants in a cartel, developed in 1996

★ Boeing/McDonnell Douglas (1997)

★ GE/Honeywell (2001)

Leading cases where mergers were authorised in the US but prohibited by the European Commission

KEY CO-OPERATION AGREEMENTS BETWEEN THE EU AND OTHER COUNTRIES ON ANTITRUST

United States	**1991**
Canada	**1999**
Japan	**2003**
South Korea	**2009**

2004

Microsoft fined for blocking interoperability for its products with non-Microsoft systems

OVER TWO YEARS (OCTOBER 2008-2010)

★ 200 decisions over state aid in the financial sector

★ 40 schemes authorised or amended

100%

Amount of EU support to eurozone crisis countries agreed at the council of ministers deemed to be compliant with state aid rules

9

Number of fines levied against cartels in 2010 which were cut because the recipient was unable to pay. 32 had appealed on these grounds

BATHROOM FITTINGS AND FIXTURES

The sinister context of a six-nation cartel coordinating prices and rebates revealed in 2011

€22 BILLION

Amount the public sector was calculated as wasting every year due to overpaying, by not making full use of public tender processes

DG ECFIN

TASKS OF DG ECFIN

★ Contribute to raising the economic welfare of the citizens in the European Union and beyond, notably by developing and promoting policies that ensure sustainable economic growth, a high level of employment, stable public finances and financial stability

€22.5 BILLION

Amount set aside under the European Financial Stabilisation Mechanism, for Ireland

€26 BILLION

Amount set aside for Portugal

€50 BILLION (€13.5 BILLION OUTSTANDING)

Balance of Payments assistance set aside for euro non-member states

€497 MILLION

Macro-financial aid set aside for euro non-member states.

Countries of current interest for EU macro-financial aid:

- ★ *Georgia*
- ★ *Moldova*
- ★ *Lebanon*
- ★ *Kosovo*
- ★ *Serbia*
- ★ *Bosnia and Herzegovina*

3 TO 15 YEARS

Length of time states can borrow from the EU pool

€40.8 BILLION

Current outstanding debt

AAA

EU's corporate credit rating (as at late 2011)

ACCESSION TO THE EURO

1999	Belgium, Germany, Ireland, Spain, France, Italy, Luxembourg, the Netherlands, Austria, Portugal and Finland
2001	Greece
2002	Launch of hard currency
2007	Slovenia
2008	Cyprus, Malta
2009	Slovakia
2011	Estonia

BAILOUT PACKAGES AGREED FOR GREECE, IRELAND & PORTUGAL

	Eurozone members	EU27 (EFSM) & non-eurozone members	IMF	Private sector	Total
Greece (May 2010)	€80bn, bilateral loans	€0bn	€30bn Stand-By Arrangement (SBA)		€110bn, three-year horizon
Ireland (November 2010)	€17.7bn (EFSF); €17.5bn (Ireland)	€22.5bn (EFSM) + bilateral loans from the UK (€3.8bn), Denmark (€0.4bn), Sweden (€0.6bn)	€22.5bn Extended Arrangement		€85bn (€67.5bn, external), three-year horizon
Portugal (May 2011)	€26bn (EFSF)	€26bn (EFSM)	€26bn Extended Arrangement		€78bn, three-year horizon
Greece (February 2012)	Including €30bn sweeteners to private sector; €23bn to recapitalise Greek banks; €35bn buy-back of bonds	Probably not	Yes, but unclear at time of writing	53.5% nominal write down of bonds. €14.5bn repayment restructured	€130bn

EFSF

European Financial Stabilisation Fund (max. €440bn), May 2010

EFSM

European Financial Stabilisation Mechanism (max. €60bn), May 2010

ESM

The permanent rescue fund, the European Stability Mechanism (ESM), is planned to enter into force in July 2012. This has been brought forward from 2013.

★ ★ ★ ★ ★ ★ ★ ★ ★ ★ ★ ★ ★

CENTRAL/EASTERN EUROPEAN COUNTRIES WHERE PUBLIC OPINION WAS MORE OPPOSED TO EUROZONE MEMBERSHIP THAN IN FAVOUR IN MID-2011 (AND RATIO)

Czech Republic (**67%/26%**)

Latvia (**55%/31%**)

Lithuania (**51%/37%**)

Bulgaria (**50%/40%**)

Hungary and Poland had numerically matched opinions

6 IN 10

Number of Estonians who noted price inflation resulting directly from the change to the Euro

	Euro area	EU-27	US
Population (millions)	317	494	300
GDP (in € trillions calculated at purchasing power parity)	8.4	11.9	11.2
Share of world GDP (% at PPP)	14.6	21	19.7

7%

Spanish cost of borrowing in November 2011 due to eurozone fears

€130 BILLION

Greek bailout funds identified by November 2011

Arguments in favour of EMU *and counter arguments*

1. **Price visibility**. It should be easier under EMU to compare the price of identical products in different EU countries. This may increase competitiveness as consumers are given the incentive to shop internationally. *It is unrealistic to suppose that this would drive prices down, as (i) it takes no account of real differences in national market costs and local price differentials (local tax differences, wages or varying local costs of manufacture) and (ii) A Single Currency already operates in the UK (the Pound) but the price of goods in London and the North can be vastly different, e.g. house prices, groceries, beer, etc.*

2. **Facilitates trans-border travel**. No need to carry traveller's cheques – the example often used is the man who changes his currency as he travels round the EU. By the 15th capital city, he has only half his original money – the rest having disappeared in translocation costs before he has the chance to spend it. *Huge advances in electronic cash card debit mean that a single currency is already in existence – the flexible friend. Anyone can draw money via a foreign bank machine (and which traveller changes his currency 15 times?)*

3. **EMU encourages tight budgetary and fiscal policy**. Maastricht criteria require strict economic management. *Maastricht criteria can be met without joining Stage 3 of EMU (the Euro) – or even without signing up to Maastricht at all. It is an issue of optional domestic policy.*

4. **Removes floating exchange rate, so businesses can better plan ahead when dealing with foreign businesses**. *This argument takes no account of the procedure by which businesses can plan transactions using a basket of currencies. Some may strengthen, but others will weaken, thereby evening out. In any case, Sterling can be strong and weak, so even this in itself averages out over time.*

5. **Helps to build an ever-closer Union closer to the hearts of the European citizen**. EMU is a visual symbol of European co-operation and integration. *Fine if you want to be part of a federal Europe.*

6. **Makes life in border areas easier**. *The UK has few of those – Northern Ireland and Gibraltar. And there, identity is important.*

7. **Creates globally strong currency to counter/complement Dollar and Yen**. *This is an argument for paranoid French government officials.*

8. **Lower interest rates in the UK, with an effect on mortgages and business investment**. *We can have zero rates right now if we wanted to. The Bank of England only sets them high if the country needs them high.*

9. **Seen as securing the City of London as a global financial centre**. *This is empty scare mongering. The City actually will do better if it is distinct and different. The UK already handles most of the trade in euro while being outside of the currency.*

10. **Fear that inward investors could pull out**. *Again, these are groundless fears. Foreign investors like Britain because of its language, skills and open work environment. Investment has continued despite the Maastricht opt-out way back in 1992.*

11. **Early entry will give the UK a greater voice in the development of the Single Currency**. *True, it will give the Bank of England one vote in the Central Bank. But Maastricht forbids Downing Street and Parliament even to lobby this single vote.*

Separate arguments against EMU

1. **A floating exchange rate acts as a safety value**. The Pound strengthens or weakens as the economy requires, thereby releasing tension on the other means of managing the economy (unemployment levels and interest rates), which have a direct impact on jobs.

2. **Asymmetric shocks**. Shocks which hit one region, industry or country hard are better absorbed if the currency takes some of the blow. It is not possible with one currency to cover different circumstances across one zone. Interest rate needs will vary from one area to another. The bigger the currency, the worse it handles a local crisis. A huge currency handles a national crisis poorly.

3. **Gold and foreign currency reserves will have to be handed over in bulk to the Central Bank – billions of pounds' worth.**

4. **EMU will lead to the centralisation of social security**. Lack of a mobile labour force due to language barriers means that regions of high unemployment would develop (as happens on a smaller scale today with Merseyside in the UK, Picardie in France and Naples in Italy). This pressure will grow for huge regional transfers to support regional/national unemployment. But the EU only has a budget ceiling of 1.27% of total national budgets, and this will have to grow and be managed centrally. So it leads to one government for Europe to handle a giant tax system.

5. **It could also lead to other policy pressures**. An independent foreign or military policy could require the backing of the Central Bank, since it might call for the use of gold reserves or commitments beyond the now-limited national ones. Managers of the euro could Veto another Suez, Falklands or Gulf War because they could breach treaty stipulations on common management of the currency.

6. **Pensions**. Huge liability and future debts exist on the continent, but there is a positive balance for the UK economy in the future because we as a country it has spent more on private and less on state pensions. Pressure will grow for a central budget to handle this European problem – at UK expense.

7. **Democratic accountability**. Concerns are expressed at who holds the Central Bank to account. The answer is simple – nobody.

8. **The European Central Bank has no track record**. It will take time to acquire one for market stability. There was a notable poor start over the selection of Wim Duisenberg as Bank President and again over Prodi's remarks about Italy leaving EMU.

9. **Costs**. Of the new computer system, tills, cash points, shop price re-jigging, minting 18 billion coins, etc. This falls heavily on small and medium businesses, who can ill afford it.

10. **Confusion**. To consumers, particularly at the time of dual pricing.

11. **Price hiking**. Shops may round up to take advantage of price confusion and recoup transaction costs for changing currencies. Consumers pay.

12. **Projected savings may be less than anticipated for business**. The UK transaction services are highly computerised. Charges for money transfer and exchange in the UK may be extremely close to the real costs involved, rather than being invented bank charges. Thus savings from joining the euro may be marginal. And most companies don't deal heavily on European business anyway.

13. **Short cuts**. Some countries, such as Belgium, were clearly running deficits and carrying debt-to-GDP shares far in excess of the Maastricht criteria. Only a federal budget plus the threat of financial punishment could stop this from continuing.

2010 figures (Eurostat)	Govt. debt to GDP	Govt. deficit	Bank assets to GDP	Avg. growth 2000-2010
Unsalvageable				
Greece	143	11	173	2.4
Cyprus	61	5	586	2.8
Banking crisis				
Belgium	97	4	182	1.4
Spain	60	9	335	2.1
Ireland	96	32	328	2.4
Competitiveness crisis				
Italy	119	5	163	0.2
Portugal	93	9	240	0.7

Source: Europe-economics.com

DG EAC

TASKS OF DG EAC

★ Foster both equity and excellence in education and training

★ Support cultural exchange and co-operation

★ Enhance the competitiveness of the audiovisual industry

★ Develop the European dimension in sport

★ Maximise the potential and well-being of young people while stimulating the mobility of individuals or works in each of these fields

1 IN 5

Proportion of designated young people in the EU

NUMBER OF EU UNIVERSITIES AMONGST THE TOP 100 IN THE WORLD

United Kingdom   **11**

Germany   **5**

France   **3**

Sweden   **3**

Netherlands   **2**

Denmark   **2**

Belgium   **1**

Finland   **1**

2 British universities are in the top ten.

54 of the top **100** are in the USA

Source: Shanghai Index, 2010

NUMBER 39

Top ranking for the first non-British university from the EU in the list. The Marie Curie Institute comes in at number 39, behind four UK institutions.

36.6%

Commission's estimate of the number of boys aged 15 who were low achievers in reading in 2009

20%

Commission estimate of the number of young Europeans (18-24) at risk of poverty in 2008

95%

English, French, German, Spanish and Russian as a proportion of taught languages

980,000

Number of non-EU nationals enrolled as students in EU colleges in 2008

NUMBER OF STUDENTS STUDYING IN ANOTHER EU COUNTRY

2000	315,000
2006	450,000
2007	480,000
2008	490,000

EU ROLE IN FACILITATING FOREIGN STUDIES (2010 FIGURES)

Erasmus: 213,266 students

Comenius: 12,500 individual mobility grants for teachers (IST action), assistants and pupils

Leonardo da Vinci: 67,873 placements

Grundtvig: 3,627 adult learners

Erasmus Mundus: 2,292 for students and 469 for academics.

Bilateral co-operation projects with Industrialised Countries: 1,900

MOST POPULAR DESTINATIONS FOR UK STUDENTS

France – 32.7%

Spain – 22.9%

Germany – 14.2%

Italy – 7.4%

Netherlands – 3.9%

€365

Monthly grant for UK students in 2009/10 under the programme

THE MOST POPULAR DESTINATIONS FOR UK STAFF

Germany

France

Spain

Italy

Finland

€459 MILLION

Budget for Erasmus activities in the 2009/10 academic year

STREETFOOTBALLWORLD

EU network behind Euroschools 2012 promoting education through football

€4 MILLION

EU grant to support the 2011 World Special Olympics Summer Games in Athens

FIVE REASONS WHY THE COMMISSION FUNDS EU STUDIES AT UNIVERSITIES

The Jean Monnet network has traditionally been playing an important leadership role in spreading knowledge and awareness on European integration in the candidate countries and new member states."

"Jean Monnet professors all over the world are greatly contributed to [sic] the European Union's visibility in the world and to the better understanding of the European integration process as a model for peaceful co-operation."

"The Jean Monnet network constitutes a meeting place for an extraordinary group of historians with a high-level reputation and is actively contributing to the historical insight that is necessary to understand the current evolution of European integration."

"The Jean Monnet network is known for its advanced research and teaching on fundamental rights and non-discrimination. Their work notably resulted in a high-level conference on Gender Equality and Europe's Future that had a concrete impact on the outcome of the European Convention."

"The Jean Monnet Programme has a tradition of being involved in the ongoing reflection on the institutional and political future of the European construction through conferences and thematic groups." [sic]

BETWEEN 1990 AND 2011, THE JEAN MONNET PROGRAMME FUNDS HAVE SUPPORTED THE ESTABLISHMENT OF:

- ★ **162** Jean Monnet Centres of Excellence
- ★ **875** Jean Monnet Chairs
- ★ **1,001** Jean Monnet Modules
- ★ In **780** universities
- ★ Involving **1,650** professors
- ★ With **200,000** students every year

Global presence of the Jean Monnet network as at 2011

" *Being the Director of the Jean Monnet Project in Chile has given me the opportunity to share my passion for European integration with the students. My long lasting relationship with the European Commission enabled me to invite distinguished speakers which have given this course the prestige that it has today. Particularly rewarding has been the increased interest of the students in the European Union as a model from which we can learn for the process of Latin American integration."*

Chilean Jean Monnet Professor

"The creation and consolidation of its Institute for European Studies and the Special Degree on European Union Law are good examples of our commitment with European integration."

Spanish Jean Monnet Professor

"Importantly, it also provides the opportunity to influence national and even international agendas regarding the EU via relations with, and training of, government negotiators and the broad public policy making community as well as civil society."

Australian Jean Monnet professor

"The Jean Monnet program has provided a great boost to my career and has been a huge encouragement to me. Without it I would have worked on the EU in any case, but with it I have greater visibility and professional recognition."

US Jean Monnet professor

"The added value of the Jean Monnet Action is in providing the teaching of European integration with an increased and lasting institutionalisation, credibility and visibility."

French Jean Monnet professor

"The Jean Monnet Action has been instrumental in the intellectual preparation of the Slovak Republic for EU membership."

Slovakian Jean Monnet professor

"Without the support of the Jean Monnet programme, EU Studies in New Zealand would not have emerged, let alone grown in the dramatic way that it has since 2000. EU Studies are now a recognised and popular area of study and research in New Zealand and the work of the NCRE is valued by the government as well as the tertiary sector. In that way, the Jean Monnet programme has had a much wider effect and impact beyond academia and has supported an outreach function as well."

New Zealand Jean Monnet professor

The Chair's visibility has opened a key interest in a different study and knowledge of the European Union in Lebanon and in the Arab world, one which is based on values and achievements typical of European soft power."

Lebanese Jean Monnet professor

€9.6 MILLION
Current budget to support the teaching of EU integration

EUROPEAN COMMISSION'S CULTURAL PRIZES

Europa Nostra (conservation)

European Union Prize for Contemporary Architecture

European Union Prize for Literature

European Union Award for Contemporary Music/European Border Breakers Award (EBBA)

2011 EU LITERATURE PRIZE WINNERS

Bulgaria: Kalin Terziyski

Czech Republic: Tomáš Zmeškal

Greece: Kostas Hatziantoniou

Iceland: Ófeigur Sigurðsson

Latvia: Inga Zolude

Liechtenstein: Iren Nigg

Malta: Immanuel Mifsud

Montenegro: Andrej Nikolaidis

Netherlands: Rodaan Al Galidi

Serbia: Jelena Lengold

Turkey: Ciler Ilhan

United Kingdom: Adam Foulds

JOOLS HOLLAND

Host of the 2012 EBBAs at an award event in the Netherlands with EU funding

SOME EU CULTURAL AMBASSADORS

European Union Youth Orchestra
European Saxophone Ensemble
Charles Aznavour
Keith Vaz

€2.6 MILLION

Cultural Ambassadors budget over the current six-year programme. Most goes towards bands and orchestras.

DG EMPL

★ Pursue policy, legislative and financial actions leading to more and better jobs

★ Combat social exclusion, and promote social justice and protection, free movement of workers, workers' rights and solidarity between generations

★ …in order to contribute to the achievement of full employment, social progress and a highly competitive social market economy in the European Union within the context of the Europe 2020 Strategy

DG EMPL'S TARGETS

Employment rate of 75% of those aged 20-64 by 2020 (currently 69%)

Early school leaving rate of 10% (currently 15%)

40% of people aged 30-34 having gone to university/equivalent (currently 31%)

20 million people fewer should be at risk of poverty

9.3%

Proportion of adults currently in education and lifelong learning

NUMBER OF ACCIDENTS AT WORK PER 100,000 WITHIN THE EU 15

2005 – **3098** accidents

2006 – **3879** accidents

The five-year objective from 2007 onwards was to get figures back down to 2005 levels

3.5%

Averaged unemployment rate in the EEC at the time of its foundation

1.7 MILLION

The Italian share of the 2.6 million EEC unemployed in 1957 – accounting for two in three

ONE MILLION

Number of Castilians who migrated into Catalonia during the last two decades of the Franco regime

DOUBLE

Increase in rate of unemployment across the EEC from 1979 to 1983, from 6 million to 12 million

8

Number of people per square kilometre for a region to qualify as sparsely populated and therefore eligible for regional aid

EXAMPLES OF EUROPEAN SOCIAL FUND PROGRAMMES, AS SELECTED AS MODELS BY THE COMMISSION:

Case Study 1: €78,677

 A project aimed at secondary school pupils, teachers and parents throughout the Piedmont region of northern Italy offered young students new perspectives and 'alternative destinations' in life.

"The 'Move up' project used a wide range of innovative activities to promote equal opportunities, focusing on respect for diversity, the prevention of violence and bullying at school, and an enhanced awareness of how to use new web technologies.

"A touring theatre workshop gave pupils the opportunity to act out and analyse their experiences, finding their own answers to problems of intolerance and aggression. Another innovative tool was a multimedia camper van, which travelled 6,590km from school to school across Piedmont. Workshops for parents and teachers explained the potential dangers lurking on the internet for ill-informed users.

"The project distributed 8,585 postcards to pupils, 4,600 leaflets to parents, and 980 manuals on teaching equal opportunities in schools."

Case Study 2: €45,902

 Tamsalu municipality in Estonia is taking on a challenge that is widespread in Europe – the employability of young mothers. Women with small children have a high risk of unemployment and employers are reluctant to take them on as their childcare obligations can mean more time off. Overall, rural female employment in Estonia is only 33% – well below national targets.

"In response the municipality launched the 'Young enterprising women for job creation' project with ESF support. Women often understand the basics of business, but they lack the confidence needed to start out – explains Ülle Kristman of the Tamsalu local government. 'So, together with our partner MTU-ETNA (Non-profit association of enterprising women in Estonia) we launched training courses to encourage a more entrepreneurial environment for women in the region'.

"Originally the project aimed for 40 participants, but altogether 60 received training in topics such as IT skills, and business and accountancy – with real success for some. These include, for example, a new company making wooden sleighs as well as jewellery and handicraft enterprises. Some women returned to higher education to get the qualifications they need for the future. Mentoring by established local businesswomen also played an important role."

Case Study 3: €887,000

The Pergolese Spontini Foundation is a promoter of music and theatre in Italy's Marche region.

In February 2010, with full ESF funding, it launched the Sipario project to train people for work in live music and theatre. Thirteen different vocational courses covered not only artistic callings like singing, dancing and orchestral conducting, but also events management and communication, plus technical skills such as costume design, lighting, sound and scenography. Each course was free and lasted 600 to 700 hours, over one year.

 The response was overwhelming, with hundreds of applications from young people all over Italy and beyond. Out of some 800

candidates, 530 hopefuls were selected and 182 finally accepted on courses, with 159 of them obtaining professional qualifications by the end.'

"*Students acquired practical experience in their chosen fields, taking part in 15 musical productions in Marche and elsewhere. And the Foundation also helped them find work after the courses finished: by September 2011, 67 of the trainees had secured contracts.*

"*Over the last decade, Italy's performing arts have suffered huge cuts in state funding, and recently even lottery resources have diminished. 'Sipario was unique,' says coordinator Germana Giorgerini. 'The world of live entertainment is in crisis in Italy at present, and yet at the same time there is a shortage of trained professionals. Thanks to the ESF, this project was able to give new hope to a whole group of aspiring young artists.' *"

€84 BILLION

Amount targeted at the ESF for the 2014-2020 programme

€575 MILLION

Amount earmarked on the Progress axis for 'social innovation and experimentation'

3,775

Number of words in Council Decision 2010/707/EU, setting out the strategic guidelines of what member state employment policy should be

PLANNED PRIORITIES FOR FUTURE ESF ENVIRONMENTAL GRANTS

★ Climate change adaptation and risk prevention
★ Water and waste sectors
★ Biodiversity including through green infrastructures
★ Urban environment
★ Low carbon economy

FLEXICURITY

Current EU buzzword on the need for the workforce to adapt to a less stable and fixed working career environment

DG ENER

★ Develop energy sectors which best meet the needs of citizens and the economy, whilst minimising damage to the environment

1:2

The DG's long-term objective for the divergence in energy prices between the cheapest and most expensive EU states

€286.5 MILLION

Money set aside for the completion of six offshore wind projects

20%

EU objective in reducing energy consumption by 2020

EU objective for the share of renewable energies in use by that year

EU POLICY ON NUCLEAR ENERGY

While it is up to the Member States to choose whether or not to use nuclear energy, the role of the EU is to develop in the interest of all Member States the most advanced EU legal framework for nuclear energy, meeting the highest standards for safety, security and non-proliferation."

€258 MILLION

Money set aside to decommission old, typically Soviet-era, nuclear reactors in 2011

35%

Amount of national electricity produced by Bulgaria's two remaining reactors in 2009

€850 MILLION

Grants provided to Bulgaria to close down its reactors. It had previously been an electricity exporter

58

Number of reactors in France, supplying 75% of its electricity

17%

Amount of national electricity currently supplied by the Cernavoda nuclear plant power in Romania. MEPs have raised its accident record and the fact that it sits in an earthquake zone as issues

DG ELARG

TASKS OF DG ELARG

★ Take forward the process of enlargement of the European Union

€259 MILLION

Budget for the current aid programme for Turkish Cypriots, who are EU citizens despite the directly applicable writ of the EU not extending to the North

NUMBER OF CHAPTERS (NEGOTIATED COMPETENCE BLOCKS) SUCCESSFULLY CLOSED, BY CANDIDATE COUNTRY, AS AT DECEMBER 2010

Croatia	**28/35**
Turkey	**1/33**
FYROM	**0**
Iceland	**0** (but **2** closed in June 2011)
Montenegro	**0**

€1.21 BILLION
2012 IPA budget – the EU's Pre-Accession assistance for applicant countries

€900 MILLION
Amount earmarked for Turkey

22% TO 25%
Amount of that total being spent on Turkish agriculture

€481.6 MILLION
Additional amount available for the pre-accession countries – Albania, Bosnia-Herzegovina, Serbia and Kosovo

€21,200
GDP per capita in Southern Cyprus in 2010

€9,500
Estimated GDP per capita in Northern Cyprus

MODEL DESIGN OF THE NATIONAL TRADEMARK FOR TURKEY-EU TRADE

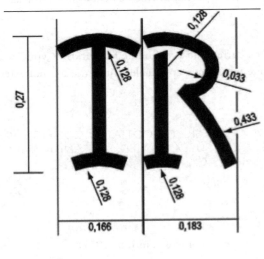

ONGOING ACCESSION ISSUES, BY APPLICANT STATE, AS SEEN BY THE COMMISSION

CROATIA

★ Judiciary and fundamental rights, in particular the independence and efficiency of the judiciary, the fight against corruption and organised crime

★ Respect for and protection of minorities, including refugee return; war crimes trials and full co-operation with the ICTY (International Criminal Tribunal for the former Yugoslavia) including settling the issue of access for ICTY to documents

TURKEY

★ Cyprus

★ Freedom of expression and of the press, freedom of religion, fight against torture and ill-treatment

★ Comprehensive structural reform

★ Fisheries, social policies, justice and home affairs

★ Longstanding trade irritants

★ Administrative capacity to implement and enforce the EU-related legislation

FYROM (FORMER YUGOSLAV REPUBLIC OF MACEDONIA)

★ Strengthen democracy and the rule of law and respect of fundamental rights

★ Sound fiscal policy and continued structural reforms

★ Administrative capacity for the implementation and enforcement of legislation

★ Maintaining good neighbourly relations, including a negotiated and mutually accepted solution to the [Macedonia] name issue, under the auspices of the UN, are essential

★ Actions and statements which could negatively affect good neighbourly relations should be avoided

ICELAND

★ The country meets the political criteria for EU membership and is considered a functioning market economy. However, the economy is still struggling with the effects of the financial crisis.

★ Iceland's overall level of preparedness to meet EU legislative requirements is good, especially in the chapters falling under the EEA Agreement.

★ However, preparations are at an early stage and structural changes are necessary in some areas such as fisheries, agriculture and rural development, environment including whaling, regional policy, as well as in food safety, veterinary and phytosanitary policy.

★ Considering the divided public opinion on accession, efforts need to be made to ensure that Icelandic citizens are properly informed about the EU.

MONTENEGRO

★ Rule of law, judicial reform, electoral reform

★ The role of parliament, public administration reform, media freedom and co-operation with civil society, addressing discrimination and the situation of displaced persons

★ The fight in particular against organised crime and corruption

★ Continue its constructive engagement in regional co-operation

★ Further enhance its administrative capacity and impartiality including in sensitive areas such as environmental protection

ONGOING ACCESSION ISSUES, BY WANNABE APPLICANT STATES, AS SEEN BY THE COMMISSION

ALBANIA

Albania needs to continue its reform process. Key priorities focus on the stability of institutions guaranteeing democracy, the rule of law, judicial reform, the fight against corruption and organised crime, electoral reform, public administration reform and the protection of human rights including property rights. Furthermore, Albania needs to overcome the current political stalemate establishing a constructive and sustained political dialogue to ensure the proper functioning of parliament.

BOSNIA AND HERZEGOVINA

Bosnia and Herzegovina has made little progress over the reporting period. The domestic political climate did not improve and the lack of a shared vision by political leaders on the direction of the country continued to block key reforms and further progress towards the EU.

SERBIA

Full co-operation with the International Criminal Tribunal remains an essential condition for membership of the EU. Judicial reform needs to continue: there were serious shortcomings in the re-appointment procedure of judges and prosecutors.

KOSOVO

Further efforts are needed to tackle successfully organised crime and corruption and to improve co-operation with all communities. Considerable reforms and investments are needed to enable Kosovo's economy to cope over the long term with competitive pressure and market forces within the Union.

DG ENTR

TASKS OF DG ENTR

★ Strengthen Europe's industry and promote the transition to a green economy

★ Promote innovation as a means to generate jobs and meet societal needs

★ Encourage the creation and growth of small businesses and promote an entrepreneurial culture

★ Ensure an open internal market for goods

★ Support the European presence in space

€1.4 BILLION

Amount available under the EU's six-year research programme into its security missions

Space systems are clearly strategic assets that demonstrate independence and the ability to assume global responsibilities. To maximise the benefits and opportunities that they can provide to Europe now and in the future, it is important to have an active, co-ordinated strategy and a comprehensive European Space Policy.

European Commission policy justification

EGNOS

The European Geostationary Navigation Overlay Service, associated with the Galileo satellites

€3.4 BILLION

Additional funding dedicated to Galileo in 2008, to run to 2013

UP TO €90 BILLION

Commission's estimate of the value of Galileo to European industry over 20 years. Galileo duplicates existing satnav systems, so the estimate is controversial

WHERE THE SATELLITE CENTRES ARE BEING BUILT

★ **Two ground-based control centres (GCCs):** Oberpfaffenhoffen and Fucino
★ **Galileo Security Centre (GSMC):** France and the UK
★ **GNSS Service Centre (GSC):** Madrid
★ **Search and Rescue Centre (SaR):** Toulouse
★ **Galileo performance centre:** to be decided
★ **In-orbit-testing station:** Rédu (Belgium)
★ **Control stations (TTC):** Kiruna (Sweden), Kourou, Tahiti, Réunion, Nouméa
★ **Quality stations (GSS):** Fucino, Svalbard, Rédu, Réunion, Kourou, Nouméa, Troll (Norway), Papeete, Kiruna, Jan Mayen (Norway), Azores, Canaries, Madeira, Kerguelen, Terre Adélie, Saint Pierre et Miquelon, Wallis, Ascension, Diego Garcia, the Falklands
★ **Upload stations (ULS):** Tahiti, Kourou, Réunion, New Caledonia, Svalbard
★ **Search and Rescue stations (SaR):** Svalbard, Toulouse, Makarios (Cyprus), Maspalomas (Spain)

2.7 MILLION

Number of logged pre-registrations for 140,000 substances for the 2008 deadline of the REACH chemicals legislation.

180,000

Number of pre-registrations that had been anticipated, involving 29,000 substances

Source: Royal Society of Chemistry (RSC)

€1.6 BILLION
2.6 MILLION ANIMALS

Original estimates of the cost of compliance with the REACH legislation

€9.5 BILLION
54 MILLION ANIMALS

Best case estimates arising from a study by toxicologists in 2009, blaming in part late amendments to the draft

Source: RSC

WHEN IS A TOY NOT A TOY?

Stated exemptions from the 2009 Toys Directive

(a) playground equipment intended for public use

(b) automatic playing machines, whether coin operated or not, intended for public use

(c) toy vehicles equipped with combustion engines

(d) toy steam engines

(e) slings and catapults

€4 MILLION

Annual budget of the EU-Japan centre, founded in 1987 and part-funded by the Commission and by the Japanese government

€14.1 BILLION

EU sum trade deficit in ores and quarrying

LEADING MINING REGIONS FOR SELECTED INDUSTRIAL MINERALS 2006

Mineral	Region	Proportion mined in region
Fuller's Earth (absorbent)	USA	72%
Graphite (steel making)	China	60%
Feldspar (glass, ceramics)	EU	60%
Barite (drilling, paper)	China	55%
Perlite (aggregate)	EU	54%
Boron (fibreglass)	Turkey	53%
Fluorspar (acids, smelting)	China	51%
Zircon (ceramics)	Australia	49%
Phosphate (cleaning, flame-retardants)	Morocco	49%
Bentonite (fillers, thickeners)	USA	44%
Vermiculite (plasters)	South Africa	43%
Talc (paper, coating, filler)	China	37%
Magnesite (slag former)	China	32%
Kaolin (as talc)	EU	31%
Diamonds (gemstones)	Russia	30%
Potash (fertiliser)	Canada	30%
Gypsum (plaster, cement)	EU	23%
Salt	EU	22%
Sulphur (stripping, bleaching, matches)	USA	19%

COUNTRIES WITH EXPORT RESTRICTIONS ON KEY RAW MATERIALS

CHINA

★ Aluminium (ores, concentrates, unalloyed unwrought metal); cokes; copper (ores, concentrates, intermediates, unwrought metal, master alloys); ferroalloys of chromium, nickel, molybdenum and tungsten;

★ High-tech metals (Rare earths, Tungsten, Indium); magnesium (ores, concentrates, intermediates, unwrought metal);

★ Manganese; molybdenum (ores, concentrates, intermediates, unwrought metal); nickel (ores, concentrates, unwrought metal, electroplating anodes); non-ferrous scrap; yellow phosphorus (chemical)

UKRAINE

Cokes; ferrous scrap

RUSSIA

Ferrous scrap; non-ferrous scrap; wood

INDIA

Iron ore; non-ferrous scrap; raw hides and skins

PAKISTAN

Non-ferrous scrap; raw hides and skins

ARGENTINA, BRAZIL

Raw hides and skins, wet-blue leather

NUMBER OF EU MINING CONSORTIA IN THE TOP TEN GLOBALLY	NUMBER EXCLUDING UK INTERESTS
3	0

450

Number of participants at the European Cluster Conference in 2010

DG ENV

★ Propose policies that ensure a high level of environmental protection in the European Union and that preserve the quality of life of EU citizens

★ Ensure that member states correctly apply EU environmental law, by investigating complaints made by citizens and non-governmental organisations, and taking legal action if it is deemed that EU law has been infringed

1973
Year DG Environment was established

200
Number of items of EU environmental legislation

€2.143 BILLION
Current six-year budget of the department's LIFE programme on the environment

732,000KM²
Designated land area under the Habitats and Birds Directives – 17.3% of total land space

174,000KM²
Designated additional marine area

620
Number of complaints made to the Commission about environmental breaches in 2010

442
Number of infringement cases opened

60
Number of cases referred to the ECJ

27 PAGES
Length of 'Ecology of Desmoulin's Whorl Snail, *Vertigo moulinsiana*', a report part-funded by LIFE looking at a snail now extinct in Luxembourg but happily present in England

Snail habitat action shot from the report

ECOLABEL

An award bearing a standard logo indicating a product or service is judged by the Commission to be environmentally friendly

TOP FIVE COUNTRIES WITH AWARDED ECOLABELS

Italy	**359**
France	**244**
Spain	**83**
Germany	**71**
Denmark	**56**

1,150

Total number of Ecolabels awarded by 2010

€200-€1,200

Cost of applying for an Ecolabel

€1,500

Limit on the annual cost of the licence once issued

SOME THINGS THAT CAN'T BE AWARDED THE ECOLABEL, FROM CASE HISTORY

★ Printed matter printed on Ecolabel paper
★ Cleaning agents in which microorganisms were deliberately added by the manufacturer
★ Cruises

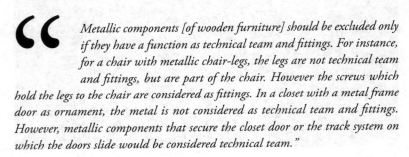

> Metallic components [of wooden furniture] should be excluded only if they have a function as technical team and fittings. For instance, for a chair with metallic chair-legs, the legs are not technical team and fittings, but are part of the chair. However the screws which hold the legs to the chair are considered as fittings. In a closet with a metal frame door as ornament, the metal is not considered as technical team and fittings. However, metallic components that secure the closet door or the track system on which the doors slide would be considered technical team."

DG DEVCO

TASKS OF DG DEVCO-EUROPEAID (FORMERLY TWO DGS, RECENTLY MERGED)

★ Design EU development policies
★ Deliver aid through programmes and projects across the world

0.42%

EU member state average of GDP committed to development aid in 2009

COUNTRIES AT OR IN EXCESS OF THE UN TARGET OF 0.7% OF GDP IN 2009

★ Denmark **0.88%**
★ Luxembourg **1.01%**
★ Netherlands **0.82%**

COUNTRIES UNDER 0.1% OF GDP IN 2009

Bulgaria	**0.04%**	Hungary	**0.09%**
Latvia	**0.08%**	Poland	**0.08%**
Slovakia	**0.08%**		

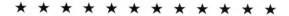

EU DEVELOPMENT SHARE OBJECTIVE

To reach a collective average of 0.7% by 2015

€11.1 BILLION

EU external assistance in 2010

€1.66 BILLION

House of Commons estimate of UK share of this

€200 MILLION

Amount of Third World climate aid that Italy decided to renege on in 2010 due to financial constraints

TEN

Number of EU states that reduced aid spending in 2010

€70 MILLION

Amount of EU aid spent on the Regional Drought Preparedness Programme for the Horn of Africa since 2006

€3.9 BILLION

EU aid to Turkey over 2007-2012

 The logical reason for executing a person who abandons Islam is the following:"

Line from a Palestinian school textbook from a department controversially discovered to be funded from EU and UK grants, as explored in a TPA paper in 2008

€130 MILLION

EU funds provided to Syria over 2007-2010 to encourage reform

COMMISSION'S PRIORITIES FOR LIBYA OVER 2011-2013, AS SET OUT SHORTLY BEFORE THE UPRISING

★ Improving the quality of human capital
★ Increasing the sustainability of economic and social development
★ Addressing jointly the challenge of managing migration

OVER HALF

Amount of EU aid paid directly into recipient country treasuries rather than directly to programme managers

ESTAT

TASKS OF EUROSTAT

★ Provide the European Union with a high-quality statistical information service, particularly with reference to EMU and candidate countries

---

1953

Year Eurostat was established, for the ECSC

1958

Year Eurostat became a DG of the Commission (named as such the following year)

1988

First policy document on statistical information

LUXEMBOURG

Location of Eurostat, putting it apart from most other Commission workforces

FREE

Cost of access to majority of Eurostat information since 2004 (confidential specific statistics are exempt)

1990

Commission establishes a directive on transferring confidential material to Eurostat

THE 64 MILLION EURO QUESTION

The operating budget for Eurostat in 2008 was €45.2 million, plus €18.5 million credits for work from other DGs

15 PRINCIPLES IN THE CODE OF PRACTICE

Principle 1:   Professional Independence

Principle 2:   Mandate for Data Collection

Principle 3:   Adequacy of Resources

Principle 4:   Commitment to Quality

Principle 5:   Statistical Confidentiality

Principle 6:   Impartiality and Objectivity

Principle 7:   Sound Methodology

Principle 8:   Appropriate Statistical Procedures

Principle 9:   Non-excessive Burden on Respondents

Principle 10:   Cost Effectiveness

Principle 11:   Relevance

Principle 12:   Accuracy and Reliability

Principle 13:   Timeliness and Punctuality

Principle 14:   Coherence and Comparability

Principle 15:   Accessibility and Clarity

TEN EXAMPLES OF EUROSTAT MAPS

★ GDP in PPS (purchasing power standards) per inhabitant
★ Total resident population in core Urban Audit cities
★ Share of population aged 65 or older in coastal regions
★ EU capitals and currencies
★ Motorway density
★ Total taxes as percentage of GDP
★ Prison population per 100,000 inhabitants
★ Percentage of the population who have never used the internet
★ Number of deaths in road traffic accidents per million inhabitants
★ Total applications to the European Patents Office

AN EXAMPLE OF ADVICE ON GOOD CARTOGRAPHICAL PRACTICE

The choropleth technique is not appropriate for the portrayal of absolute values that refer to enumeration units. Graduated point symbols, representing quantitative differences by applying the visual variable of "size", should be used instead. The variation of size is utilized along with linear or areal scaling. The point symbols appropriate for size variation through linear scaling are the bar graphs, linear graphs or other linear type graphs. Circles, squares or triangles are the most common symbols used for size variation through area scaling."

1994

First Harmonised Indices of Consumer Prices

FINANCIAL ENVELOPE

A mechanism used by certain Eurostat officials with favoured contractors to cream off surplus from an inflated contract to form special reserves in secret bank accounts. The money generated was reportedly used to fund overseas trips, lunches, a riding club, and a Commission volleyball team – all estimated at around €6 million.

Sources: EUObserver, Euractiv

€56,000

Damages awarded by the ECJ to two of the three senior officials in Eurostat who were investigated in the Eurostat fraud case. The investigating authority had referred to them publicly as guilty of criminal offences.

DG SANCO

TASKS OF DG SANCO

* ★ Empower consumers
* ★ Protect and improve public health
* ★ Ensure Europe's food is safe and wholesome
* ★ Protect the health and welfare of farm animals
* ★ Protect the health of crops and forests

€57.1 BILLION

Amount of food imported into the EU, making it as a bloc the world's biggest food importer

6,300

Number of participants in DG-supported training courses on safer food in 2011

€14 MILLION

Cost of the programme

5%

EU average rate of people acquiring infections while in hospital, around 4.1 million a year

40%

Share of the population of EU states worried that they will suffer a serious medical error

60%

Proportion of staff in an internal survey in 2010 who felt that the DG's mission and policies were clearly communicated to them

68.6%

Number of European Parliamentary Questions answered within the deadline (typically, six weeks of receipt)

£3.5 BILLION	FOUR MILLION
Ministry estimate of the cost to the British economy of the BSE Crisis	Number of British cattle culled over BSE
£27 MILLION	NINE MILLION
Cost of the UK enquiry into BSE	Total British herd

21 MAY 1996

Date John Major begins to empty chair European Council meetings over BSE policy on maintaining a ban, claimed as motivated by self-interest for their own cattle industry sales.

The policy did not apply to:

★ QMV decisions, since the empty chair could be outvoted

★ Discussions before any actual vote

★ Negotiations, although A Points would be vetoed once agreement was reached

★ The furniture, since the chair remained sat in, unlike during De Gaulle's protest

OTHER EXAMPLES OF OBSTRUCTIONISM

★ 1979 France, Denmark and the UK withhold some VAT payments over a procedural dispute over the EEC budget

★ 1981 French, German and Belgians withhold money on a budgetary dispute

★ 1984 Margaret Thatcher threatens to withhold payments after delays to address the UK rebate and refuses an advance payment

★ French threat to block planned 1995 expansion unless Strasbourg remained one seat of the EP

★ Italian veto in 1994 of an increase in the EU budget unless its illegal milk quota was retrospectively signed off and the gigantic fine was forgiven

★ Spanish threatened veto in 1994 of accession to secure regional funding

★ Spanish threatened veto in 1994 unless it gained accelerated fishing access to the Irish Box

★ French and Spanish threatened veto in 1994 over access to Norwegian fisheries

Sources: House of Commons Library; FCO accession briefing papers

620,000

Additional milk quota won by the Italian government in 2009, worth an estimated €240 million, to reduce future fines (rather than actually cutting production)

€1.85 BILLION

Level of outstanding unpaid Italian milk fines at the time of the deal

JANUARY 2012

Date on which Commission notified the Italians that ongoing deferral of repayment of these fines amounted to an illegal subsidy

SIX MONTHS

Duration of De Gaulle's empty chair, resulting in the Luxembourg Compromise

THREE MONTHS

Duration of John Major's empty chair, despite resulting in no compromise

COUNCIL DIRECTIVE 90/423/EEC

Article 13:

1. Member States shall ensure that:

– the use of foot-and-mouth vaccines is prohibited

10.8 MILLION

Meat and Livestock Commission's estimate of the number of animals culled as a result of the Foot and Mouth outbreak

£178 MILLION

Weekly loss to the UK tourist industry alone from Foot and Mouth

Source: University of Nottingham

124%

Value of livestock production in 2008 compared to that of 1996. Uruguay suffered an FMD outbreak at the same time as the UK, but elected for vaccination instead.

7 MONTHS

Time lapse from the discovery of the Uruguay outbreak to the lifting of the ban on de-boned beef

19 MONTHS

Duration of the British ban

£1.2 BILLION

Departmental assessment of the annual export value to the UK farming economy of being classified as FMD-free

DON'T DRINK THE WATER
€4 BILLION

EU funding provided over 2000-2006 to support improvements in the domestic water supply, under regional aid.

90%

Share of this funding that went to Spain, Greece, Portugal and Italy

€25 BILLION

Estimated level of spending on drinking water still needed in the 15 member states eligible for the scheme

DG HOME

TASKS OF DG HOME

★ Create, on the basis of the principle of solidarity, an area of freedom, security and justice without internal borders where EU citizens and third-country nationals may enter, move, live and work

★ Ensure that all activities beneficial to the economic, cultural and social growth of the EU may develop in a stable, lawful and secure environment

★ Develop the Union's capacity to act as a significant partner in international co-operation with third countries in the area of freedom, security and justice

42.2%

2009 deportation rate of apprehended illegal immigrants (252,785 out of 570,660)

515

Total number of terrorist attacks in the EU in 2008, excluding the UK

294

Figure for 2009

140,000

Estimated number of trafficked people in Europe in 2010, per UN estimates

$3 BILLION

Estimated money made by traffickers

32

Number of EU-chartered flights for group return of people to their country of origin

19.5 MILLION

Estimated number of third country nationals within the EU, 3.9% of the population level

19.1%

Average unemployment rate for third country nationals in the second quarter of 2009

SOME EU SECURITY NETWORKS BEING ESTABLISHED

★ European Explosive Ordnance Disposal Network (EEODN)
★ Early Warning System on Explosives (EWS)
★ European Bomb Data System (EBDS)
★ Pan-European Information System on Explosives Control to Prevent and Fight against Terrorism
★ Explosives Security Experts Task Force (ESETF)

54,689

Number of European Arrest Warrants (EAWs) issued between 2005 and 2009

11,630

Number of these warrants executed

MOST FREQUENT COMPLAINTS ABOUT EAWS

★ Limited power of domestic appeal

★ Issued for questioning only

★ Only a minor offence

★ Re-issue of warrants

★ Poor legal representation

★ Prison conditions

An amendment to EAWs was made in 2010 requiring a new box to be inserted into the form for applicants to indicate whether someone already convicted in absentia had been notified of the court proceedings

24	15
Number of countries in the Schengen system, removing border controls and adding increased police co-operation	Number of states that in 2011 voted for the temporary return of border controls to respond to a surge in illegal immigrants

NUMBER OF EAWS ISSUED BY THE UK IN 2009
220

NUMBER ISSUED BY POLAND
4,844

Source: Parliamentary Joint Committee on Human Rights

NUMBER OF PEOPLE SURRENDERED BY THE UK OVER 2009/10 UNDER EAWS
699 (of which, 425 to Poland)

NUMBER SURRENDERED TO THE UK
71

Source: Parliamentary Joint Committee on Human Rights

TOP FIVE RECIPIENT COUNTRIES OF EAWS FROM
THE UK IN 2009/10

Spain **58**

Ireland **39**

Netherlands **31**

France **25**

Poland **19**

Source: Parliamentary Joint Committee on Human Rights

RABIT

Name of the body of EU rapid deployment frontier guards available to assist in border control, as sent to Greece in 2010

64%

Population of the city of Luxembourg in 2010 that came from another country

68

Number of areas up to 2009 where the UK government decided to waive its EU opt out under asylum and immigration, and civil judicial, areas.

4

Number of occasions in comparison where Denmark, another opt out state, decided to waive its opt out

EXACTITUDE

On the cover, and on pages 2 and 3, in the title and the concluding formula:

for: '8 October 2010'

read: '7 October 2010'

Sum total of a published amendment taking up a page of the *Official Journal*, relating to an agreement on short-stay visas

Dutroux

Infamous domestic Belgian case involving a paedophile ring that shocked the country

17

Number of suspicious deaths that some journalists have pointed to in association with the case.

A number of allegations involving senior members of the Belgian establishment, around this case and others, remain unanswered.

DG ECHO

TASKS OF DG ECHO

★ Ensure goods and services get to crisis zones fast

373

Number of natural disasters in 2010

207 MILLION

Number of people affected

300,000

Number of people killed

300,000

Print run of the official comic book – *Hidden Disaster* – that attempts to popularise this DG's work, costed at €225,000

€2 MILLION

EU humanitarian aid to China in 2008

HOLIS 14 POINT REPORT

Mechanism used by member states and the DG to share information on where grants have been given

TOP FIVE HOLIS-LISTED EMERGENCY DONORS IN 2008

UK – €**342.6** million

Sweden – €**340.1** million

Netherlands – €**268.9** million

Germany – €**223.6** million

Denmark – €**178.8** million

DG HR

TASKS OF DG HR

★ Promote excellence in the practice of human resources management and in securing internal security for the European Commission

387

Number of officials since 2004 who have taken advantage of the early retirement without pension reduction scheme

THE COMMISSION'S GENERAL PRINCIPLES OF GOOD ADMINISTRATION

★ **Lawfulness**

The Commission acts in accordance with the law and applies the rules and procedures laid down in Community legislation.

★ **Non-discrimination and equal treatment**

The Commission respects the principle of non-discrimination and in particular guarantees equal treatment for members of the public irrespective of nationality, gender, racial or ethnic origin, religion or beliefs, disability, age or sexual orientation. Thus, differences in treatment of similar cases must be specifically warranted by the relevant features of the particular case in hand.

★ **Proportionality**

The Commission ensures that the measures taken are proportional to the aim pursued.

In particular, the Commission will ensure Code never leads to the imposition of administrative or budgetary burdens out of proportion to the benefit expected.

★ **Consistency**

The Commission shall be consistent in its administrative behaviour and shall follow its normal practice. Any exceptions to this principle must be duly justified.

In 2007, the Commission in Brussels occupied approximately 865,000m² of space, in 61 buildings housing 22,000 staff, of which eight buildings were larger than 20,000m². There were also other scattered buildings housing IT and archives.

These were mainly in:

★ the Quartier européen (710,000m² and 19,000 members of staff)

★ the Beaulieu (80,000m² and 2,000 members of staff)

★ Rue de Genève/Da Vinci area (56,500m² and 1,250 members of staff)

In Luxembourg, the Commission occupied around 125,000m² of office space across five office buildings for 3,740 staff

These were mainly in the Kirchberg area and the Gasperich area.

BOUNDARIES OF THE QUARTIER EUROPÉEN IN BRUSSELS

Cour St Michel to Madou Tower,
Boulevard Clovis to Square de Meeûs.

656	3,350
Number of Commission trainees inducted in the latter 2010 intake	Increase in Commission staff numbers due to the Central/ Eastern Europe accession waves

35,000M²

Increase in office space to accommodate them, in Brussels alone

450 EXTRA STAFF

Commission childcare provision increase on accessions

THE DG'S SECURITY TASKS

★ Preventing or responding to emergencies, by providing a single contact point outside office hours and monitoring the security situation in close collaboration with the national authorities

★ Raising awareness amongst staff of security issues

★ Investigating all illegal acts committed on Commission premises

★ Devising and implementing data security and secure communications measures to facilitate the secure exchange of confidential information both within and outside the Commission

★ Vetting staff

DS.1 – Protection and Crisis Management. Including deployed Health and Safety

DS.2 – Security Intelligence and External Liaison; VIP protection

DS.3 – Security Inspection and Advice

DS.4 – Guards and access (*Gardiennage*)

DS.5 – IT, coordination

DS.6 – Health and Safety at Work

"NO, MR BOND, I EXPECT YOU TO STAPLE."
MANDATE OF DS.2 COUNTER INTELLIGENCE

 DS.2 is the unit which is the point of contact with the intelligence services and national security authorities of the 27 Member States and the candidate countries. Working closely with these contacts, the unit is responsible for gathering, assessing and disseminating any relevant information concerning threats related to the security of the Commission. The unit produces frequent threat assessments and security reports based on this information. DS.2 is also responsible for carrying out security investigations in the fields of espionage, terrorism and in cases of leaks of classified or sensitive information. The unit is also in charge of providing security authorisations for staff who need to obtain access to classified information.

"DS.2 is responsible for security screening and for administrative security investigations connected with the protection of the staff and of the Commission's facilities and information."

"The threat of espionage is increasing day by day. A number of countries, information seekers, lobbyists, journalists, private agencies and other third parties are continuing to seek sensitive and classified information."

Leaked Commission memo from 2008

We are not only pointing the finger at journalists. It could be the pretty trainee with the long legs and the blonde hair."

Commission spokesman

DG DIGIT

★ Enable the Commission to make effective and efficient use of Information and Communication Technologies in order to achieve its organisational and political objectives

AT THE COMMISSION IT IS – APPROPRIATELY – ORGANISED ALONG FEDERAL LINES

Each Directorate-General has an Information Resources Manager – IRM – who is responsible for the specific needs of that DG.

DIGIT provides common (corporate) services and support

€60,000	3-5 MONTHS
Call for tender minimum threshold for the Commission, as per member states	Average length of tender process

DG INFSO

TASKS OF DG INFSO

★ Achieve the digital single market

★ Reinforce Europe's competitiveness by increasing investment in ICT research and innovation

★ Promote the access and use of ICT to the benefit of EU society

★ Implement the *acquis communautaire* in the area of Information Society and Media

'SOCIO-ECONOMIC COST OF NON-EUROPE IN TELECOMS MARKETS'

A study on pushing for a single market on the internet

. ευ

Applications to allow the Cyrillic and Greek versions of the .eu international domain name were submitted in 2010

11,000

Number of Twitter followers of the DG's Commissioner in 2010

70%

Percentage of timely legal advice to units and hierarchy in 2009

15 MILLION

Number of new people around the world estimated to have gone online over three months in 2011

DG MARKT

TASKS OF DG MARKT

★ Proposing and – once laws are adopted – control the implementing of a European legal framework in the following specific areas: regulated professions, services, company law and corporate governance, public procurement, intellectual and industrial property, and postal services

★ In the area of financial services, establish the legal framework for the integration of the Union's capital markets and the creation of a single market for financial services

€10,578,084.2 MILLION

Annual turnover of the services sector across the EU in 2009

€420 BILLION

Value of public procurement advertised in the *Official Journal* in 2009 (i.e. 3.6% of GDP)

12%

Number of defence procurement contracts in the EU published for tender, of which nine-tenths does not relate to warlike material

£11.4 BILLION

Total value of the postal market in the UK

2.15%

Commission estimate for the trade
benefit of the Single Market to EU
economies over 15 years

156%

Increase in value of UK services
between 1998 and 2008

319%

Growth over the same period of
exports of services to BRIC
countries

41%

Share of UK exports of services
that go to EU countries

DG SCIC

TASKS OF DG SCIC

★ Provide quality interpretation services

 The European Union, in its essence, can be seen as one long, on-going, intense political and technical conference."

DG perspective

46%

Amount of work provided to the Council

40%

Amount of work provided to the Commission

THE EP AND ECJ HAVE THEIR OWN INTERPRETING BODIES

50 TO 60
Number of meetings a day for which 'terps are supplied

69
Number of interpreters required to provide total symmetry interpretation between 23 languages at once

RELAY
Use of a bridge language, so language A is translated into language B then retranslated into language C

105
Number of interpreters required if direct matrix interpretation was used instead

2
Number of new booths for the Brussels Chamber that it was estimated there would in reality be space for

1997
Year in which English overtook French to become the most used language for copy in the EP

TOP 5 LANGUAGES OF EP COPY IN 1997

English – **35**%

French – **34.7**%

German – **11.4**%

Spanish – **7.4**%

Italian – **4.4**%

Use of English has further accelerated with subsequent accessions

135,000
Number of interpreter days per year

600 STAFF INTERPRETERS
300 to 400 freelance interpreters per day

3,000 accredited freelance interpreters

15

Number of staff interpreters in 1958, covering four languages

€130 MILLION

Annual interpretation cost

ONE-SIXTH

Amount of interpreter time wasted according to a Court of Auditors report in 2003, owing to the Commission cancelling meetings at the last minute

€18 MILLION

Amount of money the auditors also found was wasted on paying interpreters to hang around drinking coffee in case a meeting might take place

DG JRC

TASKS OF DG JRC

★   Provide scientific-technical advice to policymakers in other DGs

"IT LIVES!"

7

Number of research institutes

5

Number of sites (Belgium, Germany, Italy, Netherlands, Spain)

2,750

Personnel involved

- ★ Towards an open and competitive economy
- ★ Development of a low carbon society
- ★ Sustainable management of natural resources
- ★ Safety of food and consumer products
- ★ Nuclear safety and security
- ★ Security and crisis management
- ★ Reference materials and measurements

€330 MILLION
Annual budget

ASSETS
- ★ High flux reactor
- ★ Linear accelerator
- ★ Biocyclotron and reaction wall

DG JUST

TASKS OF DG JUST

- ★ Promote and enforce the Charter of Fundamental Rights of the European Union

- ★ Coordinate and promote policy developments to combat discrimination on grounds of sex, racial or ethnic origin, religion or belief, disability, age or sexual orientation. Promote awareness on gender equality and non-discrimination. Coordinate policy developments in respect of the Roma

- ★ Enhance citizenship by promoting and protecting citizens' rights in their daily lives, ensuring they fully benefit from European integration

- ★ Develop the European area of justice

- ★ Ensure legal certainty and a level-playing field for citizens, consumers and businesses in enforcing their rights within, and across, national borders, and developing citizen's access to justice through e-justice
- ★ Strengthen the single market for cross-border transactions
- ★ Develop a coherent criminal policy for the EU
- ★ Develop a global, coherent and balanced drugs policy

14%

Proportion of the Commission's work programme for 2011 made up of DG Justice's 18 Strategic and Priority Initiatives

0

Number of member states, in the Commission's eyes, currently fully and correctly applying a 2004 directive on free movement of EU citizens and their families (2004/38)

29.2 MILLION

Number of people across the EU who reported a crime in 2007

50% TO 60%

Estimated level of unreported crime

233 MILLION TO 292 MILLION

Commission's extrapolated figure for number of people affected indirectly in the family

DRUG USE ACROSS THE EU IN 2008

Cannabis – **23** million people

Cocaine – **4** million

Ecstasy – **2.5** million

Amphetamines – **2** million

Opioids (heroin) – **1.2-1.5** million

7,371

Drug related deaths across the EU in 2008

10% TO 23%

Rate of mortality amongst 15 to 49 age group attributable to opioid use

41 OUT OF 46

Number of swabs taken in toilets at the European Parliament that a German news channel took in 2005, that tested positive for cocaine

116 000

European Hotline for missing children

 I know my rights."

33%

Level of people who said they were aware of their rights in EU law on anti-discrimination grounds

17.6%

Average gender pay gap across the EU

9.1%

UK rate

Source: *FT*

OCCASIONS WHERE A RESIDENT EU NATIONAL CAN VOTE IN THE UK

★ MEP elections (in lieu of, not in addition to, a vote in the country of origin)

★ Local council elections

★ All elections, if a national of Ireland, Malta or Cyprus (a Commonwealth not an EU right)

Source: Electoral Commission

DG MARE

TASKS OF DG MARE

★ Promote long-term, sustainable development of the EU's maritime economy – creating more and better jobs for citizens – while protecting the natural ecosystems on which it depends

★ Ensure Europe's coastal communities remain attractive places to live and work

★ Implement the EU's integrated maritime policy and common fisheries policy in co-operation with local, regional, national and international partners

7.7%

Average unemployment rate in EU coastal regions in 2008, compared to the general average of 7%

SIZE OF THE FISHERIES FLEETS OF THE EU ON 30 JUNE 2009

Tonnage: **1,846,552** GT

Power: **6,767,115** kW

SIZE ON 16 NOVEMBER 2010

Tonnage: **1,797,614** GT

Power: **6,628,552** kW

39

Total number of stocks with an assessed Maximum Sustainable Yield (MSY) rate in 2010

11

Number of stock fished at MSY rate

28

Number of stock fished in excess of MSY rate

90%

Estimated maximum level of discards for beam trawls

2%

Annual average decrease in the size of fishing fleet capacity

2.5 TO 3 MILLION TONNES

North Sea catch of main species over the period 1970 to 1995

1.4 MILLION TONNES

Catch in 2007

570,000KM²

Size of the North Sea

1.8 MILLION TONNES

Catches in the Celtic Seas area in 2007

KEY DATES

1970	– Common Fisheries Policy (CFP) introduced as an EEC competence in anticipation of the entry of applicant states with rich fishing grounds
1972	– Fisheries Policy a deciding factor in encouraging Norway not to join EEC
1983	– Total Allowable Catches (TACs) introduced
1985	– Fisheries Policy a deciding factor in encouraging Greenland to withdraw from the EEC
1986	– Spanish and Portuguese entry to the EC adds huge fishing fleets
1988-90	– Factortame Case
1992	– Introduction of licensing system in order to cut down on fleets
2002	– Reform reviews the form of state aid to be allowed to upgrade fishing vessels (which had long profited Iberian vessels); reinforces the policy of governments paying skippers to scrap their ships; creates the Communities Fisheries Control Agency in Spain; and sets up cross-border talking shops called Regional Advisory Councils
2003	– Convention on the Future of Europe; proposal to end CFP does not receive any significant support
2011	– Fisheries Policy a deciding factor in encouraging the Icelandic government to slow its application to join the EU

£55 MILLION

Amount of compensation the UK government was obliged to pay out as a consequence of the Factortame Case. HMG had attempted to stop foreign owners from buying up British licenses to get around national quotas. This was deemed to be in breach of the market.

16%

Proportion of the 'UK' fishing fleet in 2003 that was still in reality foreign owned

NATIONAL WATERS

6 mile limit	National vessels only (exact distance may vary from country to country)
12 mile limit	Under national control, for fishing by local vessels, though with the UK further allowing for historic access by outside fishermen to continue. This is, however, run under a derogation that has to be unanimously renewed every ten years otherwise these waters also join the CFP
24 mile limit	Some rights in relation to national law enforcement
200 mile limit (Exclusive Economic Zone, EEZ)	Fisheries under EU control, under the CFP. Mineral rights including oil retained by member states, but under repeated pressure to relinquish

£5.6 BILLION

Estimated sum value of EU fisheries

50% TO 70%

Ranged estimate of the share of the value of the fisheries that would fall under UK sovereign jurisdiction under international law in the absence of the CFP

31 DECEMBER 2012

Date that the national 12-mile limit derogation protecting inner waters is set to expire

5

Number of times the word 'withdrawal' appears within the DG's fisheries management plan for 2011. The context however is that of products on the market

> *If you are a fisheries minister you sit around the table arguing about fishermen – not about fish. You're there to represent your fishermen. You're there to ensure that if there are ten fish you get your share and if possible a bit more. The arguments aren't about conservation, unless of course you are arguing about another country."*
>
> John Gummer, Fisheries Minister in the 1990s

> *The failure of the CFP has been due in large measure to lack of political will. The evidence of declining stocks, inappropriate control measures, inadequate enforcement and a lack of cohesion between fisheries policy and other Community policies – particularly environment and development – amounts to a tragic catalogue of misgovernment. The failure to manage the fish resource calls into question the EU's ability to manage other policies in a way which is compatible with sustainable development."*
>
> House of Lords Select Committee on the European Union, December 2000

15 MILLION

World fish catch in tons in 1938

86 MILLION TONS

Total in 1989

Source: UN

21,443

Number of fishermen in the UK in 1970

12,700

Number in 2008

X 10

True level of employment once dependent industries are included

Source: TPA Research, All at Sea

1.1 MILLION TONNES

Fish landed from British vessels in 1973

616,000 TONNES

Fish landed from British vessels in 2006

Source: TPA Research, All at Sea

20%

Drop in the number of UK fishing vessels over a ten-year period to 2007

22%

Drop in national capacity (in GT)

16%

Drop in total vessel power (kW)

Source: TPA Research, All at Sea

94,825

Tonnes of fish exported by Iceland alone to the UK market in 2007

Source: TPA Research, All at Sea

£975 MILLION

Total value of all the UK's net imports of fish in 2006, to replace lost domestic fishing capacity

Source: TPA Research, All at Sea

173 MILLION ECU

Amount of EC aid spent on upgrading the UK fishing fleet between 1994 and 1997, compared with:

248 million ECU – *Portugal*
267 million ECU – *France*
1,163 million ECU – *Spain*

1,400 – Number of obsolete Spanish vessels replaced that may not otherwise have been

1,800 – Number of existing Spanish vessels modernised, increasing catch capability

Source: TPA Research, All at Sea

MONEY SOMETIMES FOR OLD ROPE

Examples of vessels found to have received decommissioning money by the Court of Auditors:

★ A vessel without a functioning navigational system

★ A boat that had been gutted by a fire

★ A boat without a working engine

★ A smack that was sitting in a harbour and not fishing anyway

£3.58 PER WEEK

Estimated consumer cost to the average UK household of the CFP in shopping trolley terms

Source: TPA Research, All at Sea

MINISTRY FIGURES FOR DISCARDS, JUST BY BRITISH FISHERMEN, JUST FOR 2007, JUST IN THE NORTH SEA AREA, FOR COMPLIANCE WITH THE CFP

• **23,600** tonnes of cod

• **31,048** tonnes of haddock

• **6,000** tonnes of whiting

Source: TPA Research, All at Sea

70,700 TONNES

Estimated biomass of cod in the North Sea in 2009

Source: TPA Research, All at Sea

Feature of CFP		Cost to UK
Unemployment in the fleet and in support industries	–	*£138 million*
Decline in communities	–	*£27 million*
Pending damage to recreational fishing industry, low estimate used	–	*£11 million*
UK share of support to foreign fishing fleets under EU grants	–	*£64 million*
UK share of support to foreign fisheries industry under EU grants	–	*£1 million*
Redeemable UK share of EU third water fishing permits	–	*£12 million*
Loss of comparative competitiveness	–	*£10 million*
Ongoing decommissioning schemes	–	*£4 million*
Foreign flagged UK vessels	–	*£15 million*
Administrative burden	–	*£22 million*
Loss of access to home waters under 200nm principle	–	*£2.1 billion*
Higher food prices factored into social security payments	–	*£269 million*
Economic value of dumped fish	–	*£130 million*
Total estimated economic cost to the UK of the CFP	–	*£2.8 billion*

Source: TPA Research, All at Sea

9

Number of EU countries with an Atlantic coastline

27

Number of EU countries that vote on the CFP, predominantly applying to the north east Atlantic

OF THE LAST FOUR FISHERIES COMMISSIONERS DEALING
WITH THE REFORM OF THE CFP IN THE NORTH SEA:

★ 2 have come from the Mediterranean

★ 1 from the Baltic, and

★ 1 from a country with no coastline (Austria)

POINTS MAKE PRIZES

As of 2012, serious breaches of CFP rules lead to points being awarded both
to fishing vessels and to their skippers. Excess points within a three-year
period suspend fishing rights for two, four, eight or 12 months

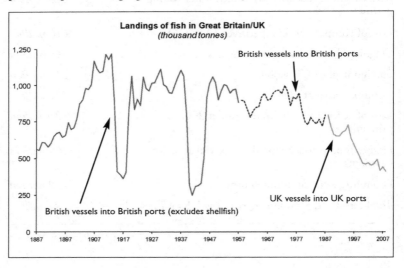

Source: House of Commons Library

CAUSES OF DECLINE IN FISHING ACTIVITY BY THE UK FLEET
IN THE TWENTIETH CENTURY

★ The Kaiser

★ Adolf Hitler

★ The Common Fisheries Policy

DG MOVE

★ Complete the European internal market: ensure the seamless integration of all modes of transport into a single competitive transport system capable of providing better services for citizens and companies at affordable cost, while safeguarding safety and security and improving the rights of passengers

★ Promote the development and roll-out of a new generation of sustainable transport technologies, in particular for integrated traffic management systems and low carbon vehicles

★ Build the EU's core trans-European infrastructure network as the backbone of a multimodal sustainable transport system capable of delivering fast, affordable and reliable transport solutions to serve Europe's transcontinental corridors as well as the needs of its urban centres

★ Project the EU's mobility and transport objectives and defend EU political and industrial interests on the world stage

SLOW CAR CRASH

31,000

Number of fatalities from road traffic accidents in the EU in 2010

3770

Number of intra-EU city to city flight routes in 2009 (down 34 on previous year)

540

Number of accidents in waters of EU states in 2009

1,214

Number of ships detained at EU ports in 2008 after an inspection by the national authority

3,537

Number of railway accidents in EU states in 2009, including level crossing incidents

158

Number of categories of information to be filled in for the EU's Register of Railway Infrastructure covering all sections of line and track

DG REGIO

★ Develop and pursue actions leading to the strengthening of the European Union's economic, social and territorial cohesion, with an objective of promoting a smart, sustainable and inclusive growth

900,000

Estimated number of jobs the Commission believes it created in 2010 as a result of having a Cohesion Policy

1.45

GDP/head disparity ratio in 2007 along either side of the borders of the EU-15/recent accession states

16

Number of industrial parks built in Slovakia over 2007-9 from EU development/regional aid (ERDF)

70%

Increase in peak journey speed for someone on the Athens Underground compared with a car, over 2000-9

4,000KM

Amount of re-laid continental rail over 2007-2013

11,400KM

Amount of re-laid continental motorways

1.2 MILLION HOURS

Estimate of annual road travel time savings to Spain from EU funds

20 MINUTES PER 100KM

Estimate of savings to Portuguese rail journey time from the input of EU funds

33KM/HR

Increased Croatian train speed target on an EU-subsidised corridor

TURKISH TOILETS

2.9 MILLION

Target number of additional population receiving integrated solid waste management systems in Turkey from EU money

€3 BILLION OR 0.6% OF GNI

Definition of the price tag attached to an incident to qualify it as a major disaster and therefore eligible for emergency Solidarity Fund aid – typically, floods

€308 BILLION

Structural and Cohesion Funds budget for 2007-2013

€9.4 BILLION

UK share of receipts

Source: BIS

€8 BILLION

Amount set aside under the 2000-2006 Structural Funds to support tourism

 The activities of persons travelling to and staying in places outside their usual environment for not more than one consecutive year for leisure, business and other purposes."

Commission definition of tourism

73%

Number of audited projects where spending had led to any increase in tourism

4.8%

Share of projects based in the UK. One-third are in Italy

EETS

European Electronic Toll Service – a unified road charging computer system authorised in 2009

DG RTD

TASKS OF DG RTD

★ Support research and innovation through European Framework Programmes

★ Coordinate and support national and regional research and innovation programmes

★ Contribute to the creation of the European Research Area by developing the conditions for researchers and knowledge to circulate freely

★ Support European organisations and researchers in their co-operation at the international level

ONE

Number of European countries outspending the US in R&D share in 2005 – Iceland

18%

EU share of world steel production. China is the world leader with 35% of the global share

40%

Coal's share of global electricity generation

0.09%

Venture capital as a 2009 share of EU countries' combined GDP

80%

Share of EU governments' total spending on R&D spent by the Big Four plus Spain

€7.6 BILLION

EU's projected R&D budget for 2012

£15.6 BILLION

UK's private sector R&D budget in 2009

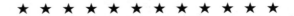

★ ★ ★ ★ ★ ★ ★ ★ ★ ★ ★ ★

Secretariat-General

★ Defines the Commission's strategic objectives and priorities and shapes cross-cutting policies.

★ Coordinates, facilitates, advises and arbitrates

★ Facilitates the smooth running of the Commission through planning, programming and operation of an efficient/modern registry

★ Acts as the Commission's interface with the other European institutions, national parliaments and non-governmental organisations and entities

ORDER OF PRECEDENCE OF HEADS OF MISSION TO THE EU, AS AT DECEMBER 2011

Holy See

Djibouti

Burkina Faso

Argentina

Mali

Niger

Morocco

Togo

Guyana

Russia

The Papal Nuncio always assumes precedence and is automatically the Doyen of the accredited Diplomatic Corps. All others are based on length of accreditation, thus China follows Nepal, and the United States Haiti, with Canada third from bottom. The longest-serving diplomat assumes the position of Vice-Doyen.

The Commission has a protocol service of 13 staff to assist.

Diplomats and their resident families enjoy diplomatic immunity, including the use of CD plates.

FLAG DAYS

> *As is customary, Diplomatic Missions accredited to the European Union fly their national flag over their chancellery building and, if they so wish, over the residence of their Head of Mission, on 9 May, Europe Day.*
>
> *Missions in Brussels also fly their flag on the following dates:*
>
> *21 July: Belgian national day*
> *15 November: Feest van de Dynastie/Fête de la Dynastie*
>
> *The national flag may also be flown for special ceremonies and other specific reasons."*

THE SECRETARIAT IS RESPONSIBLE FOR MAINTAINING AND ARCHIVING THE:

Comitology Register, listing the groups made up of people delegated by national governments to provide **formal opinions**

Register of Expert Groups, listing the consultative groups made up of specialists from outside of government with an interest or obvious expertise, to provide unbinding **advice**

Transparency Register, for lobbyists

TYPES OF EXPERT GROUPS

★ **Formal expert group** set up by a Commission decision
★ **Informal expert group** set up by an individual Commission department

"Expert groups may be composed of the following types of members:
* ★ *individuals appointed in their personal capacity;*
* ★ *individuals appointed to represent a common interest shared by stakeholders in a particular policy area; they shall not represent an individual stakeholder;*
* ★ *organisations, in the broad sense of the word including companies, associations, non-governmental organisations, trade unions, universities, research institutes, union agencies, union bodies and international organisations;*
* ★ *Member states' authorities, at national, regional or local level"*

DG TAXUD

TASKS OF DG TAXUD

* ★ Develop and manage the Customs Union
* ★ Develop and implement tax policy across the EU for the benefit of citizens, businesses and the member states

TOTAL TAX RATE BY EU COUNTRY, 2010

TTR represents total tax levels on a company as a percentage of its pre-tax profit.

21.1%	–	Luxembourg	**47.2%**	–	Greece
23.2%	–	Cyprus	**47.8%**	–	WORLD AVERAGE
26.5%	–	Ireland	**48.2%**	–	Germany
29%	–	Bulgaria	**48.7%**	–	Slovakia
29.2%	–	Denmark	**48.8%**	–	Czech Republic
35.4%	–	Slovenia	**49.6%**	–	Estonia
37.3%	–	UK	**53.3%**	–	Hungary
38.5%	–	Latvia	**54.6%**	–	Sweden
38.7%	–	Lithuania	**55.5%**	–	Austria
40.5%	–	Netherlands	**56.5%**	–	Spain
42.3%	–	Poland	**57%**	–	Belgium
43.3%	–	Portugal	**65.8%**	–	France
44.6%	–	Romania	**68.6%**	–	Italy

(The UK has the largest rate on actual profits, but a comparatively very low rate on labour and other taxes. Figures for Malta were not included in the statistics.)

Source: World Bank

PAPER TRAIL

Total business man hours spent on filling in tax paperwork, 2010.

59	—	Luxembourg	——	—	EU AVERAGE
76	—	Ireland	224	—	Greece
81	—	Estonia	243	—	Finland
110	—	United Kingdom	257	—	Slovak Republic
122	—	Sweden	260	—	Slovenia
132	—	France	277	—	Hungary
134	—	Netherlands	285	—	Italy
135	—	Denmark	293	—	Latvia
149	—	Cyprus	298	—	Portugal
156	—	Belgium	325	—	Poland
170	—	Austria	557	—	Czech Republic
175	—	Lithuania	616	—	Bulgaria
197	—	Spain			
215	—	Germany			
222	—	Romania			

(The seven economies which take the most time have on average twice as many labour taxes as the economies which take the least time.)

Source: World Bank

17/27/1

Number of hours on average required for businesses to comply/file/pay labour taxes in the UK, a total of 45 hours

60/24/24

EU average, a total of 108 hours. The EU has the highest regional level of labour taxes globally, exacerbated by multiple taxes

Source: World Bank

TOP FIVE EU COUNTRIES FOR EASE OF PAYING TAXES, AS WORLD RANKED

Ireland – **7th**

Denmark – **13th**

Luxembourg – **15th**

UK – **16th**

Netherlands – **27th**

EU average – **69th**

WORLD TOP TEN TRADE LOGISTICS PERFORMERS, 2010

Germany

Singapore

Sweden

Netherlands

Luxembourg

Switzerland

Japan

UK

Belgium

Norway

Source: World Bank

12%

Estimated level of EU VAT fraud

€107 BILLION

Estimated value of VAT fraud in 2005

€80 BILLION

Commission's estimated burden to business resulting from administering VAT

JD WETHERSPOON PLC V THE COMMISSIONERS FOR HER MAJESTY'S REVENUE AND CUSTOMS

2009 Luxembourg ruling that resolved that it was up to member states and not businesses as to whether or not to round up or down the VAT amount charged on a pint

DG TRADE

TASKS OF DG TRADE

★ Implement the common trade policy of the European Union

★ Through the EU's trade policy to secure prosperity, solidarity and security in Europe and around the globe

EU COUNTRIES IN THE TOP 20 WORLD RANKING IN BORDER ADMINISTRATION OF TRADE, 2010

2 – *Sweden*

3 – *Denmark*

4 – *Netherlands*

7 – *Ireland*

8 – *Finland*

9 – *Austria*

11 – *Estonia*

13 – *United Kingdom*

15 – *Germany*

20 – *Luxembourg*

Source: World Economic Forum

23	98.7%
Number of ongoing major trade negotiations as at 2010, including free trade agreements, between the EU and a third country	Total trade value of abolished duties, for both industrial and agricultural products, that will happen within five years from the entry into force of the FTA between the EU and South Korea

€19.1 BILLION

Estimated value of trade generated in the EU by that FTA

2.75 MILLION

Commission estimate of the jobs created by the Single Market between 1996-2006

4.3%

Increase of the volume of EU trade with third countries over the same period

218%

Increase in intra-NAFTA merchandise trade between 1993 and 2010, to $944.6 billion

£500 MILLION

Increased annual cost to UK consumers owing to EU tariffs on North American clothing

Source: WTO

1.1% TO 1.5%

European Commission estimate of EU incomes rate of rise over 1989-1993 attributed to WTO arrangements

Source: WTO

GATT TRADE ROUNDS

Year	Place/name	Subjects covered	Countries
1947	Geneva	Tariffs	23
1949	Annecy	Tariffs	13
1951	Torquay	Tariffs	38
1956	Geneva	Tariffs	26
1960-1961	Geneva Dillon Round	Tariffs	26
1964-1967	Geneva Kennedy Round	Tariffs and anti-dumping measures	62
1973-1979	Geneva Tokyo Round	Tariffs, non-tariff measures, framework agreements	102
1986-1994	Geneva Uruguay Round	Tariffs, non-tariff measures, rules, services, intellectual property, dispute settlement, textiles, agriculture, creation of WTO, etc	123
1995	WTO created		

Source: WTO

KEY WTO MEETINGS SINCE GATT

Singapore – **1996**

Geneva – **1998**

Seattle – **1999**

Doha – **2001**

Cancún – **2003**

Hong Kong – **2005**

Geneva – **2008**

"COMPARATIVE ADVANTAGE"

 Countries prosper first by taking advantage of their assets in order to concentrate on what they can produce best, and then by trading these products for products that other countries produce best."

Total permitted tonnage of frogs' legs treated by ionising radiation in approved irradiation facilities within the European Union in 2007

Belgium – **1,521** tonnes

France – **687** tonnes

Netherlands – **343** tonnes

€1 MILLION

2011 budget for the European Network of Mentors for Women Entrepreneurs

72

Number of pages of natural mineral waters recognised in the EU

THREE YEARS

Transitional period allowed for Cornish pasty manufacturers to continue to brand their products as before, if they aren't made in Cornwall

Source: WTO

£1.7 BILLION

Amount of pensions liability the UK government intended to write off from the Royal Mail Group. The Commission challenged this in 2011

EUROPEAN YEARS

Small Business was the inspiration for the first European Year. These have been continued over time to cover a wide range of themes

Year	European Year
2013	European Year of Citizens
2012	of Active Ageing
2011	of Volunteering
2010	for Combating Poverty and Social Exclusion
2009	of Creativity and Innovation
2008	of Intercultural Dialogue
2007	of Equal Opportunities for All
2006	of Workers' Mobility
2005	of Citizenship through Education
2004	of Education through Sport
2003	of People with Disabilities
2001	of Languages
1999	of Action to Combat Violence Against Women
1998	of Local and Regional Democracy
1997	against Racism and Xenophobia
1996	of Lifelong Learning
1995	of Road Safety and Young Drivers
1994	of Nutrition and Health
1993	of Older People and Solidarity between Generations
1992	of Health and Safety at Work
1990	of Tourism
1989	of Information on Cancer
1988	of Cinema and Television
1987	of the Environment
1986	of Road Safety
1985	of Music
1984	for a People's Europe
1983	of SMEs and the Craft Industry

EUROPEAN YEAR OF THE BRAIN

What the European Brain Council unsuccessfully lobbied 2013 should be designated as. They are now angling for 2014

€1 MILLION

Commission's standard European Year thematic budget

DGT

★ To operate as the European Commission's in-house translation service

---

OFFICIAL LANGUAGES OF THE EU

Dutch, French, German, Italian – **1958**

Danish, English – **1973**

Greek – **1981**

Portuguese, Spanish – **1986**

Finnish, Swedish – **1995**

Czech, Estonian, Hungarian, Latvian, Lithuanian,
Maltese, Polish, Slovak, Slovene – **2004**

Bulgarian, Irish, Romanian – **2007**

OTHER LANGUAGES
OCCASIONALLY NEEDED

Russian

Arabic

Chinese (et al.)

60

Number of regional and minority
European languages

EUROPE'S PAST LINGUE FRANCHE

★ Greek
★ Latin
★ Sabir (pidgin Italian, Mediterranean trade, aka 'lingua franca')
★ French
★ German (central and eastern Europe)
★ English

18TH CENTURY

Latin still in use as the official diplomatic language of Sweden, trying to resist the growth of French

1844

Year Latin ceased to be the official language of Hungary

ARTIFICIAL LANGUAGES (NOT USED, BUT ELIGIBLE FOR EU GRANTS)

Solresol, based on musical notes (1817)

Esperanto (1870s)

Volapük, based on German and English (1880s)

Latino sine Flexione, using simplified Latin (1903)

COUNTRIES THAT PERSECUTED ESPERANTO SPEAKERS

★ Nazi Germany
★ Japan
★ Soviet Union under Stalin
★ Spain under Franco

1,000

Number of 'native' Esperanto speakers globally

PERCENTAGE OF EUROPEANS WHO CAN HAVE A CONVERSATION IN A GIVEN LANGUAGE THAT IS NOT THEIR OWN (2005)

English – **38%**

French – **14%**

German – **14%**

Spanish – **6%**

Russian – **6%**

1%

One expert estimate of the value to UK GNP of being native English speakers

PART
FOUR

Beyond the Commissioners

MAY CONTAIN TRACES OF
SOLDIERS, LOBBYISTS
AND HIDDEN CAMERAS

PART

FOUR

Beyond the Competences

Outside of the confines of the Commission, there are a range of institutions with varying degrees of importance, fulfilling roles in areas where countries sometimes differ wildly on what they want to see achieved.

The Common Foreign and Security Policy (CFSP)

In a nutshell…

 The key institution behind the CFSP is the External Action Service, or EAS. While run by a Commissioner, it stands apart. Alongside the diplomacy, the other aspect of the CFSP is defence policy, which currently focuses on defence procurement and EU peacekeeping missions.

THE CFSP IS NOT TO BE CONFUSED WITH…

EU DG COMM staff based within the EU itself at national capitals:

★ 35 representations and offices
★ 234 Officials, 328 Contract Agents, and 55 Local Agents
★ Comprising 56% of the staff of DG Communication

34	32,949
Number of these DG COMM staff based in London, compared with 33 in Warsaw and 23 in Copenhagen	Total Commission staff

€3.9 BILLION

Annual EU budget for international relations, as run by the EAS

€63 MILLION

Annual cost of the EU embassies

€432 MILLION

2011 operating budget of the EAS

1,643

EAS civil service payroll as of 2011

5,400

Reported target number

Source: BBC

€34 MILLION

Property value of the most expensive EU embassy, in Tokyo

£24 MILLION

Reported cost of the new Europe House in central London

42

Number of times the EU flag appears in one publication from the EU embassy at Washington DC

37

Number of international organisations in which the EU has corporate membership

120

Number of EU ambassadorial residences. In Moscow, the residence is reportedly a listed eighteenth century building.

41

Number of international agreements in which the EU has declared it is the sole negotiating authority in the area

42

Number of bilateral agreements signed by the EU with other countries containing a human rights clause

456

Number of pages in the document listing the bilateral agreements signed by the EU

THREE-FIFTHS

Proportion of EU bilateral treaties signed since 2000

TOP FIVE AREAS OF EU MULTILATERAL TREATY SUBSTANCE

Environment – **24.5%**

Trade – **12.2%**

External Relations – **7.9%**

Customs – **7.4%**

Energy – **7.4%**

248

Number of pages in the document listing the multilateral agreements signed by the EU

€10 MILLION

Dedicated budget for selling EU policy abroad

"PROMOTING PEACE AND MUTUAL UNDERSTANDING."

Reason for the award in 2008 of the Peace Prize of the Children's United Parliament of the World (CUPW) to Javier Solana, CFSP High Representative

A NATURALLY GROWING ROLE: AUGUST 2011

Date of the Commission gaining Observer Status at the World Organisation for Animal Health, two experts on the Advisory Committee, and at least two experts on the Global Steering Committee covering Transboundary Animal Diseases

1890

Cut off manufacturing date for models of revolvers, pistols and machine guns that have to be notified to the EU as part of the Common Military List relating to arms exports controls

15

Number of variations of Bin Laden's name listed on the regulation banning him from travelling on an EU flight, as modified in May 2011 to accommodate the fact he was dead

148TH

Version number of the EU's no-fly list of Al Qaeda terrorists at that point

> *Notice for the attention of Abu Nidal Organisation 'ANO' – (a.k.a. 'Fatah Revolutionary Council', a.k.a. 'Arab Revolutionary Brigades', a.k.a. 'Black September', a.k.a. Revolutionary Organisation of Socialist Muslims) included on the list provided for in Article 2(3) of Council Regulation (EC) No 2580/2001 on specific restrictive measures directed against certain persons and entities with a view to combating terrorism."*

Opening lines of Council Notice 2011/C 183/02, informing Abu Nidal of changes to the paperwork behind why their funds were being frozen. It proceeds:

The group concerned may submit a request to obtain the updated Council's statement of reasons for maintaining them on the abovementioned list to the following address [...]

Such a request should be submitted within two weeks from the date of publication of this notice."

UGANDA

Host country for the EUTM Somalia, the EU Training Mission providing support for Somalian soldiers and police. It enjoys diplomatic immunity.

KEY DATES IN BUILDING A EUROPEAN DIPLOMATIC CORPS

1954 – European Coal and Steel Community (ECSC) information office opens in Washington. It is manned entirely by US nationals until 1958.

1956 – ECSC opens a liaison office for Latin America, in Santiago de Chile. First full diplomatic mission in London also opens (the UK at this stage not being a member).

1964 – New semi-autonomous non-profit agency established. The European Agency for Cooperation (EAC) is funded under a Commission grant, to recruit and manage, under renewable contracts, the heads of mission and staff to man the Commission offices in the associated countries. In this era of De Gaulle, these personnel are thus engaged as contract staff and generally do not enjoy diplomatic status.

Many of these staff are in fact former colonial administrators from member states, or development professionals from the private sector.

21 offices are run, essentially as offshoots of DG VIII rather than the whole Commission.

1971 – European Court of Justice (AETR Judgement) rules that external activity by member states is limited by internal competences and cannot outside of the EEC run counter to directives already made for within the EEC. The Commission's international role will thus automatically expand with legislation and harmonisation.

1972 – Washington legation becomes full embassy as legislation recognising full diplomatic status passes Congress.

1973 – By now, some 320 people are serving in these offices; 120 Europeans (mainly civil engineers and agronomists) and 200 local staff.

1975 – Lomé Convention. Development aid spurs representation. The number of missions in these countries (now upgraded to full delegations of the Commission) doubles to 41 in three years; diplomatic immunity for lead staff first given.

1977 – European Commission sits in on G7 meetings.

1980 – There are 50 now delegations around the world, with over 1,000 personnel working in them. This is around the same figure as the Belgian Foreign Office.

1981 – Commission opens a delegation in Australia, principally to deal with nuclear fuel and in order to defend the Common Agricultural Policy.

1982 – Report to the Council on the external competences of the Community. This contains the acknowledgement that: "The Commission has a nucleus of a foreign service. Its external delegations are doing work directly comparable to Member State embassies."

1988 – Reform: absorption of staff into the Commission mainstream. Number of officials serving in delegations rises overnight from 165 to 440. The local staff number 1,440. There are 89 missions, on all continents except Antarctica.

1990 – The majority of posts are now considered full diplomatic missions by their host countries and many heads of delegation (as the former 'delegates' were now referred to) are being accredited at Head of State level, with credentials signed by the President of the Commission, carrying the rank and courtesy title of ambassador.

1991 – The European Communities becomes the 161st Member of the Food and Agriculture Organisation (FAO), the oldest of the UN's specialised agencies. This is the first time that the future EU will enjoy a status comparable to a member nation in a UN body. EC Membership also crucially introduces the concept of the "alternative exercise of membership rights" between the EC and the member states, which applies not only to voting rights but also to speaking rights. This means that the Commission speaks, negotiates and votes on issues of Communities competence, while the presidency speaks, negotiates and votes on issues of Member State competence.

1993 – The Treaty of Maastricht specifically refers to the External Service for the first time (raising the question as to its earlier legal basis). Under the new Common Foreign and Security Policy, delegations now have a more proactive political role. Recruitment remains haphazard. Anecdotally, one senior figure recalls basing selection on performance in a staff football match.

1998 – Amsterdam Treaty creates the new post of High Representative. This effectively generates a second parallel EU foreign service, representing Council and Commission combined, as opposed to just working for the Commissioner for External Relations.

1999 – Javier Solana appointed High Representative. The position quickly accrues extra responsibilities, as existing posts are combined with his (for instance key roles at the WEU and European Defence Agency). Appointment of Special Envoys begins apace. There is a small but growing number of officials detached from member states' foreign services being placed in delegations. Meanwhile, under the policy of 'deconcentration', responsibility for implementation of assistance programmes is devolved to local offices. €6.5 billion from the EU budget is administered in this way by the European Commission.

2002 – The High Representative becomes one of the partners in the Quadripartite Commission for the Middle East (the envoy at early 2012: Tony Blair).

2003 – Delegation network is by now accredited to over 150 countries. Manned by more than 5,000 staff, it is one of the largest European diplomatic services in its own right. Embassies are often housed in more than one building, with 50-100 staff working within them. Within Europe, Commission embassies are openly involved in supporting Yes campaigns for accession countries, in other words intervening on the pro-integration side in internal democratic debates.

2005 – "It is plain from the DG External Relations website that the outcome of the referendums in 2005 in the Netherlands and France does not seem to have given the Commission pause for thought" (retrospective from House of Commons EU Select Committee, 27th Report). The number of EU staff serving abroad has gone up by a third since 2000.

2006 – Full accreditation to the Vatican (and in the following year full accreditation to the Order of the Knights of Malta) demonstrates the extent of diplomatic representation. Delegation in Iraq. Estonia is cited by the Commission as a case study of where the Commission embassy "contributed towards stimulating the debate over pros and cons of EU accession." In reality, this was achieved by the Commission battle bus driving around the country distributing pro-accession material, while being pursued by Mr Arne Otter: a hefty Estonian Eurosceptic in a clapped-out Volvo protesting at bias.

2007 – Delegations in Switzerland, East Timor, Azerbaijan, Montenegro and the African Union. Upgrading of offices in Armenia and Cape Verde. There are now 118 delegations in third countries and five delegations at centres of international organisations.

2008 – Measures for a delegation in Uzbekistan and permanent representation at the Council of Europe, as well as the upgrading of offices in Kyrgyzstan, Tajikistan, Yemen, Nepal, Togo, Djibouti and Liberia.

€932 MILLION

Sum cost of defence aspects to the EU budget (2009)

7,141	3,212
EU personnel on overseas security missions in 2009	Number deployed in uniform
	13
	Number of missions

MERGING DEFENCE PROCUREMENT

1996 – Quadrilateral Defence Agency (OCCAR)

1998 – Joint ministerial statement on defence procurement harmonisation

2004 – European Defence Agency

30	240
Staff in OCCAR in 1997	Staff in 2009

EUROPEAN DEFENCE PROCUREMENT FAILURES

★ Eurofighter
★ METEOR missile
★ A400M
★ Horizon Frigate
★ Multi-Role Armoured Vehicle
★ Trigat helicopter missile

€14 BILLION

25 year running costs for the Galileo satellite programme (2008 estimate)

EU DEFENCE INSTITUTIONS

★ **Political and Security Committee (PSC)** – ambassadorial-level working group

★ **European Union Military Committee (EUMC)** – MilReps, typically a three-star post. Provides military advice to the PSC through its Chairman

★ **European Union Military Staff (EUMS)** – advisors and planners. Has an operations centre to run a deployed battlegroup

★ **Intelligence Directorate (INTDEF)** – supports EUMS

★ **Committee for Civilian Aspects of Crisis Management (CIVCOM)** – advice on non-military crises

★ **Civilian Planning and Conduct Capability (CPCC)** – permanent Council element

★ **Joint Situation Centre (SitCen)** – monitors and assesses events and situations worldwide

★ **Civilian Intelligence Cell (CIC); General Operations Unit (GOU); Communications Unit (ComCen)** – parts of SitCen

★ **European Security and Defence College (ESDC)** – training for deployment, including media ops

★ **European Group on Training (EGT)** – trains civilian crisis management

★ **EU Institute for Security Studies (EUISS)** – EU version of Chatham House, in Paris

---

100

Reported number of SitCen staff (the actual number is classified)

SOME ARRANGEMENTS OUTSIDE OF THE EU

★ Franco-British European Air Group (FBEAG)

★ European Air Group (Belgium, France, Germany, Italy, Spain, UK)

★ Sealift Coordination Centre (UK, Netherlands)

★ St-Mâlo Accord (UK, France)

★ European Maritime Force (EUROMARFOR or EMF) (France, Italy, Portugal, Spain)

★ European Rapid Operational Force (EUROFOR) (France, Italy, Portugal, Spain)

★ Eurocorps (formerly the Franco-German Brigade) (Germany, Belgium, Spain, France, Luxembourg)

★ European Gendarmerie Force (EUROGENDARMERIE or EGF) (France, Italy, The Netherlands, Portugal and Spain)

★ European Organisation of Military Associations (EUROMIL)

★ European Airlift Centre (Belgium, France, Germany, Italy, Netherlands, Spain, UK)

★ UK-Netherlands Amphibious Force

★ European Amphibious Initiative (France, Italy, Netherlands, Spain, UK)

EU FLAGGED OPS BY 2009

★ ARTEMIS (DR Congo, 2003, **1,800** people)

★ CONCORDIA (fYROM, 2003)

★ EUPM (Bosnia, 2003, **284** people)

★ EUFOR ALTHEA (Bosnia, 2004, **1,950** people)

★ EUJUST THERMIS (Georgia, **2004-5**)

★ EUJUST LEX (Iraq/Brussels, 2005, **42** people)

★ EUBAM (Rafah, 2005, **21** people)

★ EUSEC RD Congo (2005, **44** people)

★ EUPOL Kinshasa (2005-7)

★ Support to AMIS II (Sudan/Darfur, 2005-6)

★ AMM Monitoring Mission (Aceh, 2005-6)

★ EUPOL COPPS (Palaestinian Territories, 2006, **85** people)

- ★ EUPAT (FYROM, 2006)
- ★ EUFOR RD Congo (2006, **2,300** people)
- ★ EUPOL Afghanistan (2007, **459** people)
- ★ EUPOL RD Congo (2007, **60** people)
- ★ EUMM Georgia (2008, **405** people)
- ★ EUNAVFOR – ATALANTA (Indian Ocean, 2008, **1144** people)
- ★ EUSSR Guinea-Bissau (2008, **24** people)
- ★ EULEX KOSOVO, 2008, **2,764** people)
- ★ EUFOR Tchad/RCA (2008-9, **3,700** people)
- ★ EUBAM (Moldova, Ukraine, 2010, **200** people)
- ★ EUTM Somalia (2010, **118** people)

LIST OF DESIGNATED EU BATTLEGROUPS, BY CONTRIBUTORS

1. United Kingdom
2. France and Belgium
3. Italy
4. Spain
5. France, Germany, Belgium, Luxemburg and Spain
6. Germany, Netherlands and Finland
7. Germany, Austria and Czech Republic
8. Italy, Hungary and Slovenia
9. Italy, Spain, Greece and Portugal
10. Poland, Germany, Slovakia, Latvia and Lithuania
11. Sweden, Finland and Norway
12. United Kingdom and Netherlands

EUROPE'S HIGH READINESS BRIGADES: EU MEMBERS AND BEYOND

★ **SHIRBRIG** – Stand-by High. Readiness Brigade for United Nations Operations (Austria, Denmark, Finland, Ireland, Italy, Lithuania, Netherlands, Norway, Poland, Portugal, Slovenia, Spain, Sweden; plus Canada and Argentina as non-EU contributors)

★ **SEEBRIG** – South-Eastern Europe Brigade (Greece, Italy, Slovenia; plus Turkey, Albania, Macedonia)

★ **NORDCAPS** – Nordic Coordinated Arrangement for Military Peace Support (Finland, Sweden, Denmark; plus Norway)

THE NEXT STEPS

The UK is currently vetoing proposals from the High Commissioner to:

★ Set up a permanent military and civilian crisis HQ

★ Pool defence resources within the EU structures

★ Expand the EU role within NATO HQs

★ Formalise the EU battlegroups

WEIMAR INITIATIVE

Multilateral push including France, Germany, Poland, Italy and Spain attempting to circumvent or overcome the British veto

PRE-BRUSSELS CV OF THE HIGH COMMISSIONER FOR THE COMMON FOREIGN AND SECURITY POLICY

Catherine Ashton was born in Upholland in Lancashire, from where she takes her title, Baroness Ashton of Upholland. From 1983-89 she was Director of Business in the Community, and established the Employers' Forum on Disability, Opportunity Now, and the Windsor Fellowship.

Catherine Ashton chaired the Health Authority in Hertfordshire from 1998 to 2001, and became a Vice President of the National Council for One Parent Families.

In 1999 Catherine Ashton became a life peer. She was made Parliamentary Under-Secretary of State in the Department for Education and Skills in 2001, and then Parliamentary Under-Secretary in the Department for Constitutional Affairs and subsequently Ministry of Justice with responsibilities for human rights, freedom of information and equalities. She became a Privy Councillor in May 2006.

Catherine Ashton was appointed Leader of the House of Lords and Lord President of the Council in Gordon Brown's first Cabinet in June 2007. As well as Leader of the Lords, she took responsibility in the House of Lords for equalities issues.

(The official CV excises her role in the late 1970s and 1980s for CND (Campaign for Nuclear Disarmament), culminating in a senior Executive position.)

KEY DATES IN BUILDING A EUROPEAN ARMY

1945 – De Gaulle nurses an enduring grudge over UK support for Syrian independence, though Britain does facilitate the French return to Indo-China.

1947 – Anglo-French Treaty signed at Dunkirk, targeted at future German aggression.

1948 – Treaty of Brussels expands membership of the Anglo-French Treaty, leading to the Western Union Defence Organisation.

1949 – NATO formed.

1950 – Pleven Plan mooted for a supranational European defence system (common forces, defence budget and armaments industry) incorporating Germany.

1954 – Proposal for a European Defence Community rejected by French National Assembly. Germany allowed to enter the WEDO (becoming the WEU), and focus in European integration shifts to economic issues.

1956 – Suez Crisis. Anglo-French military co-operation ends in fiasco, different strategic appreciations of the American military alliance, and divergence.

1960 – Fouchet Plan proposes wider co-operation on issues including defence and foreign policy, a more intergovernmental approach and outside of the EEC. Rejected. Major pause in European defence integration, to last three decades.

1966 – France withdraws from NATO's integrated command.

1967 – Following a British proposal, NATO forms the EUROGROUP committee to improve coordination of the continent's members.

1984 – WEU relaunched in order to improve NATO co-operation with neutral states.

1986 – Westland Affair, essentially over forming a European trade barrier for military helicopters.

1988 – Kohl and Mitterand agree in principal to closer defence structural co-operation.

1990 – Reunification of Germany as Soviet threat recedes. European defence budgets cut in the context of a world recession.

1991 – Franco-German Security and Defence Council becomes operational.

1992 – La Rochelle summit. French and Germans set up Eurocorps. Maastricht Treaty clauses on Common Foreign and Security Policy: a common defence policy which might in time lead to a common defence. Includes provisions for enhanced co-operation in the field of armaments, with a European armaments agency as a proposal to be examined further. EMU criteria place further demands on defence budgets. War in Bosnia. Alternating WEU/NATO-flagged Adriatic blockade begins. Council of the WEU sets out Petersburg tasks, effectively putting the WEU at the service of EC policy decisions.

1993 – British and French airborne and marine elements 'twinned'. WEU sets up Western European Armaments Group.

1994 – Franco-British Air Group formed. Eurocorps parades in Paris.

1995 – Ad hoc EU working group on a European Armaments Policy first formed (POLARM).

1996 – OCCAR (armaments agency) formed. Franco-German summit at Nuremburg declares, "In the European Union our two countries will work together with a view to giving concrete form to a common European defence policy and to WEU's eventual integration into the EU." It also pledges that Germany would be consulted before French nuclear weapons were used.

1997 – France's Europe Minister calls for the extension of the Franco-German "common concept" on security and defence to the whole of the EU. Amsterdam Treaty formalises the role of the WEU previously agreed and adds "peace-making" to the treaties. Principle of QMV attached. Royal Ordnance closure at Bridgwater after a takeover by a French company removes the last British manufacturer of high explosives. Meanwhile, an attempt by GEC to take over Thomson-CSF is blocked. European Commission highlights aerospace industry (including electronics and missiles) as a target for consolidation and restructuring in the face of US competition.

1998 – First common Code of Conduct on Arms Exports. Poertschach meeting: UK endorses separate European defence activity, but British policy is uncertain and ambiguous: "Cela reste a décoder". St Malo summit. Anglo-French bilateralism advanced, but at the cost of lifting the UK veto on EU defence integration. Contemporary reports explain the decision as a deliberate British concession in the context of the retreat from a commitment on joining the euro.

1999 – Cologne Council: "We [...] are resolved that the European Union shall play its full role on the international stage. To that end, we intend to give the European Union the necessary means and capabilities to assume its responsibilities regarding a common European policy on security and defence." As part of the "maintenance of a sustained defence effort" forces will adapt – particularly intelligence, strategic transport, and command and control – with more harmonisation of defence planning and procurement as states declare "We are now determined to launch a new step in the construction of the European Union." Standing

EU bodies authorised. Countries asked to 'pre-identify' deployable assets. Michael Colvin paper in the Commons on WEU options identifies six possible ways forward for the UK. Helsinki Council establishes the target of a combined 'hatted' (but not standing) resource of 60,000 men to achieve EU military policy. A Political and Security Committee, Military Committee, and Military Staff are also formed.

2000 – WEU formally incorporated into EU structures, including its satellite centre. Feira Council: 5,000 deployable Gendarmes added to the asset list. MEPs call for AWACS and carrier groups to be added and a European Security College to be founded to "foster a common culture", coupled with a specific information policy to sell this to the public in the EU and neighbouring states. Prodi gaffe: "If you don't want to call it a European Army, don't call it a European Army. You can call it 'Margaret', you can call it 'Mary-Anne', you can find any name, but it is a joint effort for peace-keeping missions".

2001 – EU Institute for Security Studies established.

2002 – European Convention first inserts Space into draft Community competences. Berlin Plus agreement creates mechanisms for EU to access NATO assets.

2004 – European Defence Agency founded. EUFOR takes over from NATO in Bosnia. Anglo-French agreement on sharing Caribbean naval patrolling duties.

2007 – Treaty of Velsen sets up a European Gendarmerie.

2009 – Lisbon Treaty expands upon EU defence institutions especially in procurement, introduces what amounts to a mutual defence clause, and greatly boosts the post and profile of the CFSP manager (currently Lady Ashton).

2011 – Libya campaign: ostensibly Franco-British but in reality heavily NATO-reliant.

> *In accordance with Article XVI, paragraph 2, of the International Rubber Study Group Constitution, this declaration indicates the powers transferred to the European Union by its Member States in the matters governed by the Constitution.*

"The European Union declares that, in accordance with the Treaty on the Functioning of the European Union, the European Union has exclusive competence with respect to international trade matters under its common commercial policy, including the production of statistics.

"The scope and exercise of the European Union competences are, by their nature, subject to continuous development, and the European Union will complete or amend this declaration, if necessary, in accordance with Article XVI, paragraph 2, of the Constitution."

Council Decision on the EU taking over governments' role on the International Rubber Study Group, an intergovernmental organisation based in Singapore with ten members, of which the EU (since September 2011) is now one.

Other significant institutions

In a nutshell...

The **Committee of the Regions** provides a talking shop for local politicians such as councillors. The **Economic and Social Committee** brings together business and union representatives for comment. The **European Ombudsman** handles complaints. The **Court of Auditors** checks the books, while **OLAF** investigates reported fraud.

COMMITTEE OF THE REGIONS (COR)

There are 344 members of the CoR

★ *"We are ambassadors of Europe in the regions, cities and municipalities and speak for them in the European debate."* **Mission statement**

★ Appointment varies from country to country, reflecting different levels of local government. Spain for instance has 8089 municipalities plus provinces and autonomous communities, as opposed to 522 districts, councils and boroughs in the UK

★ The UK has 24 delegates and 24 alternates

★ A UK member has to also be a member of a local authority or devolved assembly

★ The Local Government International Bureau (LGIB) acts as its secretariat for the UK

★ Nominations: 9 for England from English regional chambers/assemblies and GLA; 7 for England from the Local Government Association; 1 from both the Scottish Executive and MSPs; 2 nominations from the Convention of Scottish Local Authorities; 1 from the Northern Ireland Assembly; 1 from the NI Local Government Association; 1 from the Welsh Assembly; 1 from the Welsh LGA. End approval by the FCO.

★ There are (only) four political groups

★ It has a Directorate for Horizontal Policies and Networks, responsible for liaising with such movements as the Covenant of Mayors (a Commission scheme to fund town hall climate change measures) and the European Grouping of Territorial Cooperation (EGTC) – a device to provide legal sanction to cross border regional/county activity. These are pushing for the development of macro-regions that sit astride nation states.

★ Separate from the Assembly of European Regions (AER) – not an EU institution, but effectively a lobby group that is heavily funded by the EU

★ Designates members to, for instance, the Euro-Mediterranean Regional and Local Assembly (ARLEM)

★ Its draft budget for 2012 is €78.5 million

★ ★ ★ ★ ★ ★ ★ ★ ★ ★ ★ ★ ★

★ 270 member regions

★ Association of European Border Regions (AEBR)

★ Alps-Adriatic Working Community (ALPEN-ADRIA)

★ Working Community of the Western Alps (COTRAO)

★ Working Community of the Danube countries (ARGE DONAULÄNDER)

★ Working Community of the Pyrenees (CTP)

★ Conférence TransJurassienne (CTJ)

★ Working Community Galice – North Portugal

★ Working Community of the Lower and Middle Adriatic

★ Baltic Sea States Subregional Cooperation (BSSSC)

★ Channel Arc Manche

★ World Mountain People Association (WMPA)

★ Assembly of European Wine-Producing Regions (AREV)

★ Assembly of European Fruit and Vegetable Growing and Horticultural Regions (AREFLH)

★ Association of Local Democracy Agencies (ALDA)

★ European Federation of Local Government Chief Executives (UDiTE)

EUROPEAN GROUPINGS OF TERRITORIAL COOPERATION (EGTC)

Set up under Regulation (EC) No 1082/2006, this format allows county leaders and their counterparts to legally co-operate by forming a co-operative unit under the wing of the EU. This also makes them eligible for EU funding.

A highly controversial development with respect to separatist areas seeking "independence within Europe". After consultations in 2011, the programme is nevertheless being extended.

REGIONAL OFFICES

Lobbying centres in Brussels set up by regions or counties.

136

Number of pages of the handbook listing these offices in Brussels

UK OFFICES (AS AT 2008)
Cheshire (established 2001, **two** staff)

Devon (2001, **seven**)

East Midlands (1992, **five**)

East of England (1998, **seven**)

England's Northwest (2000, **two**)

Highlands and Islands (1997, **two**)

Kent (1990, **four**)

Lancashire (1990, **three**)

Liverpool (1998, **two**)

Metropolitan Glasgow (2006, **one**)

North East England (1992, **four**)

Northern Ireland (2001, **six**)

Scotland (1992, **ten** staff at Scotland Europa, **12** staff
with the Scottish government EU office)

South West UK (2001, **seven**)

Southern England (1998, **two**)

Wales (2000, **ten**)

West Midlands (2000, **eight**)

These 94 representatives are in addition to diplomatic staff at the national delegation, UKREP.

The West Midlands Regional Office also hosts the University of Birmingham's Brussels Office, which is the first lobbying/liaison centre set up (in 2010) by a British university.

TINTENBURGEN

Ink castles: German slang for consultative committees deemed to have no practical value

Source: EUObserver.com

ECONOMIC AND SOCIAL COMMITTEE (EESC)

★ There are 344 members of the EESC

★ "Committed to European integration, the EESC contributes to strengthening the democratic legitimacy and effectiveness of the European Union by enabling civil society organisations from the Member States to express their views at European level." **Mission statement**

★ The UK has 24 members

★ Members belong to one of three groups: employers, employees or various interests

★ The Employers Group has members of businessmen or people from business lobbies

★ The Workers Group has members from 80 trades unions, most affiliated to the European Trade Union Confederation (ETUC)

★ Group III is made up of members of lobbies from civil society

★ Many EU countries have a national version. As the UK doesn't, nominations are through the FCO, supported by the Cabinet Office and DTI

★ Its draft budget for 2012 is €130.5 million

EUROPEAN INVESTMENT BANK

★ The Financing Institution of the EU, based in Luxembourg

★ 26 regional offices. The London one briefly became infamous due to overspending on its marble exterior when it was set up

★ Its Board of Governors is made up of national finance ministers

★ In 2010, 88% of its €72 billion of funding went within the EU

★ Lends to support areas such as infrastructure development, support for smaller businesses and environmental work (€19 billion on climate work loans in 2010 and ongoing work supporting carbon capture through the Commission's carbon permits)

★ €26 billion of targeted support for regions hit by the eurozone crisis in 2010

★ €2.7 billion also lent to 14 city hospitals

★ Capital of €232.4 billion, of which €37.6 billion comes from each of the Big Four member states, with capital-to-asset ratio of 27.2%

★ Financially autonomous from the Commission, with a staff estimated at around 1,000

EUROPEAN OMBUDSMAN

★ Covers all EU institutions except the ECJ, the Court of First Instance, and the Civil Service Tribunal acting in their judicial role

★ He can't investigate complaints against national or local authorities, national courts, or businesses or people

★ If his attempts at conciliation fail, he can write to the European Parliament

COURT OF AUDITORS

★ Established in 1975

★ Independent external auditor – the Commission, for instance, has its own

★ It has one President, 25 members and a Secretary-General

★ Work is broken down into five chambers

★ Published 62 reports and opinions in 2010

★ 889 staff in 2010, of whom 151 were involved in translation

★ 67 directors and heads of unit

★ 2010 budget of €144.3 million

★ Its own self-audit is itself audited by external professional auditors

OLAF

★ Number of irregularities reported in 2010: Agriculture, 1,825; Cohesion Policy, 7,062; Pre-accession funds, 424; direct expenditure, 1,021; total expenditure, 10,332; own resources, 4,744

★ Total number of these cases: 25,408

★ Total estimated value of these cases: €4 billion

★ Total amount recovered: €1.83 billion

★ 90%: rate of irregularities classified by Italy and by accession countries as suspected fraud in 2010. The rate for France was 0%

★ Recent joint operations include Op Sirocco (cigarette trafficking), Fake (study of counterfeits routes), Diabolo II (Asian fakes) and Wasabi (fruit and veg declarations)

Other bodies

In a nutshell...

A number of other standalone institutions also work well below the radar. These include the Central Library, the Data Protection Officer and the Publications Office.

CENTRAL LIBRARY

★ The main building is a former convent that cost €20.7 million

★ **101,500** volumes held in Brussels, **528,000** in Luxembourg

★ **28** and **63** reading spaces respectively

★ €2.7 million – acquisitions budget

★ The Brussels site receives **239** newspaper titles

★ **4,158** visitors to the Brussels Library in 2007, including tours

★ Cost effectiveness: €711 per book loan; Brussels ratio of **1** member of staff to **67** annual visitors

★ EU institutions and the Commission DGs have their own individual libraries – **52** in total

PUBLICATIONS OFFICE

★ Publishes the *Official Journal (OJ)*, the EU record of laws

★ Prints in **22** languages, **23** if Irish required

★ It proofread **356,881** pages of the *OJ* in 2010

★ Also responsible for procurement and legal websites

* **3** million documents are available online at its EUR-Lex site
* Consolidated Treaty of Lisbon – 2010 bestseller (**1,895** total copies)
* **672** staff – one-fifth from France
* Statistically aware: total use of water in 2010 – **12,967m²**
* "The awareness campaign initiated in 2009 concerning the risks related to physical inactivity at work continued at the beginning of 2010. Conferences and workshops were organised to provide information, such as the correct position at the workstation, moving about while at work, the evolution of working conditions and their physical and psychological consequences."

HISTORICAL ARCHIVES

* Collections include: minutes of Commission, Coreper minutes, key speeches, annual general reports, bulletins and studies
* All major EU institutions have their own archives service
* Many areas are subject to the 30 years rule
* Administered by the EU Institute at Florence
* There is also an oral archive service, with tape recordings of interviews (and transcripts)

INSIDER INFORMATION

Insight on past national perspectives, from an interview from the EU archives with George Ball, a senior US diplomat and Presidential adviser heavily engaged in supporting early European integration

" *What disturbed me most at that time was that the British might slide in without taking any of the real commitments of the Rome Treaty and that it would be a kind of half-hearted sort of relationship. I was convinced that while the United States certainly should favour British membership in the EEC, it should be on the basis of ... Britain would come in as a full partner with all of the obligations. And this was something that I told Heath at that time and made it very clear to him. I think he was Lord Privy Seal. ...*

As far as Macmillan was concerned, he confused me because he pretended, his position in private conversations was extremely favorable to the idea of Europe and the need for Europe, the absolute necessity for it. In the second world war, or in the first world war, his whole battalion had been decimated and his two brothers had been wounded, one of them may have been killed and he was very eloquent about this can't be permitted to happen again, Europe must never be in a position where we could get this kind of fumble(?). So that in his private reactions he was splendid, when it came down to the problem of putting the situation to the British public he did it almost entirely on a tradesman basis. That this was a very useful necessity for Britain because of the treaty advantages it would give it, but he totally [...] He suppressed the political side of it, which I must say surprised and rather discouraged me at the time because privately he had been so enthusiastic and quite eloquent. ...

The basis of this started within a very short time after Kennedy's inauguration, I think it was about March of that year. [...] Heath had to leave to attend a meeting in the House, but I worked it out with Sir Frank Lee with whom I was completely en rapport and he was fully in accord with the fact that Britain had to come into Europe and this had to be done on the basis where if we could help them solve some of their problems, the EFTA problem, the problem with the old members of the Commonwealth, the Australians and so on. ...

Then that night at a reception at the British Embassy after I had made my speech in the morning, Macmillan came around to me in great excitement, he said this

was a great day, he said: we are going in, we made this decision this morning and he said you've got to help us but we're going in. Again I saw him a second time that night and he said exactly the same thing to me, which was very encouraging. So I had a feeling that things were pretty well set, that when he got back to England if he took strong views – I hoped he would – that it was pretty well set. But instead he took a very ... what I thought he was trying to slide in sideways like a crab rather than frontally sell the idea to the British people. ...

De Gaulle was primarily committed to a Europe of nations so that a confederation would be simply a meeting of the various presidents or heads of state. I didn't think this would constitute any kind of serious political Europe. It could be a transitory form but you had to look for something beyond that, and we weren't in a position where we could waste time on purely transitional matters unless we very clearly saw this as an intermediate step towards something that offered more possibilities of unity. ...

What seemed to me clear is that De Gaulle wasn't prepared to go beyond a very loose confederation, Monnet saw confederation as a step towards something approaching unity which I myself did. That (referring to his conversation with Couve on European confederation) was what we were saying on the ship while going down the Potomac you see. It was a serious discussion, but not in the most formal setting. I don't think Couve was talking for De Gaulle at all when he said that he foresaw a government of Europe having the life or death decision about the use of nuclear weapons.

That whole Franco-German treaty seemed to us to be just a case of a love affair between two old men, with De Gaulle exercising his entrapment over Adenauer. [...] What happened was that we got a fellow named Karl Carstens who came over from Germany and he was a kind of permanent Undersecretary of the German foreign office and I gave Karl a very very hard time. I said this is catastrophic if you go down this road because you're going to open the door for a division of Europe which is going to be fatal. So he agreed at that time that they would do something, he didn't want to be specific. So they added a preamble which nullified the treaty completely, nothing came out of it. [...] We never believed that the treaty could be expanded as a basis for the unification of Europe."

From the Historical Archives of the European Union

BUREAU OF EUROPEAN POLICY ADVISERS (BEPA)

- ★ BEPA links the Commission with "think tanks, academia, civil society, churches and communities of conviction."

- ★ It evolved from the Forward Studies Unit under Delors which acted as his personal think tank.

- ★ Under Prodi, it became GOPA, the Group of Policy Advisers, focusing on economics, foreign affairs, social affairs, and dialogue with religions

- ★ Under Barroso it became BEPA, centred on political, economic and societal teams. A further change reduced this to Outreach and Analysis

- ★ Its logo is an emerging, peering owl

- ★ A key component is the European Group on Ethics in Science and New Technologies, a barely-known body that provides direct high-level advice on cutting-edge technologies

- ★ The group has issued reports on moral issues such as animal cloning, nanomedicine, informational implants, genetic testing in the workplace, stem cell research and patenting, doping in sport and profit in blood banking.

- ★ Of the morality group's 15 members, 15 are professors, of whom only one is a cleric (Jesuit)

EUROPEAN DATA PROTECTION SUPERVISOR (EDPS)

- ★ Each EU institution is required to have its own Data Protection Officer (DPO). The Commission's is the most significant, though there are 46 others

- ★ The role (not quite yet an office) encompasses liaison across the whole institution with designated local DG counterparts

★ Each time personal data is processed by an institution, a log is kept and this is maintained online

★ The EDPS is an independent authority set up to monitor compliance. There is a Supervisor and a Deputy

★ Complaints have to be from individuals, against how data was handled by an EU institution

★ Cases for input from 2010 included: use of statistical data on pandemic prevention; privacy protection for safety suggestions; access to emails and drives belonging to absent or dead staff by the Court of Auditors; the right to dock strike pay from Commission staff; and computer forensics for fraud cases in the European Investment Bank

★ 44% of complaints in 2010 were in English, 33% in German and 15% in French

★ Complaints: access to or incorrect data (36%); objection and deletion (12%); unlawful use (16%); excessive collection of personal data (12%); violation of confidentiality (8%); data security (4%); ID thefts (4%); leaks (4%); data quality (4%)

★ €7.1 million: budget for 2010, with 47 staff

★ The EDPS has its own DPO and deputy to ensure its own data is data compliant

> " *A staff member complained against covert video-surveillance in his institution. In particular, he questioned the lawfulness of the use of a video-camera which recorded him, without his knowledge, when he entered his supervisor's office in his absence. The EDPS concluded that the institution had not demonstrated the existence of a legal basis which would explicitly allow the possibility of such highly intrusive operations and provide for specific conditions and safeguards.* "

EDPS Annual Report 2010

OFFICE FOR INFRASTRUCTURE AND LOGISTICS (OIB BRUSSELS, OIL LUXEMBOURG)

★ **Eight pages**: length of architectural guidance for Commission buildings

★ **398 pages**: length of manual building specifications for Commission offices

★ There are 16 types of named trolley identified for use in the kitchens under the building regulations, ranging from heated plate trolley to condiment trolley

★ It manages garderies (c.1,000 places, for those aged 3-6, toilet-trained and able to express themselves in their native tongue); a Study Centre (c. 550 places, for ages 6-14 in afternoons); Commission restaurants including the Foyer européen and the à la carte restaurant, and the Fitness Centre in the Jean Monnet building (swimming pool and facilities for aerobics, badminton, gymnastics, salsa, karate, judo, aikido, squash and table tennis, a weights room, a gym, two saunas and a solarium)

★ Also responsible for the Commission's display of artwork – 350 loaned from member states

★ **105 vehicles**: Commission's car pool in Brussels at the time of their last external audit, with 80 chauffeurs (another 13 in Luxembourg)

CREATING THE NIRVANA OF BUREAUCRACY: QUOTES FROM THE COMMISSION'S BUILDING MANUAL

"The building as a whole and each of its parts should be as harmonious and cohesive as possible in terms of the various elements used in its construction, which should make use of the play of volume and natural light to create an impression of spacious harmony. The colours of the facings, the textures and the various materials used should all help to create a sober but pleasant, convivial and warm atmosphere."

"As calls for tender relating to cleaning and sandblasting work explicitly require 'disposal of hazardous waste', it must be established whether the water is to be

disposed of through the drainage system to a purification plant with an adequate capacity or collected at the site for controlled disposal. Any paint sludge resulting from sandblasting work on buildings must be isolated and disposed of as hazardous waste in accordance with the usual rules."

"Wood is a renewable resource. However, some types of wood used in buildings come from regions where forests have been over-exploited, with the result that native species have disappeared and forests which would otherwise help to absorb CO_2 emissions have now vanished. The wood used in buildings represents a long-term sink for CO_2. Improved forestry-management practices can be encouraged only if invitations to tender specify that wood must come from forestry operations where the rules of sustainable development are followed. All the wood used must meet the requirements of the PEFC (Pan European Forest Certification) label, the FSC (Forest Stewardship Council) label or equivalent. **(See sections B.I.5 (Finishes) and C.II (Crèches) points 3 – Materials, and 10 – Furniture)."**

"Unless otherwise specified blinds should be of vertical design and light grey in colour, with a density of 220g per square metre. Slats should be made of a 100% fibre-glass fabric that complies with the latest standard or, if this has not been established, with the equivalent to M1 under the former standard; they should be resistant to humidity, heat and UV rays, and should not distort. The fabric used must be anti-static, non-flammable and colourfast. They should be 127mm wide unless otherwise specified."

INTERNAL AUDIT SERVICE (IAS)

- ★ The IAS is the Commission's own auditor
- ★ Directorate A covers the agencies, Directorate B the Commission itself
- ★ It only became an independent service in 2001
- ★ It falls under the general remit of the Commissioner for Taxation and Customs Union, who chairs the Audit Progress Committee

LEGAL SERVICE (SJ)

★ The SJ is an internal Commission service that reports to the President

★ It provides legal advice and, since 1959, acts as its representative in court

★ Those courts are the ECJ, national courts (typically on debt recovery) and international courts (mainly the WTO)

★ It was involved in 1,136 new litigation cases in 2010, of which 16 were EFTA cases

★ In 2009, there were 1,659 new infringement cases.

★ The top five cases brought are in issues to do with: the environment; taxation/customs; Internal Market; Justice and Home Affairs; and Energy/Transport

★ The Legal Service wins 70% of its cases before the ECJ and loses 8%

★ In 2010, it was second only to the US as instigator and defendant in WTO cases (winning and losing equally in the latter)

DISPUTING THE RULES: OPEN INFRINGEMENT CASES AS AT 31/12/09

Cases	Country	Cases	Country
368	United Kingdom	74	Bulgaria
238	Italy	72	Czech Republic
204	Greece	66	Luxembourg
197	Spain	61	Hungary
192	Belgium	60	Denmark
184	France	59	Finland
146	Poland	57	Slovakia
142	Germany	51	Romania
127	Ireland	50	Cyprus
123	Portugal	38	Estonia, Latvia, Malta
91	Netherlands	33	Lithuania
90	Austria	30	Slovenia
83	Sweden		

OFFICE FOR ADMINISTRATION AND PAYMENT OF INDIVIDUAL ENTITLEMENTS (PMO)

★ Pays staff their salaries and allowances

★ Also pays out pensions

★ Responsible for the Health Insurance Card of the European Institutions, part of the Joint Sickness Scheme (JSIS)

★ In 2009, the Commission paid out €634,000 in compensation from the insurance funds for personal injuries. A further €2,264,000 was paid out for accidental deaths, €335,000 in cases of natural deaths, and €233,000 to cover medical expenses

★ The office has an operational budget of €3.9 million, 500 staff and an administrative budget of €34 million

PART

FIVE

The Euroquangos

MAY CONTAIN TRACES OF
QUASI NONGOVERNMENTAL
ORGANISATIONS
(EUROPEAN)

Defining a European quango is not quite as straightforward as you might expect. In national government, the link between central government and the quasi-nongovernmental body is clear. Given the fluidity of staffing and of the conditions of employment, it can be more difficult to see where the Commission stops and the Euroquango begins. But we define it broadly as an institution set up at arms' length from the Commission to act on narrow areas of EU competence.

These groups (over a score are classified as Agencies, the remainder as decentralised bodies) have become increasingly important over the last decade, as the number of areas falling under EU competence in new treaties has grown. As such, their significance and relevance to individual countries can vary massively and where they are situated can sometimes reveal a lot about national priorities. The following list should not be considered as complete at the time of reading, it is designed to give a flavour of the groups.

1982

First known use of the term Euroquango, by Michael Fallon writing for the Adam Smith Institute

JACQUES SANTER

First Commission President understood to have embraced the term Eurocrat, 17 years later

€914.2 MILLION

Budget of Euroquangos in 2007

€1,183.1 MILLION

Budget of Euroquangos in 2008

3,829.5

Staff numbers in 2007

4,729

Staff in 2008

23%

Staff growth in one year, from 2007 to 2008

A WAY TO GO YET

£90 BILLION

One estimate of the budget of UK quangos at that period

AGENCY FOR THE COOPERATION OF ENERGY REGULATORS
(ACER): LJUBLJANA (SLOVENIA)

★ EU variant of national energy regulators

★ Operational since March 2011

★ Aiming at **42** staff

★ €5.1 million operating budget (2011)

COMMUNITY FISHERIES CONTROL AGENCY (CFCA): VIGO
(SPAIN)

★ Promotes and coordinates compliance with the CFP

★ **66** staff as at the end of 2009

★ Responsible for its own micro-navy – the Joint EU Inspection Vessel
Tyr, 210' long at **1,271** tonnes and with a crew of **17**. It has also chartered
vessels for joint projects

★ There are **1428** accredited Community fisheries inspectors, with **147**
from the UK, **359** from Ireland, **74** from France, **75** from Spain and
four from Belgium

★ €11 million operating budget (2011)

COMMUNITY PLANT VARIETY OFFICE (CPVO): ANGERS (FRANCE)

★ Essentially, the authority for plant 'copyright'

★ Self-financing, i.e. by levies for services rendered

★ Dealt with **2,684** applications in 2010

★ Over half of applications were ornamental, a quarter agricultural, an eighth vegetable and a fifth fruit

★ From 1995 to mid-2011, the top five applicants by country were the Netherlands (**13,336**), Germany (**5,869**), France (**5,493**), Denmark (**1,915**) and the UK (**1,795**). **4,317** came from the USA and **1,996** from Switzerland

★ €12.4 million operating budget (2011)

EUROPEAN CENTRE FOR DISEASE PREVENTION AND CONTROL (ECDC): STOCKHOLM (SWEDEN)

★ EU coordinator of national health protection bodies

★ Campaigns, for instance, on antibiotics awareness, and coordinating data on Lyme disease

★ Also the likely key agency if the Black Death reappears

★ **248** staff in 2010, a fifth of whom are Swedish

★ €56 million operating budget (2010)

EUROPEAN AGENCY FOR SAFETY AND HEALTH AT WORK (OSHA): BILBAO (SPAIN)

★ EU equivalent of national agencies

★ Notes there are **5,580** deaths at the workplace across the EU every year

★ Runs a European Risk Observatory (ERO) which analyses the data

★ Liaison office also at Brussels

- ★ Also covers harassment at work
- ★ Coordinates other EU agencies on H&S issues
- ★ Deploys a man in a cartoon workman costume, called Napo
- ★ Group photo for the 2010 annual report has the team crowded in a stairwell
- ★ €15.5 million operating budget (2010)
- ★ **66** staff

EUROPEAN CENTRE FOR THE DEVELOPMENT OF VOCATIONAL TRAINING (CEDEFOP): THESSALONIKA, GREECE

- ★ EU version of national equivalents
- ★ Work is highly statistical and theoretical, the exception being the establishment of an online EU CV system
- ★ **96** staff in December 2011; one-third of staff and two-thirds of contract agents are Greek
- ★ €18.8 million operating budget (2010)

EUROPEAN TRAINING FOUNDATION (ETF): TURIN, ITALY

- ★ Works on job skills in countries geographically fairly near to the EU
- ★ Advises the Commission DGs involved in these areas
- ★ As Cedefop is the European Centre for the Development of Vocational Training for neighbours, some deconfliction with that body takes place
- ★ **130** staff
- ★ €18 million operating budget (2010)

EUROPEAN CHEMICALS AGENCY (ECHA): HELSINKI, FINLAND

★ Deals with safety and legislation implementation across the EU in the industry

★ Mostly associated with the REACH legislation

★ Received €349.7 million in paperwork fees from the industry by 2010, as a result of the legislation requiring the registration of dangerous chemicals by European businesses

★ Top five countries of businesses putting in the paperwork and fees in 2010 (by dossiers): Germany (**4,727**), UK (**2,430**), Netherlands (**1,922**) France (1,838), Belgium (**1,676**)

★ Recruited **120** more staff in 2010 – 472 staff in total.

★ €71.3 million operating budget (2010)

EUROPEAN ENVIRONMENT AGENCY (EEA): COPENHAGEN, DENMARK

★ An EU equivalent of national environmental agencies, offering policy advice

★ Covers the EU, the EEA and Turkey

★ Partners Eionet, the European Environmental Information and Observation Network, comprising the Commission, national organisations and subsidised environmental lobbyists

★ **153** full-time staff in 2010

★ 2010 priorities included agriculture/forestry ecosystem balance; and global warming

★ Increased heating consumption of 21% in 2010 due to an abnormally cold year

★ €50.6 million operating budget (2010)

EUROPEAN FOOD SAFETY AUTHORITY (EFSA): PARMA, ITALY

★ EU level variant of national agencies

★ Covers food safety, plant health and animal welfare

★ **454** staff in 2010

★ Employees/advisers have to declare interests and stand down when there is a conflict, for instance working for a GM company

★ €74.8 million operating budget (2010)

EUROPEAN MEDICINES AGENCY: LONDON, UK

★ EU version of national authorities on human and veterinary drugs

★ Sole, central, authority for human medicines for the treatment of HIV/AIDS, cancer, diabetes, neurodegenerative diseases, auto-immune and other immune dysfunctions, and viral diseases; veterinary medicines for use as growth or yield enhancers; medicines derived from biotechnology processes, such as genetic engineering; advanced-therapy medicines, such as gene-therapy; medicines used for rare human diseases (orphan medicines)

★ 210-day turnaround period for consultations

★ National authorities licence all other drugs – for the UK, the Medicines and Healthcare Products Regulatory Agency and the Veterinary Medicines Directorate

★ Has a management board of **35**, six scientific committees drawing from **4,500** national experts, and **567** staff

★ Despite being based in the UK, fewer than one-in-ten staff are British

★ Charges fees from the industry for its work

★ Runs, amongst others, the EVVet database on negative drug reactions from animals, mostly dogs and cats

★ Stands back from the Commission's role in the Innovative Medicines Initiative (IMI), Europe's largest PFI involving the European pharmaceutical industry association, 23 projects and a match-funded €1 billion Commission budget, funding R&D

* €208.4 million operating budget (2010)
* Decided to cancel or move meetings to other countries during the 2012 Olympics owing to travel difficulties to and from London

EXECUTIVE AGENCY FOR HEALTH AND CONSUMERS (EAHC): LUXEMBOURG CITY, LUXEMBOURG

* Launched in 2005 with a three-year timeframe, extended to 2015
* EU-level equivalent of national agencies dealing with consumer protection and training for safer food
* €6.7 million operating budget (2010)
* Total staff of **100** in 2009
* €156 million budget in 2009 for funding projects (since, as with other agencies, the funds available for distribution are in addition to the costs of just running the agency)
* Some crossover with other EU agencies, for instance injury prevention, drug abuse and the major diseases

EUROPEAN FOUNDATION FOR THE IMPROVEMENT OF LIVING AND WORKING CONDITIONS (EUROFOUND): DUBLIN, IRELAND

* Set up in 1975 and as such one of the earliest Euroquangos
* Based in a seventeenth century manor house
* Runs the European Monitoring Centre for Change (EMCC), set up in 2001 to anticipate economic and social developments
* Responsible for the European Industrial Relations Observatory (EIRO), which analyses data and forms part of the Network of European Observatories (NEO)
* Also responsible for the European Working Conditions Observatory (EWCO)

- ★ Further maintains a number of surveys, such as the European Company and Quality of Life in Europe surveys
- ★ Another institution that maintains a liaison office in Brussels
- ★ €20.5 million operating budget (2011)
- ★ 121 staff

EUROPEAN INSTITUTE FOR GENDER EQUALITY (EIGE): VILNIUS, LITHUANIA

- ★ Monitors, advises and raises awareness on gender equality issues
- ★ Engaged in such projects as the Women of Europe Resource Pool, database expansion with Women Information centres, the Women Inspiring Europe 2011 calendar, the EU Gender Equality Index, a journalist task force on gender, studies on gender stereotype narratives, and finding a corporate logo
- ★ 36 staff in 2011, a quarter of whom are Lithuanian
- ★ €5.9 million operating budget (2010)

EUROPEAN UNION AGENCY FOR FUNDAMENTAL RIGHTS (FRA): VIENNA, AUSTRIA

- ★ Formerly the EU Monitoring Centre on Racism and Xenophobia (EUMC), which ran the European network on racism and xenophobia (RAXEN)
- ★ Could have an important function in that member state voting rights could potentially be suspended based on its findings
- ★ Now more tied into the treaty base of the Charter of Fundamental Rights
- ★ Runs surveys such as EU-MIDIS on treatment of immigrants and minorities
- ★ €20.2 million operating budget (2011)

* Coordinates with national level equivalents
* Staff target of **80** by 2013

EUROPEAN ASYLUM SUPPORT OFFICE (EASO): VALETTA, MALTA

* New agency established in 2010
* Facilitates exchanges, supply of interpreters, training of officials, relocation of genuine asylum seekers, and support for countries under pressure
* Contributes to the development of the Common European Asylum System
* **61** staff in 2011
* €12 million operating budget (2012)

EUROPEAN MONITORING CENTRE FOR DRUGS AND DRUG ADDICTION (EMCDDA): LISBON, PORTUGAL

* Gathers and analyses EU-level data for opinion formers
* Responsible for the Reitox and International Cooperation unit (RTX), which liaises with national data centres
* €15.8 million operating budget (2011)
* **84** posts in 2011

EUROPEAN NETWORK AND INFORMATION SECURITY AGENCY (ENISA): HERAKLION, GREECE

* Go-between for EU-level work on cybercrime, such as involves computers, banking or mobile phones
* **60** staff
* €7.9 million operating budget (2010)

EUROPEAN AGENCY FOR THE OPERATIONAL MANAGEMENT OF LARGE-SCALE IT SYSTEMS IN THE AREA OF FREEDOM, SECURITY AND JUSTICE: TALLINN, ESTONIA

★ New agency – formally established only in November 2011

★ Still recruiting: aim is **120** staff by 2013

★ Role will be to keep Schengen-related databases operational and secure 24/7

★ Tasks relating to the development and operational management of the systems to be carried out in Strasbourg, France

★ Backup system will be installed in Austria

★ Approximate budget of €54 million (2012)

EUROPEAN RAILWAY AGENCY – PROMOTING SAFE AND COMPATIBLE RAIL SYSTEMS (ERA): VALENCIENNES, FRANCE

★ Aims to integrate national rail networks

★ €26 million operating budget (2010)

★ **165** posts in 2011

★ 23% of staff are Belgian

EUROPEAN AVIATION SAFETY AGENCY (EASA): COLOGNE, GERMANY

★ Provides EU-level technical expertise, excluding security issues such as highjacking

★ Stepped in as the lead authority over the Joint Aviation Authorities, which (except for the training element JAATO) has now disbanded

★ Certifies on issues of airworthiness and environmental standards, with a future possible role in air operations and flight crew licensing

★ Charges for certification, including visits by staff members. The specs dictate that taxi claims "will be charged at the real cost"

* Around **500** staff
* 2010 budget of €61.8 million, of which (as with other EU institutions) there are support funds available for the staff: €2,173,000 is set aside for *social welfare of staff* and €162,000 for *reception and events*

TRANS-EUROPEAN TRANSPORT NETWORK EXECUTIVE AGENCY (TEN-T EA): BRUSSELS, BELGIUM

* Ten-year mandate running out in 2015
* Offshoot of DG Mobility and Transport
* Manages the running of the Trans-European Transport Networks programme, i.e. the large grants to upgrade road, rail and river routes
* **99** staff in 2011
* €9.9 million operating budget (2011)

EUROPEAN MARITIME SAFETY AGENCY (EMSA): LISBON, PORTUGAL

* Provides EU-level assistance over maritime safety, pollution and security
* Computer systems include SafeSeaNet (vessel monitoring), EU LRIT data centre (monitoring flagged vessels from EU states worldwide), CleanSeaNet (for satellite imagery of pollution) and THETIS (on port controls and monitoring ships with poor safety records)
* EMSA contracts oil spill clean up vessels that are on permanent standby to assist – **16** in 2009, accounting for around half the agency's budget
* €54.3 million operating budget (2010)
* **219** staff within the agency in 2010 and around 500 reported overall

OFFICE FOR HARMONISATION IN THE INTERNAL MARKET (TRADE MARKS AND DESIGNS) (OHIM): ALICANTE, SPAIN

★ Registers pan-EU trade marks

★ Registered **98,217** trade marks in 2010. This compares with **15,950** in the UK's Patent Office, **27,725** in the Benelux authority and **96,013** in its French equivalent

★ **705** staff in 2010, one-fifth being teleworkers

★ Business charges generated €180 million in revenue, exceeding costs by some €26 million

THE EUROPEAN GNSS SUPERVISORY AUTHORITY (GSA): BRUSSELS

★ Manages the EU's satellite programmes, especially Galileo and EGNOS (three geostationary satellites over Europe that supply GPS data)

★ Galileo is interoperable with other existing positioning systems (US GPS and Russian Glonass). The given rationale for duplication is to increase coverage in the far north, to increase connectivity for residents of cities with high buildings and in case the other countries decide they need to switch GPS off

★ Fully deployed, Galileo is intended to consist of 30 satellites (**27** at **23,222** km orbits and three spares)

★ The agency had an operating budget in 2010 of €15.9 million and a staff of **42** (a marginal fraction of the figures involved in the projects themselves)

EUROPEAN UNION SATELLITE CENTRE (EUSC): MADRID, SPAIN

★ Provides analysis of satellite imagery releasable at EU level or commercially available

★ Supports EU military deployments, crisis planning, verification tasks and stability monitoring

* **97** posts in 2010
* €16.4 million operating budget (2010)

> *I solemnly undertake to exercise in all loyalty, discretion and conscience the functions entrusted to me as employee of the European Union Satellite Centre, and to discharge these functions with only the interests of the Centre in view. I further undertake not to seek or accept instructions in regard to the performance of my duties from any government or from any authority other than the Centre."*

Declaration required from staff at the EUSC on joining

EUROPEAN DEFENCE AGENCY (EDA): BRUSSELS, BELGIUM

* Works to expand central EU crisis management capability and joint procurement
* Designed to save money but also as an integrator for building a common defence
* €7 billion of European equipment procurement is spent on European collaborative ventures, €25 billion through national procurement and only €1 billion beyond Europe. This latter is predominantly advanced tech US partnerships, involving privileged UK access (2008 figures)
* **109** staff in 2009
* €29.6 million operating budget (2009)

EUROPEAN UNION INSTITUTE FOR SECURITY STUDIES (EUISS): PARIS, FRANCE

* EU defence policy think tank
* Has nine in-house research fellows, plus visiting fellows and temporary places for young researchers

★ Hosts an annual forum to help extend corporate EU-US defence relations
★ Funded from member states' budgets rather than directly from the EU budget due to legality issues under the treaties

EUROPEAN SECURITY AND DEFENCE COLLEGE (ESDC): NETWORK, HEADQUARTERED IN BRUSSELS

★ A virtual college, with courses set up in five countries
★ Intended to generate common instruction for future joint deployment – for instance on the law of armed conflict – and promote a European security culture
★ Supports young officer exchanges

EUROPEAN POLICE COLLEGE (CEPOL): BRAMSHILL (HAMPSHIRE), UK

★ Organises **60-100** courses and seminars annually
★ Main activities take place in the police institutes of member states
★ 2011 budget of €8.3 million
★ Has a secretariat of **30** – about the same size as its actual governing board
★ Subject to severe early criticisms by MEPs in 2008, claiming mismanagement and a breakdown of working relations that were suppressed to maintain a positive public image
★ May be the prototype for a proposed College of European Diplomacy

EUROPEAN POLICE OFFICE (EUROPOL): THE HAGUE, NETHERLANDS

★ Coordinates nations' police forces on cross-border issues such as counterfeiting, trafficking and terrorism

★ Coordinates analysis of shared intelligence, for instance through the SIENA system

★ **174,459** objects and **35,585** people entries on the Europol database by 2011

★ 26% of cases relate to drug trafficking and 24% people trafficking

★ Early warning cases have included alerts relating to the spread of the Hell's Angels to the Balkans and use of light aircraft in smuggling

★ Worked on data from an arrest by Greater Manchester Police to identify a cross-border radical preacher

★ Heavily involved in euro counterfeiting cases

★ **698** HQ staff, including **129** liaison officers

★ €92.8 million operating budget (2010)

> *In some cases the immigrants illegally sold commodities, such as cigarettes, to finance their onward journey to western Europe – mainly France and the United Kingdom. According to reports from some of the smuggled immigrants, the UK is considered a dream destination by the Vietnamese as they can readily earn money as gardeners tending and protecting illegal cannabis plantations."*

Europol annual report for 2010

CRIMINAL HUBS AS DEFINED BY THE EU ORGANISED CRIME THREAT ASSESSMENT

Source: Europol

THE EUROPEAN UNION'S JUDICIAL COOPERATION UNIT (EUROJUST): THE HAGUE, NETHERLANDS

★ Facilitates cross-border investigations and prosecutions

★ Key role with European Arrest Warrants

★ Secretariat of the European Judicial Network (EJN) is co-located

★ Run by a college, with one member from each member state

★ €31.7 million operating budget (2011)

★ **186** staff

EUROPEAN AGENCY FOR THE MANAGEMENT OF OPERATIONAL COOPERATION AT THE EXTERNAL BORDERS (FRONTEX): WARSAW (POLAND)

★ Supports border forces, with special reference to the external border of the Schengen Area

★ Liaises with EUROJUST and EUROPOL

★ Schengen has 42,672km of sea borders and 8,826km of land borders, monitored by 400,000 national border personnel

★ Supplies the Rapid Border Intervention Teams (RABITs)

★ FRONTEX has **289** staff

★ **5,707** joint operations in 2010

★ Jointly established a number of entities, such as the European Patrols Network (EPN), Heads of EU Coast Guards Forum, International Border Police Conference and the Baltic Sea Region Border Control Cooperation (BSRBCC)

★ Role was increased in October 2011. It now maintains centralised lists of national assets, standing teams of deployable border guards, a risk analysis system (intelligence cell), a role in scientific development, and a role in coordinating rules and procedures

★ €92.8 million operating budget (2011)

EUROPEAN EXTERNAL BORDER SURVEILLANCE SYSTEM (EUROSUR): NOT YET AGREED, BUT LIKELY TO BE IN AN EAST EUROPEAN STATE ON THE EU'S EXTERNAL BORDERS

★ Projected agency for sharing border intelligence and for research in surveillance technology

★ Set out in a 2008 document and a 2011 working paper

★ May be an expansion of the existing FRONTEX centre

★ Aim is to be operational in 2013

EDUCATION, AUDIOVISUAL AND CULTURE EXECUTIVE AGENCY (EACEA): BRUSSELS

★ Coordinates a large number of EU budget areas dealing with these themes

★ Many areas of activity are controversial and have been criticised for being PR for European integration

★ **432** posts in 2010

★ €49 million operating budget (2010)

EUROPEAN RESEARCH COUNCIL EXECUTIVE AGENCY (ERC EA): BRUSSELS

★ Manages the 'scientific curiosity-driven frontier research' fund for the European Research Council

★ The value of the fund is €7.5 billion over 2007-2013, covering 15% of the overall research funds

★ The UK was the lead recipient of these grants in 2010, and the largest attractor of grant-receiving researchers moving to another country, with a high proportion of non-UK nationals attracting ERC grants while working in the UK

★ **330** staff in 2010, a quarter of whom are Belgian

★ €36 million operating budget (2010)

RESEARCH EXECUTIVE AGENCY (REA): BRUSSELS

★ Handles a separate tranche of research grants to those looked after by the ERC, worth another €6.5 billion

★ **205** cases in 2010 where proposals needed to be re-evaluated due to mistakes of lack of qualifications by the assessor

★ **408** staff in 2010

★ €33.6 million operating budget (2010)

CLEAN SKY JOINT UNDERTAKING: BRUSSELS

★ Partnership between the Commission and the airline industry rather than an agency

★ A governing board is above an Executive Team, providing overview of the programmes. MEPs provide budgetary discharge

★ Aims to cut emissions

★ A €1.6 billion research project (over 2008-2013)

★ Provides an example of how multilateral arrangements can form working groups with large budgets that fall short of becoming official quangos

★ Joint Undertakings (JUs) provide a new and developing form of semi-institution. Another example is the Fuel Cells and Hydrogen Joint Undertaking (FCH-JU), a PPP working on cleaner fuel cell technology with a budget in the order of €1 billion up to 2017

★ The Single European Sky Air Traffic Monitoring Research (SESAR) joint undertaking is a €2.1 billion PPP programme on increased safety in air traffic control

★ The ARTEMIS JU is a PPP on microchips, with a grants budget for 2010 of €93.3 million

EUROPEAN JOINT UNDERTAKING FOR ITER AND THE DEVELOPMENT OF FUSION ENERGY (FUSION FOR ENERGY): BARCELONA, SPAIN

★ A joint undertaking that has taken semi-agency status

★ Set up to support fusion research over 35 years, following on from EURATOM work

★ Italy, France and Germany benefit most from grants

★ Manages EU contribution to the multinational ITER programme, an experimental fusion device being built at Cardarache, France

★ The nuclear programme assumed administrative control over a number of Euratom staff, who were discovered to have been paid discriminatory rates based on nationality for decades. Extremely large compensation payouts are reported to have followed

- ★ The fusion device is so experimental it is currently reportedly running at 12 years behind schedule
- ★ Has tried to popularise fusion using drummers and doughnuts
- ★ **302** staff in 2010
- ★ €41.5 million operating budget (2012)

EUROPEAN INSTITUTE OF INNOVATION AND TECHNOLOGY (EIT): BUDAPEST, HUNGARY

- ★ Aims to generate more entrepreneurs
- ★ Intends to create Kitemarks for educational establishments
- ★ €24.6 million operating budget (2010)
- ★ **29** staff

EUROPEAN INVESTMENT FUND: LUXEMBOURG

- ★ Specialist provider of European Investment Bank support to Small and Medium Enterprises (SMEs)
- ★ Therefore, not an agency of the Commission but an offshoot of the EIB
- ★ **200** staff

EXECUTIVE AGENCY FOR COMPETITIVENESS AND INNOVATION (EACI): BRUSSELS

- ★ Supports renewables in energy, the environment, business support, multi-modal transport, communication and finance
- ★ €16.2 million operating budget (2011)
- ★ **119** staff

EURATOM SUPPLY AGENCY (ESA): BRUSSELS

★ Nuclear industry round table at an EU level, to monitor the nuclear market

★ ESA has the right of first refusal for the purchase of nuclear materials produced in the member states

★ Staff comprise delegated Commission personnel under a Director-General

★ Euratom itself operates under a budget of €126.5 million (2011). While legally distinct from the EU, it has slowly been administratively merged over the years

INTERINSTITUTIONAL BODIES: BRUSSELS AND LUXEMBOURG

★ Not agencies, but with an element of distance from the Commission

★ Computer Emergency Response Team (CERT), a pilot project in 2011

★ European Personnel Selection Office recruits EU staff

★ European Administrative School trains staff

★ Translation Centre for the Bodies of the European Union (CdT) translates for the agencies and assists during peaks for the main institutions

★ The Publication Office prints matter

EUROPEAN UNIVERSITY INSTITUTE: FLORENCE, ITALY

★ Set up in 1972, just prior to second wave accession

★ Offers PhDs or Masters in Law

★ Also offers Jean Monnet, Max Weber and Fernand Braudel Fellowships. Some Marie Curie Fellows (from a mobility research science grant) also attend

★ First mooted by Hallstein to create a pan-European elite, but blocked for that reason by de Gaulle

- ★ Campus is spread over 14 sites and hosts 85 teaching staff with 154 administrative staff

- ★ **600** registered students

- ★ Locations include the Robert Schuman Centre for Advanced Studies, the Department of Political and Social Sciences, the Academy of European Law, and the Department of History and Civilisation

- ★ Regular visits from Commissioners

- ★ Hosts very large numbers of conferences

- ★ Runs Cadmus, a repository for published papers by members and former members of the Institute: 943 in 2010

- ★ Also houses the EU historical archives

- ★ **137** doctoral vivas in 2010

- ★ €52 million operating budget (2010)

- ★ €9.4 million external funding for research projects typically on pan-European themes

- ★ President's official hat looks like a lamp stand

THE BANKING STRUCTURES: FRANKFURT, PARIS AND LONDON

- ★ Sharing office space in Frankfurt with the ECB is the European Systemic Risk Board (ESRB), set up in late 2010 and incorporating three key sub-entities

- ★ In Paris, the European Securities and Markets Authority (ESMA) covers securities markets, derivatives and short selling

- ★ In London, the European Banking Authority (EBA) covers broad areas such as banking, corporate governance and payments

- ★ In Frankfurt, there is also the European Insurance and Occupational Pensions Authority (EIOPA)

- ★ Combined with the European Supervisory Authorities, these make up the European System of Financial Supervision (ESFS)

- ★ The scope and future role of these organisations, particularly as concerns the City, remains an issue of high controversy

BAGSY THAT QUANGO

National priorities are suggested by areas where countries have successfully lobbied for the siting of EU agencies

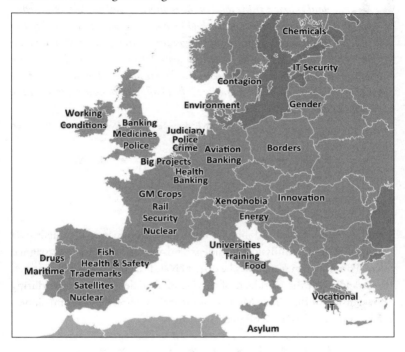

4.4%

Increase in administrative costs of the EU in 2011, i.e. during the financial crisis and national cut backs

2.9%

Increase in administrative costs of the Commission in 2011

25%

Pay cut the Romanian government had tried to impose on its central bank employees as a symbolic austerity measure in 2010, triggering a warning letter from the ECB

A WORD ON DUPLICATION OF NATIONAL AGENCIES

> *Politicians and taxpayers have assumed (with occasional phases of doubt) that a rising total in the number of civil servants must reflect a growing volume of work to be done. Cynics, in questioning this belief, have imagined that the multiplication of officials must have left some of them idle or all of them able to work for shorter hours. But this is a matter in which faith and doubt seem equally misplaced. The fact is that the number of the officials and the quantity of the work to be done are not related to each other at all."*

From *Parkinson's Law*, by Cyril Northcote-Parkinson

IN COMPARISON: MEMBER STATES AND THE KEY COMMISSION JOBS

A considerable amount of lobbying takes place from national capitals over who gets to be Commission President and which key roles are assigned where. Portfolios can sometimes be extremely indicative of national priorities, for instance with the workload of the German trade commissioner during the expansion of the Single Market, or the lack of reform by commissioners in charge of the CAP or CFP over the years.

PORTFOLIO OBTAINED BY A GIVEN COUNTRY'S COMMISSIONERS OVER THE LAST TWO COMMISSIONS

Austria –Trade; Regional Policy

Belgium – Development and Humanitarian Aid; Trade

Bulgaria – Consumer Protection; Humanitarian Aid

Cyprus – Health; Education, Culture, Multilingualism and Youth

Czech Republic – Employment, Social Affairs and Equal Opportunities; Enlargement and Neighbourhood Policy

Denmark – Agriculture and Rural Development; Climate Action

Estonia – Administration and anti-fraud; Transport

Finland – Enlargement; Economic and Monetary Affairs and the Euro

France – Transport, Justice, Freedom and Security; Internal Market and Services

Germany – Enterprise and Industry; Energy

Greece – Environment; Maritime Affairs and Fisheries

Hungary – Taxation and Customs; Employment, Social Affairs and Inclusion

Ireland – Internal Market and Services; Research, Innovation and Science

Italy – Justice, Transport; Industry and Entrepreneurship

Latvia – Energy; Development

Lithuania – Budget; Taxation and Customs Union, Anti-fraud

Luxembourg – Information Society and Media; Justice, Fundamental Rights and Citizenship

Malta – Maritime and Fisheries; Health and Consumer Policy

Netherlands – Competition; Digital Agenda

Poland – Regional Policy; Budget

Portugal – Commission Presidency

Romania – Multilingualism; Agriculture and Rural Development

Slovakia – Education, Training, Culture and Youth; Administration

Slovenia – Science and Research; Environment

Spain – Economic and Monetary Affairs; competition

Sweden – Institutional Relations and Communications; Home Affairs

UK – External Trade, External Relations

P A R T

S I X

Recurring Themes and Controversies

MAY CONTAIN TRACES OF
PERKS, WHISTLEBLOWERS,
FREEMASONS AND
ACCOUNTANTS

Sometimes it is not a competence or power that the EU holds that commands the newspaper headlines, or even a country's position, or a budget line. Sometimes it is a feature of the system itself and such reports can colour how citizens view the European project.

How much red tape is there in Brussels?

In a nutshell...

Overregulation is a recognised feature of EU legislation, though estimates vary on its effect from bad to extremely bad.

ESTIMATES OF EU RED TAPE COST, RISING THROUGH TIME

IAN MILNE, CIVITAS (1994)

Most likely £20 billion annually

PETER MANDELSON (2004)

4% of EU GDP, i.e. €421 billion across the EU economies

UK share at 2004 prices: £49 billion

DUTCH THINK TANK CPB (2005)

Cutting 25% of EU red tape would generate 1.4% of growth – and one quarter of the EU's red tape costs €150 billion

GÜNTER VERHEUGEN, EU COMMISSIONER FOR TRADE (2006)

EU red tape is equivalent to €600 billion across the EU economies

UK share at 2006 prices: £56 billion

... LEADING TO ...

25%

Headline target for reduction of EU red tape, agreed by heads of government, at 2007 rates

€150 BILLION

The amount the Commission itself reconfirmed was at stake

... BUT NOTING ...

FOI'd Treasury Report on the Drivers of Productivity and Growth referencing the CPB report and indicating that this transferred to growth specifically for the UK of 1.8% rather than 1.4%, which would mean total EU red tape costs specific to the UK of…

£72 BILLION

BEAUDOUIN, REVIEW OF COSTS APPLYING TO FRANCE (2008): TWO-THIRDS OF TOTAL FRENCH COST RANGE OF

€52 billion to €63 billion

BRITISH CHAMBERS OF COMMERCE (2010)

£7.4 billion annually, £62 billion since 1998

BRITISH GOVERNMENT ESTIMATE OF EU INPUT INTO UK RED TAPE OVER 2010-11 (PARLIAMENTARY QUESTION)

31% of range of £27.8 billion to £30.3 billion, i.e. a median EU input of…

£9 billion new EU red tape in one year

… MEANING …

69%

Amount of red tape estimated to be generated nationally for which the EU was not to blame and which could be addressed unilaterally. The UK used to have a reputation for being relatively deregulated compared with other EU countries.

A RECOGNISED COST OF IMMENSE SCALE: ONE ASPECT REVIEWED

> *In October 2009, the Commission finalised its measurement of the administrative burdens that businesses incur in meeting EU legal obligations to provide information on their products or activities, either to public authorities or to private parties. This study estimated the costs imposed by the 72 acts covered by the action programme and its 13 priority areas at 123.8 billion euro in 2005. The Commission has identified a total of 486 EU information obligations, and more than 10,000 national obligations which transpose or implement these EU obligations (of which more than 700 go beyond EU legal requirements). Based on this analysis, and in addition to measures that are under its own responsibility, the Commission has initiated a number of legislative proposals to remove or reduce administrative burdens: so far, the European Parliament and the Council have adopted 33 acts (with an estimated reduction of 5.7 billion euro) proposed by the Commission. A further 18 measures that could bring an estimated reduction of 30.7 billion euro are still pending."*

European Court of Auditors review of Impact Assessments, 2010

TEN CAUSES OF EU RED TAPE

★ Successful lobbying by competitors seeking to hamstring competition

★ Input by national governments seeking to hamstring business in other countries (the *level playing field*)

★ "Something must be done"

★ Lack of business awareness amongst legislators

★ Gold plating by national civil servants adding to original EU laws when putting into national law

★ Application of the Precautionary Principle "just in case"

★ Ambiguity requiring later legal clarification

★ Lack of scrutiny, including ministers not being informed/not paying attention until negotiations are over

★ Drive to politically seize an 'occupied field' by legislating to secure a competence

★ Measures to monitor compliance

Source: Brussels bars

Staff pay

In a nutshell...

EU staff can be extremely well-remunerated, though the menial support staff are on much lower wages.

€7,807

MEPs' monthly salary

€4,299

MEPs' Monthly General
Expenditure allowance

€152

MEPs' daily subsistence allowance
outside the EU

€4,243

MEPs' annual travel allowance for
semi-official work

£1,000 PER MONTH

Amount MEPs could over-claim
prior to changes to the system
requiring proof of purchase of plane
tickets at the cost claimed – as
estimated by a fraud-busting MEP

PATRICELLO CASE

ECJ ruling in 2011 which allowed
national courts to decide if an MEP
enjoyed diplomatic immunity
outside of the Chamber, if the link
was direct and obvious; the EP's
own position would only count as a
guiding opinion.

€5.9 BILLION

Annual wage bill for the three
major EU institutions

€220 MILLION

Pay rise sought by staff in 2009

€27 MILLION

Amount saved on salaries each day
EU staff go on strike

€0

Amount saved if customary
practice of not docking pay is
included in any wage settlement

1,023

Number of EU civil servants in
2010 on a higher pay scale than
the British Prime Minister, as
discovered by journalist Bruno
Waterfield. After privileges, the
figure may be double that.

90

Number of British EU officials
surpassing the British PM's income

Source: *Daily Telegraph*

€19,709

MEPs' monthly staff budget

31

Number of MEPs' assistants earning over £70,000 a year

Source: *Daily Telegraph*

6%

Budget increase in administration costs sought by the EU institutions for 2011

4.5%

Budgeted rise

€216,301.08

Reported annual salary of the AD 16 grade civil servant in charge of the European Parliament

AD 99

The grade invented to cover him, in the absence of an AD 16 grade in the EP

Source: *Daily Telegraph*

1 PER 5

Ratio of the 149 top earning (AD 14+) civil servants in the EP to the actual number of MEPs they serve

Source: *Daily Telegraph*

€1.235 BILLION

EU staff pension costs in 2010

83%

Increase in this bill by 2059

63

Pensionable age after recent reforms

0.9% OF FINAL SALARY PER YEAR OF SERVICE

Pension rate after recent reforms

£60,602

Average annual pensions on the current scheme

€26 BILLION

2004 estimate of the EU's total pensions liabilities, largely unfunded. The figure was up €3 billion on the previous year, which itself had already surpassed the 1997 estimates for 2020, but predated expansion.

€302

Average salary in Bulgaria in 2010

Source: EurActiv

ONE GRADE PER TWO YEARS

Rate of promotion in the Commission

8% TO 45%

Tax rate applied to Commission staff, historically better than rates in their home country

20 WEEKS

Maternity leave on full salary, with six months' parental leave on basic salary, per child

10 DAYS

Paternal leave granted on full salary

 The Commission takes a holistic approach to all aspects of well-being at work: there are also many leisure, sports and cultural clubs open to Commission staff and their families, including athletics, dance, theatre, art and language exchange."

Source: Commission recruitment website

MONTHLY SALARY GRADES FOR THE EU CIVIL SERVICE AS AT JULY 2010 (EURO)

Staff grade tier	Grade 1	Grade 2	Grade 3	Grade 4	Grade 5
16	16,919.04	17,630.00	18,370.84	-	-
15	14,953.61	15,581.98	16,236.75	16,688.49	16,919.04
14	13,216.49	13,771.87	14,350.58	14,749.83	14,953.61
13	11,681.17	12,172.03	12,683.51	13,036.39	13,216.49
12	10,324.20	10,758.04	11,210.11	11,521.99	11,681.17
11	9,124.87	9,508.31	9,907.86	10,183.52	10,324.20
10	8,064.86	8,403.76	8,756.90	9,000.53	9,124.87
9	7,127.99	7,427.52	7,739.63	7,954.96	8,064.86
8	6,299.95	6,564.69	6,840.54	7,030.86	7,127.99
7	5,568.11	5,802.09	6,045.90	6,214.10	6,299.95
6	4,921.28	5,128.07	5,343.56	5,492.23	5,568.11
5	4,349.59	4,532.36	4,722.82	4,854.21	4,921.28
4	3,844.31	4,005.85	4,174.18	4,290.31	4,349.59
3	3,397.73	3,540.50	3,689.28	3,791.92	3,844.31
2	3,003.02	3,129.21	3,260.71	3,351.42	3,397.73
1	2,654.17	2,765.70	2,881.92	2,962.10	3,003.02

EXAMPLES OF PERKS AND PRIVILEGES

★ Sickness and pension rights

★ Parental and maternity leave

★ €313 monthly child allowance

★ Ill widow bonus

★ Orphan's pension

★ Adoption leave

★ Childbirth or adoption grant of €200

★ General preferential rate of taxation

EU DIPLOMATIC STAFF MAY IN PARTICULAR QUALIFY FOR

★ Extra leave (distance allowance on top of a higher rate of 3.5 days per month)

★ First class travel to and from role, including family

★ Annual leave family travel payments

★ Long distance family ticket bonus

★ Health insurance for all family

★ Increased education allowance for school children (up to €1900 per month)

★ Increased education allowance for children not yet old enough to be in education (up to €380, from €64 per month normally)

★ Removal expenses

★ High Risk insurance

★ Accommodation – either supplied, or accommodation bills covered

★ Standard household allowance (family or marriage/partner allowance)

★ Daily subsistence allowance when the official has moved into an official residence, €27 to €33, lasting four to six months

★ Daily subsistence allowance when in the field

- ★ Furniture removal or storage allowance
- ★ Shift bonus
- ★ Standby allowance if on call
- ★ Difficult posting weighting
- ★ Understaffing weighting
- ★ Expatriation allowance, not less than €40 per month, for staff living in a foreign country
- ★ Entertainment allowance
- ★ Cumulative bonus for each consecutive difficult posting (*dump allowance*)
- ★ Choice of currency of payment: euro or local; or if there is an exchange rate collapse, in any currency chosen
- ★ Installation/resettlement allowance, one or two months' salary with the option of payment in local currency with extra weighting (where labour and resources will be cheap)
- ★ Staff car or generous mileage allowance
- ★ Own car annual allowance of €892 for senior personnel without an official car
- ★ Extra per diem payments if role is mission-orientated

Note that the existence of grants does not mean all staff will claim, or even in some cases be aware of them.

€110 PER DAY
Living allowance in a harsh posting

€160 PER DAY
Accommodation allowance in a harsh posting

€190,000

Estimated salary of an EU Ambassador to Africa, pre-bonuses

€87

Daily allowance to UK-based EU staff, where eligible

€149

Hotel allowance for UK-based EU staff, where eligible

Perks of the job

In a nutshell...

Across the EU, journalists occasionally identify areas where the job brings its own reward. These range from indirect benefits to status symbols, where there is ongoing debate over whether they are necessary in order to carry out the work.

€5.25 MILLION

Value of the MEPs' limousine budget. Committee chairmen, political group leaders, the President, and even for a set period past Presidents of the Parliament, are eligible for their own car and driver.

£2.3 MILLION

Cost of the EP gym

£4 MILLION

Amount spent on i-mobility for MEPs, after having first provided MEPs with an incompatible laptop

KEY FEATURES OF A 'JUNKET'

★ Accommodation is five star

★ First class travel

★ Limited official work

★ Lack of clear tangible benefit

★ Sunny

★ Beaches

★ VIP treatment, e.g. limousines and outriders

★ Special assistance, e.g. tours/visits laid on

★ Paid for by the taxpayer or by a foreign party

★ Oversubscribed

THREE

Number of defibrillators in Commission buildings, leading union leaders to demand more after the death of a colleague:

> *If a defibrillator had been available in the building, this colleague could have benefited from a substantive opportunity for reanimation and survival. This drama appears thus the unfortunate result of scandalous lack of means!*

"Following official statistics, each second working day, one of us may be struck by a heart attack and be in need of immediate reanimation at the work premises."

1962

Year of foundation of the European Civil Service Federation, campaigning for better conditions

Full title: FFPE – Federation of European Civil Servants Section "European Commission Brussels and Out of the Union"

1974

Protocol first agreed between the Commission and the unions, providing for such items as membership, conference leave, due notice for strikes, and participation on boards. Among the roles listed for minimum provision of services during industrial action are security staff, those dealing with perishable goods at frontiers, and those printing laws relating to agriculture

6

Unions that signed across the EU institutions, of which 3 were at Euratom

7

Number of trades unions in the European Parliament

TO BE A PILGRIM: EP UNION TERMS

Unions in the EP are governed by a framework agreement dating from 1990.

Each organisation winning at least 15% of the seats at the Staff Committee over the previous two elections receives:

★ part-time services of a civil servant
★ individual office in Luxembourg
★ shared office in Brussels and in Strasbourg

An organisation winning at least 5% of the seats at the Staff Committee receives an office in Luxembourg; an organisation winning more than half of the seats receives double the above rate.

Source: Public Service Europe

"Europe has always had dramatic moments; all those who have fought and still fight thoughtlessly against European integration put the blame for the difficulties on the institutions which have produced unprecedented social development in Europe.

"The European Civil Service Foundation is the staff association for these officials; its aim is to defend not only the interests of officials but also the idea of a united and federal Europe capable of ensuring peace on the continent and in the world.

"The purpose of this document is not only to introduce the European Civil Service Federation to those who do not yet know it, but also to make it clear that without a civil service freed from national mentalities, we cannot work together on building Europe. History has shown and still shows that associations of states without civil servants independent of national allegiances never reach the critical threshold where it can really be seen that strength comes through unity: the results obtained by organisations such as COMECON, EFTA, etc., prove this point."

Introduction to the *FFPE Yearbook* c. 2000

1962

Founding year of the FFPE

ITEMS SPECIFICALLY EXCLUDED FROM MEPS' HEALTH INSURANCE COVER

★ Spectacles with non-corrective lenses
★ Mountain search and rescue
★ Air-sea rescue

€11,840

Average cost per pupil in a
European School

€155.4 MILLION

Commission's contribution to the
European Schools' budget in 2010

€130,188

2010 Budget of the European
Schools' Board of Governors, of
which €81,755 went on travel and
subsistence, and €56,944 on
interpretation

€236,005

Litigation costs arising for the
Schools in 2010

LOCATIONS OF EUROPEAN SCHOOLS

★ Alicante

★ Bergen

★ Brussels (four, fifth pending)

★ Culham, Oxfordshire (some reduction as a plan to become an Academy
was halted)

★ Frankfurt

★ Karlsruhe

★ Luxembourg (two)

★ Mol, Antwerp

★ Munich

★ Varese

1953

Year first school was opened in Luxembourg

STATEMENT ON PARCHMENT SEALED INTO THE FOUNDATION STONES OF EVERY SCHOOL

> *Educated side by side, untroubled from infancy by divisive prejudices, acquainted with all that is great and good in the different cultures, it will be borne in upon them as they mature that they belong together. Without ceasing to look to their own lands with love and pride, they will become in mind Europeans, schooled and ready to complete and consolidate the work of their fathers before them, to bring into being a united and thriving Europe."*

37.5 HOURS

Commission's basic working week

1967

Last time that Commissioners' own pensions and salary scales were modified

ARTICLE 49

Section of the founding ECSC Treaty that from the outset declares of the High Authority, "it may receive gifts"

REGISTER OF GIFTS OVER €150, RECEIVED BY MEMBERS OF THE CURRENT COMMISSION; LIST AS DECLARED AND COMPILED AT DECEMBER 2011

Received	Description	From (in their own words)	To
2/2010	Vase	Diplomats/Brussels mission	José Manuel Barroso
3/2010	Silver medal	Head of State	José Manuel Barroso
17/03/2010	Miniature Georgian Towers	National government	José Manuel Barroso
23/03/2010	Replica of a painting	National government	Cecilia Malmström
25/03/2010	Carpet	Diplomats/Brussels mission	Štefan Füle
25/03/2010	Plate	National government	László Andor
9/04/2010	Pen + holder and golden calling card case	Industry et commerce (firms)	Günther Oettinger
10/04/2010	Ceramic plan	Local	José Manuel Barroso
26/04/2010	Crystal vase	Diplomats/Brussels mission	John Dalli
29/04/2010	Tie chain	National government	José Manuel Barroso
26/05/2010	Pen	N/A	Cecilia Malmström
26/05/2010	Jewel box in crystal and silver	N/A	Cecilia Malmström
20/07/2010	Silver plate (copy)	Religion	Maria Damanaki
9/08/2010	Handmade jug	National government	Štefan Füle
9/09/2010	Handy storage bowl	Parliament	José Manuel Barroso
13/09/2010	Leather suitcase	National government	José Manuel Barroso
13/09/2010	Tapestry	Head of state	José Manuel Barroso
11/11/2010	Leather Delvaux tie holder	National government	José Manuel Barroso
31/01/2011	Traditional costume and one silk scarf	President of Uzbekistan	José Manuel Barroso
31/01/2011	Silver cutlery	President of Uzbekistan	José Manuel Barroso
13/12/2010	Mauve carpet (handwoven)	National government of Libya (The timing could have been better)	Cecilia Malmström

Received	Description	From (in their own words)	To
31/01/2011	Gilded holder with two gilded spoons	National government of Turkmenistan	José Manuel Barroso
22/10/2010	Blue/orange porcelain vase	National government	Štefan Füle
13/07/2010	Decorative cup	National government	Štefan Füle
22/11/2010	Painting	National government	Štefan Füle
13/12/2010	Silvered statuette/sculpture	PM of Nepal	José Manuel Barroso
9/03/2010	Mustard yellow/ mauve tapestry (handwoven)	Kirghiz government	José Manuel Barroso
25/01/2011	Men's watch (This mirrors the peculiarly large collection of watches and jewellery acquired by Tony Blair from his meetings with Silvio Berlusconi)	National government of Italy	Antonio Tajani
25/01/2011	Men's watch	National government of Italy	Antonio Tajani
17/05/2011	Statuette in black marble (mother and child)	Diplomats/Brussels mission	José Manuel Barroso
20/05/2011	"A" shaped silver cuffs	Mayor of Antwerp	José Manuel Barroso
N/A	Silver amphora vase	President of Cyprus	José Manuel Barroso
9/06/2011	Samovar tea set in copper/brass and silver	President of Russia	José Manuel Barroso
10/06/2011	Baccarat crystal candle holder	President of France	José Manuel Barroso
21/06/2011	Oil painting of three-mast sailing ship	Head Fed Fishery Agency of Russia	Maria Damanaki

Fraud, waste and their enemies

In a nutshell...

 OLAF is the official anti-fraud unit. The Court of Auditors conducts the checks on the books. But occasionally it is the whistleblowers who do all the running. Sometimes stories relate to mismanagement of spending or lack of results rather than deliberate fraud.

36%

Frequency of errors found in the Court of Auditors annual report for the 2010 budget

10.7%

Upper end of the error range assessed by the Court of Auditors to apply to Cohesion, Energy and Transport

3.3% TO 3.7%

Court of Auditors' estimate of the error rate across the EU budget

€785 MILLION

Amount of Fontainebleau Rebate discovered to have been accidentally overpaid by the EU to the UK since 2006, requiring repayment in 2010/11

152

Number of ongoing cases as at end 2010 where VAT statements from member states were challenged as wrong

INVENTIVE ACCOUNTING

93,500 tonnes:
level for which aid was granted for a French sugar producer to dismantle a plant

72,000 tonnes:
production capability that the producer had immediately beforehand been awarded a grant to upgrade capability from

60,000 tonnes:
actual capability

10%: number of recipients in this grant case who had never delivered sugar beet to the facility

---

21.7%

Share of errors found in final payments for an organic cashew project in Nicaragua in 2010

0%

Number of errors detected by the Commission at the stage of final payment

€235 MILLION

Level of payments out of the European Council's Residence Palace building project that the Court of Auditors noted did not match payments to the progress of the building work

---

OFFICIAL DEFINITION OF A WHISTLEBLOWER IN 2007

" *An EU official or other EU staff member (temporary, auxiliary, local, or contract staff, or special advisers) who comes forward to OLAF with information they have discovered in the course of or in connection with their duties concerning matters which may be within OLAF's competence; in which they have a legal responsibility and duty.* "

OFFICIAL DEFINITION OF A WHISTLEBLOWER IN 2006

"A member of staff of a Community body."

OLAF today distinguishes between *whistleblowers* and *informants* depending on how the fraud gets reported. Around half of cases are triggered by the latter and one in ten by the former (with which are statistically grouped journalists and anonymous free-phone calls)

ONE

Number of submissions to the Convention on the Future of Europe addressing the issue of EU fraud

DE MINIMIS

"1 million euro in the customs, cigarettes and trade sectors; 100,000 euro in the agriculture and structural funds sectors; 50,000 euro in direct expenditure and external aid cases."

Official definition of fraud that merits priority investigation by OLAF (sometimes meaning any investigation)

OTHER FACTORS THAT DETERMINE WHETHER A CASE WILL BE PROPERLY INVESTIGATED

★ Reputational risk

★ Indications of systematic fraud

★ Whether there are other competent investigative bodies

---

25 MONTHS

Average length of a given OLAF investigation

> *It is difficult to form an overview of OLAF's performance. The information provided is to be found in different documents, which are prepared for different purposes and addressed to different audiences. Additional, more comprehensive information available in CMS is not presented. The Annual Activity Report does not enable the reader to make comparisons of OLAF's performance over time because there is no summary of key statistics for previous years. The Annual Operational Report provides comparisons with previous years for a number of indicators relating to activity (information received, initial evaluations carried out, opening decisions and average duration of cases), potential results (% of cases closed with follow-up) and real results (funds actually recovered). However, it does not make the important link between OLAF's activity (number of cases closed in a year) and the ensuing results, both potential (e.g. amounts identified for recovery) and real (e.g. amounts actually recovered)."*

Auditors' reservations on reviewing the work of OLAF

€60 MILLION

Amount a Court of Auditors' investigation concluded was mafia profit from EU tobacco policy in Southern Italy

FLAVOUR COUNTRY 40 YEARS

Duration of the EU's tobacco subsidy, introduced in 1970 and at its height costing €1 billion to support sub-standard crop that could only be exported at discount rates to Russia and Africa

---

TYPES OF EU FRAUD

As defined in the whistleblower paper at the European Convention

★ **Administrative** (breach of treaty law)
★ **Structural** (fraudulent contracts)
★ **Systematic** (paying relatives, bulk theft of printer cartridges, false claims of allowances)

STANDARD EU WHISTLEBLOWER (WB) PROCESS

★ WB spots fraud
★ WB reports fraud (repeatedly)
★ WB recognises the problem is not being addressed
★ WB attempts other routes to address the fraud
★ WB's identity is leaked
★ Encouragement to recant/apologise, in writing
★ Suspension (perhaps on half pay)
★ Transfer to a department to *count light bulbs*
★ Negative press briefing
★ Internal isolation
★ Deprivation of support staff
★ Intimidation by security personnel
★ Close monitoring of daily activity and meetings
★ Illicit office and computer searches
★ Legal proceedings
★ Pay stoppage
★ Stress/illness
★ Sacked/induced to quit
★ Threat to pension entitlements

 Financial accountability underpins political accountability; and when neither the accounts nor the audit are reliable, the financial and the political legitimacy of the European endeavour is undermined."

Robert (Dougal) Watt, whistleblowing auditor

97%

Longstanding average of the proportion of the EU accounts the Court of Auditors would not sign off

162

Number of words used in 2010 by the Accounting Officer of the Commission to sign off the accounts

17 YEARS

Number of times in a row (by 2011) the Court of Auditors has disagreed

TWO

Number of EU-funded river patrol boats for Romania's border force that breached tender requirements by not being useable in winter

THREE TIMES

Price differential between Russian vehicles and more expensive Western vehicles on offer for Bulgaria's border police. The more expensive version was bought under the EU tender, requiring each vehicle to leave the country in order to be serviced.

NIL

Amount of ecological impact assessment that went into a Kiribati seaweed project, failing to spot that wooden posts would need to be cut from vital mangrove swamps and that seaweed farmers would be incentivised to kill protected turtles.

EXAMPLES OF REVERSE INTENT

★ Water pollution arising from a Mali rice programme
★ Fijian fishery polluted by a new bridge
★ Deforestation in Brazil accelerated by identifying areas that weren't to be protected
★ A subsidised nature reserve where locals turned to poachers when promised tourism failed to materialise, because the star attraction gorillas were nervous of visitors and hid

€2.75 MILLION

Amount left in a Congolese bank account, a country in which the Commission had no presence, for which it lost the paper trail. The money was subsequently 'rediscovered'

100'

Size of a steel viewing tower built in Brandenburg with a €380,000 grant, but with no noticeable impact on local tourist figures

98%

Amount of a €3 million grant intended for irrigation and greenhouses in Spain but spent on cardboard boxes instead

€200 MILLION

Accounting gap visible in the published EU accounts in 2001

Source: Marta Andreasen

234 PAGES

Size of the fraud dossier submitted to OLAF by whistleblower Paul van Buitenen

£2 MILLION

Amount of state money siphoned off by Jacques Barrot to his political party. His conviction was quashed by French Presidential decree and Barrot later became Commissioner for Justice

5%

Ballpark estimate of the level of EU money lost on fraud, de facto offered by EU press officers justifying it as no worse than the level of national social security fraud

SIX MONTHS

Duration the Santer Commissioners remained running the Commission after resigning en masse following a fraud scandal

FOUR

Number of Commissioners from the disgraced Santer Commission who took office as Commissioners under his successor, Prodi. One (Neil Kinnock) was put in charge of trying to reform work on fraud

PEOPLE COVERED BY THE POLITICALLY EXPOSED PERSONS DIRECTIVE

Directive 2005/60/EC by which certain people are subject to increased scrutiny, as potential money launderers, when abroad

★ Heads of State, heads of government, Ministers and deputy or assistant Ministers

★ Members of parliaments

★ Members of supreme courts, of constitutional courts and of other high-level judicial bodies whose decisions are not generally subject to further appeal, other than in exceptional circumstances

★ Members of courts of auditors and of the boards of central banks

★ Ambassadors, *chargés d'affaires* and high-ranking officers in the armed forces

★ Members of the administrative, management or supervisory bodies of state-owned enterprise

€10 MILLION

Reported ransom claimed by a Commission official after staging his own kidnap in Colombia. According to the Spanish press, he had been in the country to perform a social assessment study on the country's poor.

Source: EUObserver

£30,000

Amount of allowance reported ended for Commissioner Kinnock and other senior personnel after it was pointed out he was ineligible for currency weighting of his salary

DR ANTONIO QUATRARO

Commission official dealing with Italian tobacco grants whose suspicious death in 1993 remains the subject of claims of mafia fraud and in-house cover up. Not helped by the original auditor reportedly being the same person who tried to suppress the story going public and who had earlier invited the whistleblower to become a freemason

ONE DIRECTOR AND TWO HEADS OF DIVISION

Staff who took the Court of Auditors to court alleging irregularity in the appointment of a new Secretary General

205

Number of Court of Auditors staff who, in a staff committee election in 2002, backed a candidate alleging "a regime of nepotism, venality and mismanagement."

 Thank you for contacting the Serious Fraud Office (SFO) and for the information you have provided to us. We welcome all information that will assist us in our fight against serious and complex fraud."

Intro to the standard automated reply from the SFO on reporting a case of fraud. As British taxpayer money is involved, the SFO has an interest in the finances and the institutions.

5

Total number of SFO staff reportedly assigned to cover EU fraud

Source: ThisisMoney.co.uk

SPENDING FOR ITS OWN SAKE: AN EXAMPLE OF SPENDING ON AN AREA OF QUESTIONABLE VALUE – THE INTERREG IVA FRANCE (CHANNEL) ENGLAND PROGRAMME

Cases of funding that are being used primarily to develop cross-border identity

Agissons autour des déchets

The Waste in Action project aims to develop sustainable actions encouraging an optimisation of waste management and enhanced environmental practices. This cross-border, multi-sectors partnership between France and England is managed by stakeholders presenting different approaches and experiences regarding waste management

AlcoBinge

This projects looks specifically into the biological effects of binge drinking, more precisely on brain development of young people.

CAMIS -EMDI+

The aim of this project is to develop and implement an integrated maritime policy in the Channel area whilst fostering concrete co-operation between stakeholders.

CHAIN

The partners want to create a network of business incubators, science parks and BIC in France and England.

Channel Circus Arts Alliance

The Channel Circus Arts Alliance project aims at spreading circus works on both sides of the Channel, while creating a durable network of circus professionals in order to expand their distribution and production possibilities. The project will implement different actions to widen potential audiences, to allow them to better understand and appreciate new forms of circus. These actions will also target an audience unaware of the cultural offer.

Côte to Coast

The Côte to Coast micro-project aims to study the feasibility of the implementation of a home exchange programme for people living less than one hour away from the sea by public transport and within the co-operation zone. The project offers to remove the budget and accommodation obstacles and to encourage people joining in sport and cultural activities as well as practising languages during their stay.

CRESH

The CRESH project aims to encourage a sustainable management of cephalopods in the Channel area.

CROIS

The main aim of this project is to encourage the access to higher education to young people and to develop their social mobility in the Kent and Somme areas.

CROSS-CHANNEL FILM LAB

Aims to develop cinematographic projects of full-length films specific to two regions: Finistère and Cornwall. The project offers to implement a new European model for script and project development

CYCLE

The CYCLE project aims to enhance the touristic opportunities of the Channel area by developing a joint network of cycle routes and greenways linking South East England to North West France.

[The cycle networks unhelpfully need to stop and start at either end of the Channel Tunnel and at other ports.]

DocExplore

The DocExplore project aims to enhance cultural and historical links present on both sides of the Channel by facilitating the access to and understanding of major historical documents.

ECOfab

A trans-Channel think tank to create theme-based networks which will propose methods of prospecting for projects and schemes involved in eco-renovation and eco-building.

IFORE

Aims to implement a regional joint strategy for the eco-refurbishment of social housing.

INTRAMES

To improve in the short term the care of patients struck down by cerebral hydro-dynamical disorders.

IS:CE

To establish a leading scientific training programme in the field of molecular chemistry (synthesis and materials), in order to substantially increase the attraction of the Channel region for training students in Europe.

LiCCo

To empower Channel communities to adapt to coastal climate change and to create better places and better public services.

LIN/flax

To create a virtual cross-border centre of excellence dedicated to increasing the production value of flax

MISCO[2]

To develop a greater understanding of the business language and the corporate culture of the UK and France in order to facilitate international trade by SMEs in East Anglia and Trégor (Brittany, France).

Moments inoubliables

Magic moments offers to provide a strategic, co-ordinated approach to developing and marketing festivals and events.

Monc

Monc aims to encourage primary schools from both side of the Channel to learn the language and culture of their neighbour. [Portsmouth and Caen]

Nuit blanche

The White Night project aims to enhance jointly and sustainably the cultural and tourist offer of two major cities: Brighton and Amiens. Inspired by the Paris-based concept, a White Night will be organised each year, in October, on both sides of the Channel. The objective is to offer the audience sound, visual and choreographic performances, concerts and exhibitions in meaningful places of both cities. The artistic programming and communication will be designed to target particular disadvantaged audiences.

Patrimoine numérique

The *digital heritage* project aims to exploit the extensive film archives of East Anglia and Upper Normandy and create ways for the visitors and communities of the two Channel regions to enjoy greater access to these collections, in order to increase the cultural understanding of common heritage.

VegeDurable

Aims to provide farmers with integrated management solutions for vegetable cultures, in order to keep the use of chemical products to a minimum and replace them by biological practices when possible.

WAVES

This project aims to strengthen social cohesion and social inclusion of populations from both regions through artistic practices based on puppet construction.

EXAMPLES OF CLAIMS OF FRAUD RAISED

★ An official was accused by his boss of committing a crime in saying that fraud is rife within one of the institutions.

★ One employee allegedly received invalidity benefit after spending time regularly asleep on her office floor, though was fit enough to work on an election campaign team.

★ An employee got caught stealing. He then had a seizure and was kept on the books.

★ A staff member decided "to start acting like the majority of *fonctionnaires*" by coming in late, leaving early and taking long lunches, because his salary was reduced when he was found to be overpaid.

★ One of the institutions uses a temping agency which is reportedly run by the daughter of the head of the typing pool.

★ An ex-boyfriend of an employee was said to be regularly flown in to be employed as a permanent member of staff in his own right. One official was overheard complaining that the regular staff never get sent to Strasbourg because of all the fake officials working there. So he and others just hang around cafés back in Brussels and Luxembourg.

★ There are reports of individuals being ostracised for refusing to sign off doctored accounts.

★ Instances of petty fraud in the offices of the most senior personnel are rife.

★ Car rental procedures are routinely abused.

★ Staff pull 'sickies' by regularly using up the full regulation 16 days uncertified sick leave allowed every year.

★ Building contracts have been awarded to the husband of someone working in the team of a very senior official.

★ Senior staff have planted false allegations about whistleblowers' private lives in the press in order to discredit them.

★ Where a whistleblower has been identified, management has failed to use the correct disciplinary procedure.

★ Hard evidence of fraud handed over by whistleblowers has been suppressed and incriminating evidence has mysteriously gone missing or been stolen.

★ A senior official took a job transfer and bought a house, but then was given his old job back with a pay hike – which he took while still collecting an allowance for accommodation in the house which was now being rented out.

★ Contracts awarded to partners of senior personnel through blackmail relating to personal medical data.

" It is a heart-warming comedy set in the beautiful Welsh countryside. The film will tell the story of what happens when you give a small town £250,000 to 'play with' … Enter the so-called "Pontycel Players", who suddenly find themselves entangled in a nightmare of their own making and are led 'unto the breach' by their Mayor, Eric Jenkins. For the last five years the council of Pontycelwyddau have been sent large sums of money from Brussels to fund cultural development in their town. Instead they have used the money to fund holidays, a pool table, a fashionable car, one new bathroom with Jacuzzi, strip weekends in Amsterdam, two new building extensions, forty five crates of Bollinger champagne, four hundred and twenty boxes of scampi fries and a bondage weekend in Cheltenham that nobody talks about."

Funding bid for the film *Bridge of Lies* (subsequently released as *Caught in the Act*)

26.5%

Percentage of applications for OLAF to investigate fraud that were considered *prima facie non-cases* and closed before they were even opened

267

Number of *prima facie non-cases* in 2009, out of 1,007 evaluations made

END RESULT OF NEW CASES IN 2009

Non-cases (not pursued)	**66%**
Coordination	**5%**
Criminal assistance case	**5%**
External investigation case	**13%**
Internal investigation case	**7%**
Monitoring case	**4%**

43 MILLION CIGARETTES

Number of smokes seized as part of a Miami smuggling ring, for which OLAF claims some credit

3,400 TONNES

Volume of sugar re-exported from Kaliningrad to Croatia and therefore discovered by OLAF and the relevant authorities to be ineligible for €2.7 million grants

NEW CASES BY AREA

Agriculture – **39**
Cigarettes – **12**
Customs – **22**
Direct Expenditure – **24**
EU institutions/EU bodies – **73**
External Aid – **29**
Structural Funds – **21**

TOP FIVE COUNTRIES UNDER INVESTIGATION IN 2009, BY NUMBER OF CASES

Bulgaria – **68**
Belgium – **48**
Italy – **36**
France – **22**
Germany – **22**

| 4

Number of staff employed in the Commission's Disciplinary Office

FINDINGS OF THE INVESTIGATION AND DISCIPLINARY OFFICE OF THE COMMISSION (IDOC)

2005

Penalties and warnings for four staff involved in:

★ Paedophile acts

★ Depraved behaviour

★ External activity (not declared)

★ Failure to meet the requirements of the Staff Regulations

2006

Disciplinary measures for eight staff involved in:

★ Unauthorised absences

★ Improper/inappropriate remarks with an outside person in an email

★ Acts of violence against a colleague

★ Negligence in monitoring the performance of a contract

★ Leaking information to an outside contractor

2007

Seven staff received official warnings for the following:

★ As a member of a selection panel, of having omitted to report an indirect situation of conflict of interests.

★ Repeatedly addressing emails and telephone messages of an insulting and pornographic nature to a former partner. In this case, however, apologies were made and were accepted.

★ Conduct at work with a sexual connotation that was unwanted by the person to whom it was directed.

★ The use of the mail facilities of the Commission to send a large volume of private mail.

Plus seven disciplinary decisions relating to the following cases

★ Driving a service car in a state of inebriation and causing an accident, as established and punished by a criminal court, judged contrary to the dignity of the function.

★ Forging documents with the intention to distort several public tender procedures in a Member State, as established and punished by a criminal court. In view of the circumstance that the facts were old and in the absence of any personal enrichment of the official concerned, a reprimand was imposed on the former official in question.

★ The acquisition, in full knowledge of the facts, of a day hotel, located in a street frequented by prostitutes, which is used to receive private customers in search of discretion – and no doubt many other types of customers – and the fact of deriving profits from the services offered by this hotel.

★ Repeated and extended unauthorised absences, after several unsuccessful attempts to offer the official concerned a post corresponding to his/her qualifications, experience and physical condition.

★ The preparation of false invoices by a person responsible for financial tasks intended to remunerate non-statutory personnel without personal enrichment.

2008

FOUR STAFF RECEIVED WARNINGS FOR THE FOLLOWING INCIDENTS:

★ **Filing claims for undue reimbursement of medical expenses for a low amount.** The AA decided, however, not to open disciplinary proceedings against the official concerned because the medical claims in question concerned a very small amount (€150), which had been reimbursed, and the official concerned had committed no previous breaches of the Staff Regulations.

★ **Financial irregularities in award and performance of study contracts.** The facts, which dated back to a dozen years earlier, had been investigated by OLAF, which found that the procedures established by the old Financial Regulation for selecting successful bidders and awarding contracts had not been fully observed. However, the board decided not to open disciplinary proceedings against the official concerned because the facts dated back a long time, had no impact on the Community budget and had led to no personal advantage for the person concerned and also because the rules applicable at that time were not totally clear and were not backed up by a vade-mecum in the DG concerned.

★ **Online advertising of consultancy services in a field of activities directly linked to the tasks performed by the member of staff in the department where he is employed.** This conduct by an agent in active employment, who was mentioning his status in his online CV, was considered to reflect adversely on his position. However, the board decided not to open disciplinary proceedings against the person concerned, considering the apology made by him and that the website in question had never really worked.

★ **Irregular use of the diplomatic bag to send undeclared personal belongings.** This misuse of the immunity conferred on the diplomatic bag under the Vienna Convention of 18 April 1961, following reminders contained in several notes sent to Commission staff, would normally have triggered disciplinary proceedings. However, the board considered that it was not appropriate to open a disciplinary proceeding against an official who had recently retired and whose conduct in the service had always been irreproachable.

PLUS THREE CASES OF DISCIPLINARY ACTION

★ **Failure to inform the AA of a conflict of interest.** A written warning for the chairperson of an evaluation committee who, in the course of a procurement procedure, participated in a selection process in which one of the bidders was a firm belonging to the chairperson's partner.

★ **False information provided at the time of recruitment and failure to inform the AA of a conflict of interest.** The temporary agent concerned had omitted, at the time of his recruitment, to declare his previous activities within a state security service. His previous employer had dismissed him for the same reason.

★ **A prolonged irregular absence.** This resulted in the removal from work of an official who had been absent from work, without explanation, for several years. The person concerned had stopped providing medical certificates and had no longer been in touch with the European Commission, without providing the slightest explanation, for a very long time.

A SUGGESTED CATEGORISATION OF EU WASTE

A. ORGANISATIONAL WASTE

Administrative

★ Administrative costs, such as bids by universities that cost more than the grants, or the existence of a second European Parliament seat

★ Strategic failure

   a. Cost-benefit failure, i.e. building items with little appreciable return such as observation towers in the Brandenburg woods

   b. Failed incentives, i.e. investments where money would have been spent anyway, such as where farmers admit they would have built fences regardless of receiving any grant

★ Dysfunctional planning, such as the border bridge over the River Prut which had a road running to only one side

FRILLS

★ Areas that are not key or even necessary, such as money spent on PR for the EU

Duplication

★ Unnecessary waste, such as the 6,000 wasted man hours involving hired-in interpreters, or EU agencies duplicating the work of national counterparts

B. FRAUD

Local fraud

★ Organised fraud at a national level, such as half of Slovenia's suckler cows found to be imaginary, Albanian roads that were narrowed to save on tarmac, and organisations such as the Greek farming union whose computer files had been tinkered with

★ Ad hoc petty fraud, with local grants being redirected locally, such as hiring out grant-aided farm machinery or building swimming pools as purported tourist attractions

EU level fraud

★ Fraud within the EU institutions, such as the delegation that kept interest payments with which to buy cars, or instances of nepotism, expenses fiddling or insider dealing

C. POLICY BURDENS

Extra costs

★ Burdens to business that arise, both:

a. Direct regulatory and administrative costs of new laws, such as compliance costs with health and safety laws

b. Gold plating that is added on to EU laws by national civil servants

★ Policy consequential, i.e. the costs that arise from the impact of the policy itself, such as the CFP forcing British boats alone to dump the equivalent of 6 billion fish fingers back into UK waters annually, and the impact this has both on stocks and on port economies

★ Direct costs of subsidies, e.g. cost to the taxpayer in a protected industry

★ Secondary costs of subsidies, e.g. the increase in EU food prices at the till due to CAP protectionism and the impact in turn upon developing world farmers unable to export their goods

A CHANCE FOR MASSIVE REFORM

The Court of Auditors in 2012 proposed a major shift in EU thinking to stop competence creep

> *Expenditure programmes which do not add European value are by definition unlikely to be an effective and efficient use of the EU taxpayer's money. It has therefore recommended articulating the concept of European added value in a suitable political declaration or in EU legislation in order to provide guidance to the EU's political authorities to be used when choosing expenditure priorities. A favourable opportunity for the Legislative authorities is to do so when putting in place the legal framework for the 2014-20 period."*

What this means in practice

> *A fundamental prerequisite of EU spending added value is that it must offer clear and visible benefits for the EU and for its citizens which could not be achieved by spending only at national, regional or local level. In that perspective, the Court has suggested recasting expenditure programmes in terms of acceptable outputs; with programmes based on a set of concrete objectives, and disbursements linked to the achievement of results."*

★ ★ ★ ★ ★ ★ ★ ★ ★ ★ ★ ★

Marta Andreasen

(The first qualified) Chief Accountant, European Commission
Highlighted major auditing flaws

Guido Strack

European Commission
Reported contractual irregularities

Paul van Buitenen

DG auditor
Indicated fraud was widespread and covered up institutionally

Robert McCoy

Financial Controller, Committee of the Regions
Repeatedly pushed for conducting investigations into fraud cases

Bart Nijs

Translator at the Court of Auditors
Pursued a case of suspected nepotism

Christine Sauer

Joint Research Centre
Reported lax handling of nuclear materials

Dougal Watt

Auditor, Court of Auditors
Reported cases of nepotism, soliciting bribes for jobs,
misclaiming of allowances and cover up

Dorte Schmidt-Brown

Eurostat
Flagged up flawed tender process leading to failed contract

Bernard Connolly

Head of Monetary Affairs, Commission
Wrote about treaty breaches in pursuit of EMU

Carol Thompson

European Parliament
Persistently warned of systemic fraud and nepotism

Honorary mention

Hans-Martin Tillack

Investigative journalist
Harassed for his work including a dawn raid by Belgian police at
OLAF's request. His personal files were returned four years later

How much power does the EU have over national laws?

In a nutshell…

The precise figure, though important in understanding how to change any bad laws, is not known but is very significant. The figures depend on how an EU rule is transposed, and vary hugely across competences since some areas like agriculture and trade are decided more at Brussels than others.

666,879

Number of pages of printed EU law, 1957-2005

170,000

Estimated pagination of the laws still in force in 2005

Source: Open Europe

3,836

Number of votes in the European Parliament in 2010

TYPES OF EU LAW

★ **Treaty law**: the underlying international basis for everything

★ **Regulations**: directly applicable in all countries

★ **Directives**: general rules to be turned into national law as countries choose, within a time limit

★ **Decisions**: binding judgements on a specific issue and named individuals or organisations

- ★ **Case law**: precedent set by the ECJ interpreting the application of the above
- ★ **Recommendations**: suggestions (not in a sergeant major sense)
- ★ **Opinions**: non-binding views

ALSO KNOWN AS...

- ★ **Primary legislation** – the treaties
- ★ **Case law** – the ECJ rulings
- ★ **Secondary legislation** – everything else

TYPES OF EU COMPETENCE

Exclusive competences

The EU alone is able to legislate and adopt binding acts in these fields. The member states' role is therefore limited to applying these acts, unless the EU authorises them to adopt certain acts themselves

Shared competences

Member states may exercise their competence only in so far as the EU has not exercised, or has decided not to exercise, its own competence

Supporting competences

The EU can only intervene to support, coordinate or complement the action of member states. Consequently, it has no legislative power in these fields and may not interfere in the exercise of these competences reserved for member states

Special competences

- ★ EU broad direction and coordination of national economic and social policies
- ★ EU competence across all of CFSP, but no legislative competence and no ECJ rights
- ★ Flexibility clause

ARTICLE 352: THE FLEXIBILITY CLAUSE

★ The *Rubber article* in the treaty.

★ Formerly covered by articles 94, 95 and 308, it allows the EU to have a competence in an area not mentioned in the treaties, if member states agree.

★ An example is the authority granted for the EU Presidency to communally negotiate a legally binding agreement on forests in Europe at the Sixth Ministerial Conference on the Protection of Forests in Europe in Oslo in June 2011.

★ Historically used ostensibly to complete the Single Market but in practice useful to justify activity where no clear treaty basis can be found. As such, it is controversial.

AN AUDIT OF EU INPUT BY COMPETENCE INTO UK LEGISLATION, FROM 2001

100%
★ Customs Union
★ DTI – Other Internal Market
★ Monetary (for eurozone countries on launch)

90%
★ Fisheries
★ DTI Nuclear Safeguards
★ Trade
★ Agriculture

80%
★ Environment

60%
★ Transport

50%
★ Public Health, Consumer Protection
★ International Development

★ Regional Policy
★ Social Policy

40%
★ Employment

30%
★ Foreign Affairs
★ Defence

20%
★ Taxation
★ Fiscal/economic

10%
★ Health
★ Culture and Media

Under 10%
★ Sport
★ Home Office

Source: Research paper by Nirj Deva MEP with Gawain Towler, Bow Group

THE EU IN A NUTSHELL

> *Whenever those states which have been acquired as stated have been accustomed to live under their own laws and in freedom, there are three courses for those who wish to hold them: the first is to ruin them, the next is to reside there in person, the third is to permit them to live under their own laws, drawing a tribute, and establishing within it an oligarchy which will keep it friendly to you."*

Nicolo Machiavelli

ESTIMATES OF THE AMOUNT OF EU LEGISLATION AS A PERCENTAGE OF NEW NATIONAL LAW (WITH YEAR)

54% (1993) – French Conseil d'État

70% (1998) – Chairman of the Austrian Parliament Finance Committee

"Well below 50%" – Chairman of the Austrian Parliament

55% (2001) – Audit by Nirj Deva MEP (est. 70% if eurozone)

40% (2002) – OECD assessment of new regulations with significant business impact

9.6% (2003) – Danish academics, as a share of all legislation in force

12.4% (2003) – Austrian academics, as a share of all legislation in force

26% (2004) – Share of CBI consultation responses relating to EU regulations

40% (2004) – HM Better Regulation Taskforce estimate of legislation affecting businesses

42% (2004) – British Chambers of Commerce estimate of legislation affecting businesses

60% (2004) – Dutch junior minister for EU affairs

9% (2005) – Government estimate based on the proportion of Statutory Instruments

50% of significant new regulations come from EU (2005) – From a report by the Cabinet Office (RIU/BRU), briefly referenced in an FOI'd Treasury document

51.8% (2005) – Belgian government parliamentary question, on incorporating directives

Around half (2006) – Government estimate of legislation impacting upon business, charities and voluntary sector

80% (2006) – German Federal Department of Justice, on laws or regulations 1998-2006

Around half (2006) – Government estimate of those "with a significant economic impact"

84% (2007) – German President, on laws in Germany between 1998-2004

50% (2007) – Official German government view that followed

31.5% (2007) – German academic reappraisal

38.6% (2007) – German academic study on EU-influenced law 2002-5

Nearer 20% than 80% (2009) – French academic study

(2009) – Government obliged to clarify the 9% figure estimated in 2005 counts only SI's and excludes EU laws with direct impact

75% (2009) – President of the EP, on legislation in which MEPs had an input

20% down from 30% (2009) – British Chambers of Commerce on a drop in regulations that year

Roughly half (2009) – Institute of Directors, on regulations affecting business

17% to 53% (2009) – Range offered by the Commons Library once one includes the regulations that are incorporated outside of legislation, e.g. by court interpretations or by changing the implementing guidelines

27.97% (2009) – Fine Gael European election manifesto

18% (2010) – Dutch academics, after including amending EU acts

Source: House of Commons Library

PART SEVEN

Aspirations and Directions

MAY CONTAIN TRACES OF
RESOLUTIONS,
FOUNDING FATHERS, AND
EVER-CLOSER UNION

PART SEVEN

Aspirations and Directions

Across the world, and even across Europe, countries have chosen a variety of different ways of co-operating. The EU structures that exist are not the only possible format.

In assessing what countries get out of the EU, it is important to remember that there is an inherent current that pulls countries to an intended destination. Some countries will benefit more than others from political and economic integration. Others will have enduring democratic difficulties since they have different motivations. Not all see the solution to their problems as a federal Europe.

The principles of ever closer union

In a nutshell...

Many of the key people pushing for the ECSC and the early EEC were passionate supporters of full political integration, who sought a country called Europe to stop what they saw as centuries of European civil war. This was particularly felt by those who had come off worst in the second world war.

1923

Foundation of the Pan-European Union by Count Koudenhove-Kalergi, seeking political unification of the continent

1929

French foreign minister, Aristide Briand, proposes a federal Europe at the League of Nations

1948

Foundation of the European Movement

CURRENT OBJECTIVE OF THE EUROPEAN MOVEMENT

"To contribute to the establishment of a united, federal Europe founded on the principles of peace, democracy, liberty, solidarity, and respect for basic human rights."

PREAMBLE SEGMENT FROM THE ECSC TREATY

RESOLVED to substitute for age-old rivalries the merging of their essential interests; to create, by establishing an economic community, the basis for a broader and deeper community among peoples long divided by bloody conflicts; and to lay the foundations for institutions which will give direction to a destiny henceforth shared

PREAMBLE SEGMENTS FROM THE EEC TREATY

DETERMINED to lay the foundations of an ever-closer union among the peoples of Europe

RESOLVED by thus pooling their resources to preserve and strengthen peace and liberty, and calling upon the other peoples of Europe who share their ideal to join in their efforts

"ANY EUROPEAN STATE"

Countries eligible to apply to join the ECSC

INITIAL NUMBER OF DELEGATES TO THE ECSC COMMON ASSEMBLY

Germany – **18**
France **18**
Italy – **18**
Belgium – **10**
Netherlands – **10**
Luxembourg – **4**

"IN PARTICULAR, WITH THE BRITISH GOVERNMENT"

Priority instructions for the new ECSC High Authority for opening negotiations with third parties

TWO

Number of pages of the published ECSC text dedicated to the exchange of letters between the French and German governments indicating that the ECSC did not settle disagreements over who ran the Saar

FOUNDING FATHERS
KONRAD ADENAUER

Nationality	German
Background	Rhinelander and therefore, like other fathers of Europe, a frontiersman. Mayor of Cologne until removed in **1933** by the Nazis. Arrested by the Gestapo in **1944** in the wake of the failed Valkyrie bomb plot. First Chancellor of the Federal Republic of Germany, **1949-1963**.
Motivation	Uncertain of US and UK political reliability with regard to East German and West Berlin matters. Conscious of German war guilt and its impact on the new West German state.
Special role	Key figure in Franco-German rapprochement in the context of post-war and cold war shifted geopolitics – the man who won over de Gaulle after Suez.
Key quotes	*"An atmosphere of peace in Europe should be attained again and it seems that political economy must pave the way for it."* (**1924**) *"It is my deepest belief that the United States of Europe can finally bring peace to this continent which has been ravaged by war so often."* (**1946**) *"The first period of European integration has ended. Its purpose was to ensure that a war may never break out between the European people [...] The objective of the second period of European integration is to ensure that Europe and the European countries retain their value, relevance and their standing in the world."* (**1956**) *"Let us not forget that dams have been built up in over two thousand years of European history; they cannot be taken down quickly. Deeply-rooted views have to be abandoned. The overall political education of the European people, which is geared towards the idea of the nation as the last value of political decision-making, has to be changed. This will not happen overnight."* (**1963**)

Source: Konrad Adenauer Foundation

Nationality	French
Background	Cognac dealer, then banker. Senior administrator dealing with food supply during WWI and arms supply during WWII (despite early issues with de Gaulle's status). Reportedly the inspiration behind the briefly mooted 1940 union of Britain and France. Commissioner responsible for modernisation in 1945.
Motivation	Experience in the political integration of essential stocks
Special role	Proposed the Monnet Plan behind the Coal and Steel Community. First President of the ECSC. Resigned when the European Defence Community was blocked in Paris and went on to help set up the Action Committee for the United States of Europe.
Key quotes	*"Patience is certainly something that I learned from where I grew up. The people of Cognac were not nationalist, at a time when France was."* *[On the League of Nations] "Bringing governments together, getting national officials to co-operate, is well-intentioned enough; but the method breaks down as soon as national interests conflict, unless there is an independent political body that can take a common view of the problem and arrive at a common decision."* *"There will be no peace in Europe if the States rebuild themselves on the basis of national sovereignty, with its implications of prestige politics and economic protection. The countries of Europe are not strong enough individually to be able to guarantee prosperity and social development for their peoples. The States of Europe must therefore form a federation or a European entity that would make them into a common economic unit."* *"Once a common market interest has been created, then political union will come naturally. We are not forming coalitions between States, but union among people."* (1957)

ROBERT SCHUMAN

Nationality	Born in Luxembourg
Background	Lawyer in Metz. Arrested by the Gestapo 1940. Went on the run from house arrest **1942**. Subsequently joined the French Resistance. French Foreign Minister **1948-52**.
Motivation	Personal experiences in Nazi Europe. A little known fact relates to his time in southern France, where he had fled when he was on the run. He had not reckoned on the German reaction to the North African landings and Hitler's decision to close down Vichy. Schuman had barely arrived at a quiet town when a Panzer regiment rolled in, forcing him to take refuge with Trappists. A fellow fugitive was from Alsace, named Émile Baas and together they wiled away the time by discussing how postwar Europe might look Source: Madeleine Baas
Special role	Worked with Monnet on what became the Schuman Plan, proposing ECSC principles. President of the European Assembly **1958-60**.
Key quotes	*"Europe will not be made all at once, or according to a single plan. It will be built through concrete achievements which first create a de facto solidarity. The coming together of the nations of Europe requires the elimination of the age-old opposition of France and Germany. Any action taken must in the first place concern these two countries."* *"By pooling basic production and by instituting a new High Authority, whose decisions will bind France, Germany and other member countries, this proposal will lead to the realization of the first concrete foundation of a European federation indispensable to the preservation of peace." (Schuman Declaration, **1950**)*

Nationality	Italian
Background	Born in South Tyrol, which originally made him an Austrian subject before WWI. Parliamentarian in Imperial Vienna before becoming one in Rome.
Motivation	In WWI, worked on food relief for the Trentino, which had become a battlefield and much of the population of which was forcibly removed. Imprisoned by Mussolini between 1926-9. Very strong links to the Catholic Church, which sheltered him from the fascists. Driven by regionalism, and as a politician conscious of Italy's weak post-war position and territorial losses. Increasingly pushed for accelerated European integration which he saw as being secured by monetary or military union.
Special role	Italian Minister for Foreign Affairs, and Prime Minister, over 1945-1953. Elected President of the ECSC Assembly in 1954.
Key quotes	*"How could we not react and not protest when our call for local autonomy was opposed by a centralising and levelling bureaucracy."* (1919)
	"Supranational institutions will not be enough and may well become no more than a playing field in which particular interests are competing, if the men assigned to them do not feel that they represent higher and European interests. Without this European mentality, any formula upon which we decide may well be no more than an empty legal abstraction." (1952)

Source: EPP Group biography

PAUL HENRI SPAAK

Nationality	Belgian
Background	From a political dynasty. Prisoner of War for two years in WWI. Foreign Minister during WWII. Following the German invasion, he was initially interned but then escaped to England.
Motivation	Interested in European co-operation in the **1920s**. Revisited through personal wartime experiences. Pushed towards collective security through his personal failure to maintain Belgian independence by neutrality.
Special role	Foreign Minister and Prime Minister after WWII, in which he was able to put into action his wartime proposal for a Benelux union. President of the working committee for the Messina Conference. A founder of the European Movement. His son, in **1977**, became the first functionary to head the EEC delegation to Washington.
Key quote	*"Making Europe means realizing that we shall certainly have to sacrifice a number of things, perhaps even some legitimate interests, with the intention or, better, the certainty that in time the whole European community to which we belong will find in the new system greater prosperity, happiness and well-being."* **1949** speech to the Council of Europe

WALTER HALLSTEIN

Nationality	German
Background	Professor of Law (some critics controversially accuse him of excessive membership of Nazi trade organisations). German foreign minister under Adenauer.
Motivation	Post-war German self-interest, then Commission self-interest
Special role	First President of the European Commission. President of the European Movement.
Key quotes	*"Integration is thus a process and not a static thing, and this process is one that tends towards complete federation, that is, to the federal state. Of course, a European state does not exist until the final position has been attained – and this is in conformity with our concept of a confederation."* *"The community must also be responsible for defence and non-economic foreign policy based on a federal constitution."* 1969 Speech to the British Council of the European Movement

Nationality	Italian
Background	Communist who was imprisoned by the fascists.
Motivation	Idealism, founded on opposition to nationalism, regime-dominated unions, and big business
Special role	Founder of the federalist movement in post-war Italy. Intellectual godfather as author of the Ventotene Manifesto, written while in internal exile. Advisor, Commissioner and MEP. Authored the Spinelli Plan for further integration in the 1980s.
Key quotes	*"The collapse of the majority of the States on the continent under the German steam-roller has already placed the destinies of the European populations on common ground: either all together they will submit to Hitler's dominion, or after his fall, all together they will enter a revolutionary crisis, and they will not find themselves adamantly distinct in solid, States structures. The general spirit today is already far more disposed than it was in the past towards a federal reorganisation of Europe. The hard experience of the last decades has opened the eyes even of those who refused to see, and has matured many circumstances favourable to our ideal."* *"The European Federation is the only conceivable guarantee that relationships with American and Asiatic peoples can exist on the basis of peaceful co-operation, while awaiting a more distant future, when the political unity of the entire globe becomes a possibility."* *"Private property must be abolished, limited, corrected, extended: according to the different situations and not according to principle. This guideline is easily inserted into the process of forming a European economic life freed from nightmares of militarism or national bureaucratism."* Ventotene Manifesto, 1941

WINSTON CHURCHILL

Nationality	British
Background	Wartime premier
Motivation	Fear of another French-German conflict triggering a nuclear war
Special role	Called for European integration in a speech in Zurich in **1946** and was an early sponsor of European institutions. However, he was uncommitted on whether a federal structure should apply and was persistently clear that this entity would act as just one regional pillar supporting the United Nations – alongside the "elastic" British Empire/Commonwealth, the United States and the Americas, and a future South East Asian association. The UK would not be part of the United Europe but be a sponsor along with the USA and, hopefully, Russia.
Key quotes	*"If Europe were once united in the sharing of its common inheritance, there would be no limit to the happiness, to the prosperity and glory which its three or four hundred million people would enjoy."* (Zurich, **1946**) *"It is necessary that any policy this island may adopt towards Europe and in Europe should enjoy the full sympathy and approval of the peoples of the Dominions."* (**1947**) *"We should not hesitate to accept with the greatest cordiality ever closer ties of unity with the United States."* (**1948**) *"I cannot conceive that Britain would be an ordinary member of a Federal Union linked to Europe in any period which can at present be foreseen."* (**1950**) *"We genuinely wish to join a European Free Trade area, and if our continental friends wish to reach agreement, I am quite sure that a way can be found and that reasonable adjustments can be made to meet the essential interests of all."* (**1957**)

THE CULT OF EUROPE

SCHUMAN ONE N, MONNET TWO NS

How to distinguish between Fathers of Europe and celebrated artist(e)s – an error even the Commission can make

EUROPEAN HOUSES

Museums and EU cultural centres based in the former homes of Fathers of Europe

 The Jean Monnet and Robert Schuman houses are meeting places for the people of Europe, the aim being to set the pioneers and pioneering activities of European integration in the context in which two of the founding fathers of Europe lived and worked, and to provide information on today's and tomorrow's Europe; as such, these organisations pursue an aim of general European interest."

Decision 2004/100/EC

MAISONS DE L'EUROPE

A set of (predominantly French) EU cultural centres, sponsored by the EU, but confusingly not based in any historical figure's occupancy. One grant recipient in the UK was found to be someone's front room.

HOUSE OF EUROPEAN HISTORY

An entirely different project again. 4,800 square metres of museum in Brussels dedicated to the history of European integration

£136.5 MILLION

Latest estimate of the spiralling costs of the project

Source: *Daily Telegraph*

A DIVISIVE HISTORY

1946

Year the house of European
History begins at, in order to
avoid disputes over how to portray
the war

1945

Date the joint Franco-German
school history textbook begins

HISTORY OF THE BALTIC COUNTRIES

As a comparison, a joint history project that failed when Lithuania's chronological approach followed traditional lines and therefore diverged into a separate narrative

BLACK SEA, A HISTORY OF INTERACTIONS

Joint historical project described as a "fiasco" where the authors failed to interact to create a linked narrative

THE HISTORY OF EUROPE

Major attempt to create a common EU school textbook. However, the texts and figures quoted change across different language versions. The reviewer joked even the French version and the French master version were different.

Source: paper by van der Leeuw Roord, President, Euroclio

€255,000

EU grant to the Jean Monnet
House in 2005

€128,000

EU grant to the Robert Schuman
House in 2005

IN MEMORIAM: SOME EU PROJECTS IN HONOUR OF SCHUMAN

★ Europe Day (to commemorate his 1950 speech)
★ EU Funding of national Schuman centres
★ Funding of Schuman committees and associated projects, such as dance
★ A medal from the European Peoples Party and Diploma of Honour
★ Commemorative gold/silver euro
★ Schuman/Monnet memorial papers

IN MEMORIAM: SOME EU PROJECTS IN HONOUR OF MONNET

★ Jean Monnet European centres of excellence
★ Jean Monnet professors/chairs
★ Jean Monnet conferences
★ Jean Monnet academic thematic groups
★ Jean Monnet scholarships
★ Jean Monnet public lectures
★ Special commemorative ceremonies at the EP

SOME PAST RECIPIENTS OF THE ROBERT SCHUMAN MEDAL

★ Pope John Paul II
★ Chris Patten
★ Mario Monti
★ Nicole Fontaine
★ Franz Fischler
★ Sir Edward Heath
★ Jacques Santer
★ Valéry Giscard Estaing
★ Jacques Delors
★ Hans-Gert Poettering

PURPOSE OF THE SCHUMAN MEDAL

> *To pay tribute to public figures who have advanced the cause of peace, the construction of Europe and human values through their public activities and personal commitment."*

1990

Year in which the Bishop of Metz opened beatification proceedings for Robert Schuman

50KG

Weight of the dossier sent to Rome in 2004

PRAYER FOR THE GLORIFICATION OF THE SERVANT OF GOD ROBERT SCHUMAN AND TO ASK FOR GRACES THROUGH HIS INTERCESSION

> *Lord, you willed that your creatures should reflect your love, and that peoples should develop between themselves bonds of peace and solidarity.*
>
> *Your servant Robert Schuman was a faithful peacemaker. He carried out his secular actions as a vocation. He worked to build the first community of nations, expressing the wish "that Europe prefigure universal solidarity in the future". His active life showed that politics may be a way of holiness. In the image of your Son, he was gentle and humble of heart (Mt 11, 29).*

Grant that your Church soon honour Robert Schuman, disciple and imitator of Jesus Christ. Let him be a model for lawmakers and those who govern, so that they also may become servants of their own peoples and work for justice between nations.

Through the intercession of your servant Robert Schuman, give us the grace (indicate here the grace that is asked for).

Grant, loving Father, that we be instruments of your divine will during our earthly pilgrimage through the most beautiful struggle of faith, in order to gain eternal life, to which we are called (1 Tim 6, 12). And according to the example of Robert Schuman, may we always be able ever to live in accordance with your love. Amen."

Models for Europe

In a nutshell…

Other models for European co-operation exist beside the EU, such as UNECE, the OECD, EFTA and the EEA. The intergovernmental approach of the Council of Europe indeed predates the EEC and works as a parallel model of how European co-operation can work.

47
Number of countries in the Council of Europe in 2011

800 MILLION
Total population

FIVE
Countries with observer rights – the Vatican, Canada, USA, Mexico, Japan

4,892 MILES
Distance from Reykjavik to Vladivostok, both in Council of Europe countries

FOUNDING FATHERS OF THE COUNCIL OF EUROPE

Sir Winston Churchill

Konrad Adenauer

Robert Schuman

Paul-Henri Spaak

Alcide de Gasperi

Ernest Bevin

The Council of Europe is, to be sure, the laboratory in which experiments in European co-operation are conducted, until such time as it is transformed into an organic institution of European unity."

Schuman's caveat on the limits of the Council of Europe as the forum for European integration (1951)

1949

Date of the founding of the Council of Europe by the Treaty of London

10

Number of original CoE members: Belgium, Denmark, France, Ireland, Italy, Luxembourg, the Netherlands, Norway, Sweden and the United Kingdom

1955 – creation of the CoE flag

1972 – adoption of a European anthem, the prelude to Ode to Joy from Beethoven's 9th

1986 – Both 'Strasbourg' symbols appropriated by 'Brussels'

1999 – Strasbourg adopts a distinct logo, an 'e' with 12 stars

KEY COUNCIL OF EUROPE INSTITUTIONS

★ Committee of Ministers: makes decisions on policies, activities and budget

★ Parliamentary Assembly

★ Congress of Local and Regional Authorities

★ European Court of Human Rights (ECHR)

★ The Commissioner for Human Rights

★ The Conference of International Non-governmental Organisations

★ The Secretary General

★ The Secretariat

★ The Council of Europe Development Bank

FOUR

Number of times a year the Parliamentary Assembly sits

SOME COE GROUPS AND THEIR THEMES

ECRI (European Commission against Racism and Intolerance) – racism

GRETA (Group of Experts on Action against Trafficking in Human Beings) – trafficking

MONEYVAL – money laundering

Pompidou Group – drugs and narcotrafficking

Venice Commission – constitutional standards

GRECO (Group of States against Corruption) – corruption

EPAS (Enlarged Partial Agreement on Sport) – sport

Dosta! – Roma and travellers

€217 MILLION

Total CoE budget for 2011

€1,557,000

Operating budget of the CoE's European Court of Human Rights in 2011

€309,000,000

Budget of the EU's European Court of Justice for 2012

1959

Foundation of EFTA by "the Seven" in response to the founding of the EEC by "the Six"

80%

Total amount of EFTA trade covered by preferential trading arrangements

4

Number of states currently in EFTA: Norway, Iceland, Switzerland and Liechtenstein

> *"EFTA comes close to realising the dispensation that most British voters always wanted from Europe: free trade without unnecessary regulation or political union. Its rude prosperity is embarrassing to British Euro-sophists, who have been telling us for 30 years that the EU is vital to our economic survival."*

Dan Hannan, MEP

12.7 MILLION
Total EFTA population today

€664 BILLION
Total EFTA GDP

€19.1 MILLION
EFTA operating budget for 2011

100
Number of EFTA staff

6
Number of EU countries that used to be in EFTA: Denmark, UK, Portugal, Austria, Finland, Sweden. Membership of both is incompatible

20
Number of Free Trade Agreements between EFTA and 29 non-EU countries. Sixteen more are being pursued.

€357.7 MILLION
Current annual contribution from EEA states to the EU under the EEA agreement

30
Number of countries in the EEA (the EU plus three).

From 2004 to 2007, pre-accession countries joined the EEA before joining the EU.

EU AREAS EXCLUDED FROM THE EEA

★ Common Agriculture and Fisheries Policies (except some aspects of trade in agricultural and fish products)

★ Customs Union

★ Common Trade Policy

★ Common Foreign and Security Policy

★ Justice and Home Affairs

★ Monetary Union

UNANIMITY

Mechanism by which EEA countries approve agreements, i.e. each country has a veto

1972
First EFTA agreement with the EEC

1984
European Economic Space (EES)

1994
EEA launched

1992
Year Switzerland voted against EEA membership, choosing to adopt a different, bilateral, approach instead

SIZE OF THE EEA AGREEMENT

★ **129** articles
★ **22** annexes
★ **49** protocols

THE EEA PAY OFF

Can only input into the Commission's drafting stage of EU legislation (no seats at the Council or EP); but a veto on whether to implement the end agreement nationally

EEA BODIES

★ **EEA Joint Committee** – representatives from EEA countries and the Commission, for management meetings
★ **EEA Council** – EEA Foreign Ministers, for political impetus
★ **EEA Joint Parliamentary Committee** – national parliamentarians
★ **EEA Consultative Committee** – social partners quango
★ **EFTA Surveillance Authority** – monitors compliance
★ **EFTA Court** – judges on infringements and appeals

11

Number of EU agencies in which there is direct EEA participation

56

Number of countries in UNECE (United Nations Economic Commission for Europe), founded in 1947. It is one of five regional commissions for the UN

AIM OF UNECE

To promote pan-European economic integration through the following means:

★ Policy dialogue

★ Negotiation of international legal instruments

★ Development of regulations and norms

★ Exchange and application of best practices as well as economic and technical expertise

★ Technical co-operation for countries with economies in transition

UNECE SUCCESSES

★ The network of 'E' roads linking all European countries

★ Harmonisation of road signs and signals

★ Safety and anti-pollution standards for motor vehicles

★ Standards for the transport of dangerous goods by road

★ Agreement for the development of combined transport

★ Standards for perishable agricultural produce

★ Agreements on customs procedures and various trade regulations

★ Standards for the electronic exchange of trade and transport data

★ Conventions on transboundary air pollution, the protection of watercourses and the transboundary effects of industrial accidents

★ Authoritative analyses and statistics on regional economic development, especially for helping transition following communism

Many of these were achieved despite the cold war

GENEVA
Location of UNECE

$53 MILLION
UNECE budget for 2011

234
Total number of staff at UNECE

1961
Foundation of the OECD
(Organisation for Economic Co-
operation and Development) in
Paris

34
Number of OECD countries

€342 MILLION
OECD budget

2,500
Number of OECD staff

CURRENT NON-EUROPEAN OECD MEMBERS

Australia

Canada

Chile

Japan

Korea

Mexico

New Zealand

United States

OECD MISSION STATEMENT

 To promote policies that will improve the economic and social well-being of people around the world."

56

Number of countries in the OSCE, an organisation dedicated to crisis and conflict prevention in Europe

550

Number of staff at the OSCE secretariat. Another 2,330 work in the field

€150.9 MILLION
OSCE budget for 2011

OSCE WORKING AREAS

★ Arms control
★ Border management
★ Combating human trafficking
★ Combating terrorism
★ Conflict prevention and resolution
★ Economic activities
★ Education
★ Elections
★ Environmental activities
★ Gender equality
★ Good governance
★ Human rights
★ Media freedom and development
★ Military reform and co-operation
★ Minority rights
★ Policing
★ Roma and Sinti
★ Rule of law
★ Tolerance and non-discrimination

CEFTA (CENTRAL EUROPEAN FREE TRADE AGREEMENT) MEMBERSHIP

Albania, Bosnia and Herzegovina, Croatia, Macedonia, Moldova, Montenegro, Serbia, Kosovo

A SHIFTING FREE TRADE AREA

CEFTA originally covered the EU applicant states of central and eastern Europe. When these joined the EU, the FTAs of the Balkan states that weren't in the EU were effectively shifted to the CEFTA framework. Management costs are not known, but administrative costs for Kosovo's entry were estimated at €100,000 annually.

BAFTA

- ★ Award ceremony for thespians
- ★ Baltic Free Trade Area for the former Soviet Baltic States, operating prior to EU accession

NORDIC COUNCIL

87
Number of representatives on the Nordic Council

They represent Denmark, Finland, Iceland, Norway, Sweden, the Faroe Islands, Greenland and Åland.

PRESIDIUM
The governing body of the Nordic Council

THE SESSION
The parliamentary meeting

1952
Founding year

900 MILLION DANISH KRONE
Annual operating budget of the Nordic Council (around £105 million)

NORDIC COUNCIL SUPPORTED BODIES

★ NordForsk (research and researcher training)
★ Nordic Atlantic Cooperation (NORA) (intergovernmental collaborative agency)
★ Nordregio (regional studies)
★ Nordic Centre for Welfare and Social Issues (NVC)
★ Nordic Council for Reindeer Husbandry Research (NOR)
★ Nordic Council on Disability
★ Nordic Culture Fund
★ Nordic Culture Point
★ Nordic Energy Research
★ Nordic Environment Finance Corporation (NEFCO)
★ Nordic Film & TV Fund
★ Nordic Game Program (access to quality Nordic computer games for children and young people)
★ Nordic Gender Institute (NIKK)
★ Nordic Gene Resource Centre (NordGen)
★ Nordic House in the Faroe Islands (FO)
★ Nordic Information Centre for Media and Communication Research (NORDICOM)
★ Nordic Innovation
★ Nordic Institute for Advanced Training in Occupational Health (NIVA)
★ Nordic Institute for Theoretical Physics (NORDITA)
★ Nordic Institute of Asian Studies (NIAS)
★ Nordic Institute of Dental Materials (NIOM)
★ Nordic Institute of Maritime Law
★ Nordic Joint Committee for Agricultural Research (NKJ)
★ Nordic Journalist Centre
★ Nordic Medico-Statistical Committee (NOMESKO)
★ Nordic Project Fund (Nopef) (small and medium sized Nordic enterprises)
★ Nordic Sámi Institute (NSI)
★ Nordic Social-Statistical Committee (NOSOSCO)
★ Nordic Summer University (NSU)
★ Nordic Volcanological Center (NORDVULK)
★ Nordjobb (Nordic Work Exchange Programme)
★ The Nordic Development Fund (NDF)
★ The Nordic Forest Research Co-operation Committee (SNS)
★ The Nordic House in Reykjavik (NOREY)
★ The Nordic School of Public Health (NHV)

NORDEN ASSOCIATIONS

Independent, non-party organisations that promote closer Nordic co-operation, open borders in the region and a deeper sense of cultural affinity

8

Number of countries participating in the Nordic Investment Bank

120

Total number of staff at the three secretariats

SOME OTHER NORTHERN COUNCILS
Barents Euro-Arctic Council
Barents Regional Council
Council of Baltic Sea States
Arctic Council

BRITISH-IRISH COUNCIL

Priority areas of work

★ agricultural issues

★ health

★ regional issues

★ consideration of inter-parliamentary links

★ energy

★ cultural issues

★ tourism

★ sporting activity

★ education

★ approaches to EU issues

★ minority and lesser used languages

★ prison and probation issues

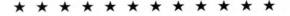

SECONDHAND STEEL COMMUNITY

One mooted proposal instead of EU accession was for post-Soviet Ukraine, Baltics, Poland and Belarus to combine to form their own trading bloc.

DON'T MENTION THE WAR

Some past attempts at European union

Holy Roman Empire	The Founding Six, less southern Italy
Charles V	Holland, Belgium, Luxembourg, Germany (notional/partial), Austria, Spain, much of Italy, parts of France (his son did not inherit eastern Europe but added Portugal and, briefly by marriage, England, Wales and Ireland)
First French Empire	France, Holland, Belgium, parts of Spain, Italy, Croatia; dependent states in Spain, Germany, Switzerland, Italy, Poland
Austro-Hungarian Empire	Austria, Hungary, Czech Republic, Slovakia, Slovenia, Croatia, Bosnia and parts of six other modern countries
COMECON	USSR, Bulgaria, Czechoslovakia, Hungary, Poland, Romania, East Germany (plus Mongolia, Cuba, Vietnam); Albania to 1961

KEY COMECON INSTITUTIONS

★ Conference of First Secretaries of Communist and Workers' Parties and of the Heads of Government: unofficial guide to COMECON policy

★ Session of the Council for Mutual Economic Assistance – reviewed socialist integration and directed the secretariat. Delegations headed by national prime ministers. Liaison in the meantime was through a permanent representative.

★ Executive Committee of the Council. Developed and followed through on policy.

★ Council Secretariat

- Four council committees, for: Planning (coordinating economies); Scientific and Technical Cooperation; Material and Technical Supply; and Cooperation in Machine Building. Headquartered in Moscow.
- 24 standing commissions (in 1986)
- Six interstate conferences, for: water management; internal trade; legal matters; inventions and patents; pricing; and labour affairs.
- Two scientific institutes
- Associated institutions, including the International Bank for Economic Cooperation and the International Investment Bank.

Source: Sonu Trivedi, *A Handbook of World Organisations*, 2005

COMECON OPERATIONAL PRINCIPLE

Decisions were made in theory by unanimity. However, there was no veto but instead countries could elect not to participate – the principle of disinterest.

PAST ATTEMPTS AT CURRENCY PARITIES AND UNIONS IN EUROPE

- Latin Monetary Union (a Franc parity zone – France, Belgium, Italy, Switzerland and Greece)
- Scandinavian Monetary Union
- The Gold Standard (originally mooted to have had separate but interchangeable currencies)
- Austro-Hungarian monetary union
- Occupation currencies
- The Snake (to 1977)
- Irish Pound parity
- ERM I
- The Rouble
- Czech-Slovak monetary union

AD 928

Statute of Greatley makes provision for a national English coinage, modelled on Carolingian standards – themselves possibly modelled on an earlier English penny

ACP (African, Caribbean, and Pacific Group of States)	Angola, Antigua and Barbuda, Belize, Cape Verde, Comoros, the Bahamas, Barbados, Benin, Botswana, Burkina Faso, Burundi, Cameroon, Central African Republic, Chad, DR Congo, Republic of the Congo, Cook Islands, Côte d'Ivoire, Cuba, Djibouti, Dominica, Dominican Republic, Eritrea, Ethiopia, Fiji, Gabon, Gambia, Ghana, Grenada, Republic of Guinea, Guinea-Bissau, Equatorial Guinea, Guyana, Haiti, Jamaica, Kenya, Kiribati, Lesotho, Liberia, Madagascar, Malawi, Mali, Marshall Islands, Mauritania, Mauritius, Micronesia, Mozambique, Namibia, Nauru, Niger, Nigeria, Niue, Palau, Papua New Guinea, Rwanda, Saint Kitts and Nevis, Saint Lucia, Saint Vincent and the Grenadines, Solomon Islands, Samoa, Sao Tome and Principe, Senegal, Seychelles, Sierra Leone, Somalia, South Africa, Sudan, Suriname, Swaziland, Tanzania, Timor Leste, Togo, Tonga, Trinidad and Tobago, Tuvalu, Uganda, Vanuatu, Zambia, Zimbabwe (created to facilitate bilateral action with the EU as the other single party)
ACS (Association of Caribbean States)	Antigua and Barbuda, the Bahamas, Barbados, Belize, Colombia, Costa Rica, Cuba, Dominica, Dominican Republic, El Salvador, Grenada, Guatemala, Guyana, Haiti, Honduras, Jamaica, Mexico, Nicaragua, Panama, Saint Kitts and Nevis, Saint Lucia, Saint Vincent and the Grenadines, Suriname, Trinidad and Tobago, Venezuela
ALADI (Latin American Integration Association) Replaced LAFTA (Latin American Free Trade Association)	Argentina, Bolivia, Brazil, Chile, Colombia, Ecuador, Mexico, Paraguay, Peru, Uruguay, Venezuela, Cuba
Andean Community	Bolivia, Colombia, Ecuador and Peru
APEC (Asia-Pacific Economic Cooperation)	Australia, Brunei Darussalam, Canada, Chile, People's Republic of China, Hong Kong/China, Indonesia, Japan, Republic of Korea, Malaysia, Mexico, New Zealand, Papua New Guinea, Peru, Philippines, Russia, Singapore, Taiwan, Thailand, USA, Vietnam
APTA (Asia-Pacific Trade Agreement) Previously Bangkok Agreement	Bangladesh, China, India, South Korea, Laos, Sri Lanka
ASEAN (Association of Southeast Asian Nations)	Brunei, Cambodia, Indonesia, Laos, Malaysia, Myanmar, Philippines, Singapore, Thailand, Vietnam
BAFTA (Baltic Free Trade Area)	Estonia, Latvia, Lithuania (to 2004)

BSEC (Black Sea Economic Cooperation)	Albania, Armenia, Azerbaijan, Bulgaria, Georgia, Greece, Moldova, Romania, Russia, Turkey, Ukraine
CAFTA-DR (Central American Free Trade Area) Successor to the moribund CACM (Central American Common Market)	Costa Rica, Dominican Republic, El Salvador, Guatemala, Honduras, Nicaragua, United States
CARICOM (Caribbean Community) Formerly CARIFTA (Caribbean Free Trade Area)	Antigua and Barbuda, the Bahamas, Barbados, Belize, Dominica, Grenada, Guyana, Haiti, Jamaica, Montserrat, Saint Lucia, Saint Kitts and Nevis, Saint Vincent and the Grenadines, Suriname, Trinidad and Tobago. Associate Members: Anguilla, Bermuda, British Virgin Islands, Cayman Islands, Turks and Caicos Islands
CELAC (Community of Latin America and Caribbean States) Expanded from the Rio Group, a more neutralist subgroup of the Organisation of American States (OAS)	Argentina, Bolivia, Chile, Colombia, Costa Rica, Cuba, Dominican Republic, Ecuador, El Salvador, Guatemala, Honduras, Mexico, Nicaragua, Panama, Paraguay, Peru, Uruguay, Venezuela, Brazil, Antigua and Barbuda, the Bahamas, Barbados, Belize, Dominica, Grenada, Guyana, Jamaica, Saint Lucia, Saint Kitts and Nevis, Saint Vincent and the Grenadines, Trinidad and Tobago, Haiti, Surinam
CEMAC (Economic and Monetary Community of Central Africa)	Cameroon, Central African Republic, Chad, Republic of the Congo, Equatorial Guinea, Gabon
CER/ANZCERTA (Closer Economic Relations Agreement) Following from NAFTA (NZ-AUS Free Trade Agreement)	Australia, New Zealand
CIS (Commonwealth of Independent States)	Armenia, Azerbaijan, Belarus, Georgia, Kazakhstan, Kyrgyzstan, Moldova, Russia, Tajikistan, Turkmenistan, Ukraine, Uzbekistan
COMESA (Common Market for Eastern and Southern Africa)	Burundi, Comoros, DR Congo, Djibouti, Egypt, Eritrea, Ethiopia, Kenya, Libya, Madagascar, Malawi, Mauritius, Rwanda, Seychelles, Sudan, Swaziland, Uganda, Zambia, Zimbabwe
EAC (East African Community)	Kenya, Uganda, Tanzania, Rwanda, Burundi
EAEC (Eurasian Economic Community)	Belarus, Kazakhstan, Kyrgyzstan, Russian Federation, Tajikistan
ECO (Economic Cooperation Organisation)	Afghanistan, Azerbaijan, Iran, Kazakhstan, Kyrgyzstan, Pakistan, Tajikstan, Turkey, Turkmenistan, Uzbekistan
ECOWAS (Economic Community of West African States)	Benin, Burkina Faso, Cape Verde, Gambia, Ghana, Guinea, Guinea Bissau, Ivory Coast, Liberia, Mali, Niger, Nigeria, Senegal, Sierra Leone, Togo

THE EU IN A NUTSHELL

IBSA (India-Brazil-South Africa Dialogue Forum)	India, Brazil, South Africa
GCC (Cooperation Council for the Arab States of the Gulf)	Bahrain, Kuwait, Oman, Qatar, Saudi Arabia, UAE
GSTP (Global System of Trade Preferences among Developing Countries)	Large number of signatory states and trade groups
MERCOSUR/MERCOSUL (Mercado Comun del Cono Sul)	Argentina, Brazil, Paraguay, Uruguay, Venezuela. Associate Members: Bolivia, Chile, Colombia, Ecuador, Peru
MSG (Melanesian Spearhead Group)	Fiji, Papua New Guinea, Solomon Islands, Vanuatu
NAFTA (North American Free Trade Agreement)	Canada, Mexico, USA
Pacific Community	American Samoa, Cook Islands, Fiji Islands, French Polynesia, Guam, Kiribati, Marshall Islands, Micronesia, Nauru, New Caledonia, Niue, Northern Mariana Islands, Palau, Papua New Guinea, Pitcairn Islands, Samoa, Solomon Islands, Tokelau, Tonga, Tuvalu, Vanuatu, Wallis and Futuna, Australia, France, New Zealand, USA
PATCRA (Papua-Australia Trade and Commercial Relations Agreement)	Australia, Papua New Guinea
SAARC (South Asian Association for Regional Cooperation)/SAPTA (preferential trading agreement)	Afghanistan, Bangladesh, Bhutan, India, Maldives, Nepal, Pakistan, Sri Lanka
SADC (Southern Africa Development Community)	Angola, Botswana, DR Congo, Lesotho, Madagascar, Malawi, Mauritius, Mozambique, Namibia, Seychelles, South Africa, Swaziland, Tanzania, Zambia, Zimbabwe
SPARETECA (South Pacific Regional Trade and Economic Cooperation Agreement), emerging from the South Pacific Forum	Australia, Cook Islands, Fiji, Kiribati, Nauru, New Zealand, Niue, Papua New Guinea, Solomon Islands, Tonga, Tuvalu, Western Samoa
UNASUR/UNASUL (Union of South American Nations)	Andean Community, MERCOSUR, plus Chile, Guyana, Surinam
WAEMU (West African Economic and Monetary Union)	Benin, Burkina Faso, Cote d'Ivoire, Guinea-Bissau, Mali, Niger, Senegal, Togo

DIFFERENCES IN OBJECTIVES AND END STATES

★ **ACS**: "The strengthening of the regional co-operation and integration process, with a view to creating an enhanced economic space in the region; preserving the environmental integrity of the Caribbean Sea which is regarded as the common patrimony of the peoples of the region; and promoting the sustainable development of the Greater Caribbean."

★ **NAFTA Treaty**: "Eliminate barriers to trade in, and facilitate the cross-border movement of, goods and services between the territories of the Parties."

★ **Andean Community**: "An integral integration process that will contribute effectively to sustainable and equitable human development, in order to live well, with respect for the diversity and asymmetries that agglutinate the different visions, models and approaches and that will converge in the formation of the Union of South American Nations (UNASUR)."

Where co-operation extends beyond economics, areas chosen vary from the environment amongst islanders, to post-colonial regional cultural identities, via joint measures against Malaria or water supplies (or strategic actions such as support for the Frontline States during Apartheid). The Latin American countries in particular occasionally express Bolivarian dreams of unification, while differing over the amount of free trade integration that would accompany it – the reverse of the EU experience.

TIR CONVENTION

★ UN agreement (through UNECE) allowing for the transportation of goods across Europe and well beyond, without repeated intermediary frontier checks. It has 66 contracting parties.

★ Originally set up in a small number of European countries in 1949, the Tir Convention was established in 1960 and reworked in 1975 to take into account the development of the container system. It remains the only existing universal customs transit system.

★ 2.8 million carnets were issued in 2010 allowing for long-distance transit

PRT
EIGHT

The View from the Member States

MAY CONTAIN TRACES OF
COSTS, BENEFITS AND
THE NETHERLANDS
DISTORTION

In this book, we have been able to see how the EU functions and in many cases identified areas where some countries fare better than others. Now, it is possible to make an assessment whether individual nations benefit, or not, fron the EU.

The costs and benefits of the EU

In a nutshell..

The realities of membership vary from state to state. Regulatory burdens hit Eastern Europe harder, because they affect their low labour costs and underdeveloped industries. On the other hand, Germany's geographic position means that it was the main beneficiary from enlargement of the Single Market. Comparing trade benefits and red tape costs within each country, what is clear is that countries with a high share of their national GDP coming from trade with other EU countries won't feel the red tape costs as much. Countries with more internal trade, or trade outside the EU, will feel regulations just as additional costs.

In the following there is key data on each EU member, so readers can dip in and review for themselves countries that have a particular interest for them.

Note, with respect to the following tables, that regulatory cost (red tape) figures are highly debated. While we use the more conservative of the Commission's figures here, a direct assessment of costs in each member state is speculative given the variable impact of legislation in differing national circumstances. Whereas one country may enjoy a derogation from a given law, and another have no large factories to be affected, another country may be home to a large proportion of the EU-wide industry. This area was explored more in Part Six of this book.

The figures for the total positive view of EU membership relate to Eurostat's standard Eurobarometer poll conducted in spring 2011, in which people are asked whether they have a very positive, positive, neutral, fairly negative or very negative image. The first two categories make up the positive response percentage, for which the EU average is 40%.

GDP variation is a simple check of the country's GDP change over the year contrasted with the EU average, with the difference added up over a ten-year period (2001 to 2010). While not definitive, and clearly more of an issue if persistently demonstrating underperformance, it provides some indication of the extent to which a country's economic cycle has been significantly out of kilter with other EU states. This is particularly important for economies locked into the eurozone that cannot benefit from exchange rate fluctuation. A fuller study would set out the extent to which cycles trend towards being higher or lower, and compare the cycle with other key economies, particularly that of the United States (which is historically considered to run more closely to the economies of UK and Ireland).

Austria

Form of government	**Republic**
Population (2010)	**8.4 million**
Population as a share of EU population	**1.7%**
Date joined Community	**1995**
Key motives for joining	**Freer trade, emergence from cold war isolation**
Eurozone membership	**1999**
GDP (2010)	**€284 billion**
Level of public debt (2010)	**€205.2 billion (72.3% of GDP)**
Annual budget deficit (2010)	**€13.2 billion (-4.6% of GDP)**
Exports by country (2010)	**Germany 32.1%, Italy 7.9%, Switzerland 4.8%, France 4.2%, Czech Republic 4.1%**
Total exports to EU (2009)	**€70.8 billion**
Total exports to EU as a share of GDP (2009)	**25.8%**
Gross payments to EU (2009)	**€2.3 billion**
Net EU payments (2009)	**€0.5 billion**
Per capita payment (2009)	**€60 per head**
Ten years' sum variation from EU mean GDP change	**6.3 points**
Previous membership of trade groups	**EFTA**
Estimated additional EU regulatory costs	**€11.4 billion**
Extrapolated annual EU regulatory burden per capita	**€1360**
Level of inward Foreign Direct Investment from outside the EU (2010)	**€700 million disinvestment**
Government's declared political priorities in 2011	**National debt limits**
Referenda held on EU issues	**1994 – Accession**
Opt outs	**No**
Voting strength at council of ministers	**10/345 (3%)**
Voting strength at European Parliament (as at close 2011)	**19/753 (2%)**
Ongoing border issues	**No**
Polling of people with positive view of EU	**31%**

Belgium

Form of government	**Federal constitutional monarchy**
Population (2010)	**10.9 million**
Population as a share of EU population	**2.2%**
Date joined Community	**1952**
Key motives for joining	**Historical occupations by Germany**
Eurozone membership	**1999**
GDP (2010)	**€353 billion**
Level of public debt (2010)	**€341 billion (96.8% of GDP)**
Annual budget deficit (2010)	**€14.4 billion (-4.1% of GDP)**
Exports by country (2010)	**Germany 19.1%, France 17%, Netherlands 12.2%, UK 7.2%, US 5.3%, Italy 4.7%**
Total exports to EU (2009)	**€201.2 billion**
Total exports to EU as a share of GDP (2009)	**59.4% (Note, this figure is skewed by the Antwerp effect, counting re-exports through the port originating from elsewhere.)**
Gross payments to EU (2009)	**€4.7 billion**
Net EU payments (2009)	**€1.0 billion receipts**
Per capita payment (2009)	**€90 per head receipt**
Ten years' sum variation from EU mean GDP change	**5.6 points**
Previous membership of trade groups	**BENELUX**
Estimated additional EU regulatory costs	**€14.1 billion**
Extrapolated annual EU regulatory burden per capita	**€1,290**
Level of inward Foreign Direct Investment from outside the EU (2010)	**€2.4 billion disinvestment**
Government's declared political priorities in 2011	**Actually forming a government**
Referenda held on EU issues	**No**
Opt outs	**No**
Voting strength at council of ministers	**12/345 (3%)**
Voting strength at European Parliament (as at close 2011)	**22/753 (3%)**
Ongoing border issues	**No**
Polling of people with positive view of EU	**47%**

Bulgaria

Form of government	**Republic**
Population (2010)	**7.5 million**
Population as a share of EU population	**1.5%**
Date joined Community	**2007**
Key motives for joining	**Regional aid, economic backwater**
Eurozone membership	**No**
GDP (2010)	**€36 billion**
Level of public debt (2010)	**11.4 billion BGN (16.2% of GDP)**
Annual budget deficit (2010)	**2.2 billion BGN (-3.2% of GDP)**
Exports by country (2010)	**Germany 10.9%, Italy 9.9%, Romania 9.5%, Greece 8.1%, Turkey 7.9%, France 4.1%**
Total exports to EU (2009)	**€7.6 billion**
Total exports to EU as a share of GDP (2009)	**21.7%**
Gross payments to EU (2009)	**€0.4 billion**
Net EU payments (2009)	**€0.6 billion receipts**
Per capita payment (2009)	**€77 per head receipt**
Ten years' sum variation from EU mean GDP change	**33.4 points**
Previous membership of trade groups	**COMECON, CEFTA**
Estimated additional EU regulatory costs	**€1.4 billion**
Extrapolated annual EU regulatory burden per capita	**€190**
Level of inward Foreign Direct Investment from outside the EU (2010)	**€200 million**
Government's declared political priorities in 2011	**Economic growth, improving quality of government**
Referenda held on EU issues	**No**
Opt outs	**No**
Voting strength at council of ministers	**10/345 (3%)**
Voting strength at European Parliament (as at close 2011)	**18/753 (2%)**
Ongoing border issues	**No**
Polling of people with positive view of EU	**55%**

Cyprus

Form of government	**Republic**
Population (2010)	**0.8 million**
Population as a share of EU population	**0.2%**
Date joined Community	**2004**
Key motives for joining	**Relative isolation, North Cyprus**
Eurozone membership	**2008**
GDP (2010)	**€17 billion**
Level of public debt (2010)	**€10.6 billion (60.8% of GDP)**
Annual budget deficit (2010)	**€926 million (-5.3% of GDP)**
Exports by country (2010)	**Greece 24.5%, Germany 10.5%, UK 8.6%**
Total exports to EU (2009)	**€0.6 billion**
Total exports to EU as a share of GDP (2009)	**3.5%**
Gross payments to EU (2009)	**€0.2 billion**
Net EU payments (2009)	**€0.03 billion**
Per capita payment (2009)	**€34 per head**
Ten years' sum variation from EU mean GDP change	**17.4 points**
Previous membership of trade groups	**(Commonwealth)**
Estimated additional EU regulatory costs	**€680 million**
Extrapolated annual EU regulatory burden per capita	**€850**
Level of inward Foreign Direct Investment from outside the EU (2010)	**€2.4 billion**
Government's declared political priorities in 2011	**Preparing for EU Presidency**
Referenda held on EU issues	**No**
Opt outs	**No**
Voting strength at council of ministers	**4/345 (1%)**
Voting strength at European Parliament (as at close 2011)	**6/753 (1%)**
Ongoing border issues	**Northern Cyprus**
Polling of people with positive view of EU	**42%**

Czech Republic

Form of government	**Republic**
Population (2010)	**10.5 million**
Population as a share of EU population	**2.1%**
Date joined Community	**2004**
Key motives for joining	**German trade**
Eurozone membership	**No**
GDP (2010)	**€145 billion**
Level of public debt (2010)	**1.4 trillion CZK (38.5% of GDP)**
Annual budget deficit (2010)	**172.8 billion CZK (-4.7% of GDP)**
Exports by country (2010 est.)	**Germany 31.7%, Slovakia 8.7%, Poland 6.2%, France 5.5%, UK 4.9%, Austria 4.7%, Italy 4.5%**
Total exports to EU (2009)	**€68.6 billion**
Total exports to EU as a share of GDP (2009)	**50%**
Gross payments to EU (2009)	**€1.4 billion**
Net EU payments (2009)	**€1.6 billion receipts**
Per capita payment (2009)	**€150 per head receipt**
Ten years' sum variation from EU mean GDP change	**21.4 points**
Estimated additional EU regulatory costs	**€5.8 billion**
Extrapolated annual EU regulatory burden per capita	**€550**
Previous membership of trade groups	**COMECON (as Czechoslovakia), Visegrad, CEFTA**
Level of inward Foreign Direct Investment from outside the EU (2010)	**€200 million**
Government's declared political priorities in 2011	**Consolidate and improve public finances**
Referenda held on EU issues	**2003 – Accession**
Opt outs	**Application of Fundamental Rights**
Voting strength at council of ministers	**12/345 (3%)**
Voting strength at European Parliament (as at close 2011)	**22/753 (3%)**
Ongoing border issues	**Minor dispute with Poland**
Polling of people with positive view of EU	**29%**

Denmark

Form of government	**Constitutional monarchy**
Population (2010)	**5.6 million**
Population as a share of EU population	**1.1%**
Date joined Community	**1973**
Key motives for joining	**UK leaving EFTA, impasse in Nordic Free Trade area**
Eurozone membership	**No**
GDP (2010)	**€234 billion**
Level of public debt (2010)	**760.7 billion DKK (43.6% of GDP)**
Annual budget deficit (2010)	**47.4 billion DKK (-2.7% of GDP)**
Exports by country (2010)	**Germany 17.6%, Sweden 13.8%, UK 8.1%, US 5.9%, Norway 5.6%, Netherlands 4.8%, France 4.7%**
Total exports to EU (2009)	**€45.1 billion**
Total exports to EU as a share of GDP (2009)	**20.3%**
Gross payments to EU (2009)	**€2.5 billion**
Net EU payments (2009)	**€1.2 billion**
Per capita payment (2009)	**€211 per head**
Ten years' sum variation from EU mean GDP change	8.9 points
Previous membership of trade groups	**EFTA, Nordic Council (social, workforce and travel links)**
Estimated additional EU regulatory costs	**€9.4 billion**
Extrapolated annual EU regulatory burden per capita	**€1,680**
Level of inward Foreign Direct Investment from outside the EU (2010)	**€1.9 billion**
Government's declared political priorities in 2011	**EU Presidency, balancing the books**
Referenda held on EU issues	**1972 – Accession, 1986 – Single European Act, 1992 – Maastricht (No), 1993 – Maastricht, 1998 – Amsterdam, 2000 – euro (No)**
Opt outs	**EMU, JHA aspects, CFSP aspects**
Voting strength at council of ministers	**7/345 (2%)**
Voting strength at European Parliament (as at close 2011)	**13/753 (2%)**
Ongoing border issues	**Continental shelf issues over Faroes**
Polling of people with positive view of EU	35%

Estonia

Form of government	**Republic**
Population (2010)	**1.3 million**
Population as a share of EU population	**0.3%**
Date joined Community	**2004**
Key motives for joining	**Split with Soviet past, ongoing Russian issues**
Eurozone membership	**2011**
GDP (2010)	**€15 billion**
Level of public debt (2010)	**€951 million (6.6% of GDP)**
Annual budget deficit (2010)	**€18 million surplus (+0.1% of GDP)**
Exports by country (2010)	**Finland 18.5%, Sweden 17%, Russia 10.4%, Latvia 9.8%, Germany 5.7%, Lithuania 5.3%**
Total exports to EU (2009)	**€4.5 billion**
Total exports to EU as a share of GDP (2009)	**32.1%**
Gross payments to EU (2009)	**€0.2 billion**
Net EU payments (2009)	**€0.6 billion receipts**
Per capita payment (2009)	**€416 per head receipt**
Ten years' sum variation from EU mean GDP change	**50.9 points**
Previous membership of trade groups	**COMECON (as USSR), Baltic Free Trade Agreement**
Estimated additional EU regulatory costs	**€600 million**
Extrapolated annual EU regulatory burden per capita	**€460**
Level of inward Foreign Direct Investment from outside the EU (2010)	**Under €50 million**
Government's declared political priorities in 2011	**Strengthening the Single Market, especially with regard to digital services, patents, and SMEs**
Referenda held on EU issues	**2003 – Accession**
Opt outs	**No**
Voting strength at council of ministers	**4/345 (1%)**
Voting strength at European Parliament (as at close 2011)	**6/753 (1%)**
Ongoing border issues	**Russian border**
Polling of people with positive view of EU	**38%**

Finland

Form of government	**Republic**
Population (2010)	**5.4 million**
Population as a share of EU population	**1.1%**
Date joined Community	**1995**
Key motives for joining	**Break with Finlandisation**
Eurozone membership	**1999**
GDP (2010)	**€180 billion**
Level of public debt (2010)	**€87.2 billion (48.4% of GDP)**
Annual budget deficit (2010)	**€4.4 billion (-2.5% of GDP)**
Exports by country (2010)	**Sweden 11.6%, Germany 10.2%, Russia 8.5%, US 7%, Netherlands 6.9%, China 5%, UK 4.9%**
Total exports to EU (2009)	**€25 billion**
Total exports to EU as a share of GDP (2009)	**14.5%**
Gross payments to EU (2009)	**€1.8 billion**
Net EU payments (2009)	**€0.6 billion**
Per capita payment (2009)	**€114 per head**
Ten years' sum variation from EU mean GDP change	**14.5 points**
Previous membership of trade groups	**COMECON (Non-Socialist Co-operant status only), EFTA, Nordic Council**
Estimated additional EU regulatory costs	**€7.2 billion**
Extrapolated annual EU regulatory burden per capita	**€1,330**
Level of inward Foreign Direct Investment from outside the EU (2010)	**€100 million disinvestment**
Government's declared political priorities in 2011	**Limiting sovereign debt crisis**
Referenda held on EU issues	**1994 – Accession, 1994 – Accession of the Åland Islands**
Opt outs	**No**
Voting strength at council of ministers	**7/345 (2%)**
Voting strength at European Parliament (as at close 2011)	**13/753 (2%)**
Ongoing border issues	**Lost Karelia and other territory to the Soviet Union, but no official claims stated**
Polling of people with positive view of EU	**31%**

France

Form of government	**Republic**
Population (2010)	**65.1 million**
Population as a share of EU population	**13.0%**
Date joined Community	**1952**
Key motives for joining	**Secure French agriculture, hobble Germany, tariffs vs US**
Eurozone membership	**1999**
GDP (2010)	**€1,933 billion**
Level of public debt (2010)	**€1,591 billion (81.7% of GDP)**
Annual budget deficit (2010)	**€136.5 billion (-7% of GDP)**
Exports by country (2010)	**Germany 16.4%, Italy 8.2%, Belgium 7.7%, Spain 7.6%, UK 6.8%, US 5.1%, Netherlands 4.2%**
Total exports to EU (2009)	**€215.9 billion**
Total exports to EU as a share of GDP (2009)	**11.4%**
Gross payments to EU (2009)	**€20.1 billion**
Net EU payments (2009)	**€6.5 billion**
Per capita payment (2009)	**€100 per head**
Ten years' sum variation from EU mean GDP change	**5.7 points**
Previous membership of trade groups	**No**
Estimated additional EU regulatory costs	**€77.3 billion**
Extrapolated annual EU regulatory burden per capita	**€1,190**
Level of inward Foreign Direct Investment from outside the EU (2010)	**€8 billion**
Government's declared political priorities in 2011	**Fiscal union to strengthen the eurozone**
Referenda held on EU issues	**1972 – Enlargement, 1992 – Maastricht, 2005 – Constitutional Treaty (No)**
Opt outs	**No**
Voting strength at council of ministers	**29/345 (8%)**
Voting strength at European Parliament (as at close 2011)	**74/753 (10%)**
Ongoing border issues	**No**
Polling of people with positive view of EU	**41%**

Germany

Form of government	**Federal Republic**
Population (2010)	**81.8 million**
Population as a share of EU population	**16.3%**
Date joined Community	**1952**
Key motives for joining	**Larger home export market, war guilt**
Eurozone membership	**1999**
GDP (2010)	**€2,499 billion**
Level of public debt (2010)	**€2,079.6 billion (83.2% of GDP)**
Annual budget deficit (2010)	**€81.6 billion (-3.3% of GDP)**
Exports by country (2009)	**France 10.1%, US 6.7%, UK 6.6%, Netherlands 6.6%, Italy 6.3%, Austria 5.7%, Belgium 5.2%, China 4.7%, Switzerland 4.5%**
Total exports to EU (2009)	**€508.4 billion**
Total exports to EU as a share of GDP (2009)	**21.2%**
Gross payments to EU (2009)	**€20.5 billion**
Net EU payments (2009)	**€8.8 billion**
Per capita payment (2009)	**€107 per head**
Ten years' sum variation from EU mean GDP change	**9.4 points**
Previous membership of trade groups	**COMECON (East Germany)**
Estimated additional EU regulatory costs	**€100 billion**
Extrapolated annual EU regulatory burden per capita	**€1,220**
Level of inward Foreign Direct Investment from outside the EU (2010)	**€14.5 billion**
Government's declared political priorities in 2011	**Stronger controls over elastic eurozone public sector spenders, no German bail out**
Referenda held on EU issues	**No**
Opt outs	**No**
Voting strength at council of ministers	**29/345 (8%)**
Voting strength at European Parliament (as at close 2011)	**99/753 (13%)**
Ongoing border issues	**No but some groups campaign over post-WWII Eastern European expulsions, in the context of the Polish and Czech borders**
Polling of people with positive view of EU	**38%**

Greece

Form of government	Republic
Population (2010)	11.3 million
Population as a share of EU population	2.2%
Date joined Community	1981
Key motives for joining	Secure democracy post-Colonels, cold war support
Eurozone membership	2001
GDP (2010)	€230 billion
Level of public debt (2010)	€328.6 billion (142.8% of GDP)
Annual budget deficit (2010)	€24.2 billion (-10.5% of GDP)
Exports by country (2010)	Germany 10.9%, Italy 10.9%, Cyprus 7.3%, Bulgaria 6.5%, Turkey 5.4%, UK 5.3%, Belgium 5.1%, China 4.8%, Switzerland 4.5%, Poland 4.2%
Total exports to EU (2009)	€9.0 billion
Total exports to EU as a share of GDP (2009)	3.8%
Gross payments to EU (2009)	€2.4 billion
Net EU payments (2009)	€3.0 billion receipts
Per capita payment (2009)	€267 per head receipt
Ten years' sum variation from EU mean GDP change	20.2 points
Previous membership of trade groups	No
Estimated additional EU regulatory costs	€9.2 billion
Extrapolated annual EU regulatory burden per capita	€810
Level of inward Foreign Direct Investment from outside the EU (2010)	€100 million
Government's declared political priorities in 2011	Deficit/public debt
Referenda held on EU issues	No
Opt outs	No
Voting strength at council of ministers	12/345 (3%)
Voting strength at European Parliament (as at close 2011)	22/753 (3%)
Ongoing border issues	Issues with Turkey, definition of Macedonia
Polling of people with positive view of EU	31%

Hungary

Form of government	Republic
Population (2010)	10 million
Population as a share of EU population	2%
Date joined Community	2004
Key motives for joining	Reorientate trade, de-Sovietise
Eurozone membership	No
GDP (2010)	€98 billion
Level of public debt, 2010	21.7 billion HUF (80.2% of GDP)
Annual budget deficit, 2010	1.1 billion HUF (-4.2% of GDP)
Exports by country (2010 est.)	Germany 25.5%, Italy 5.5%, UK 5.4%, Romania 5.3%, Slovakia 5.1%, France 4.9%, Austria 4.7%
Total exports to EU (2009)	€47.3 billion
Total exports to EU as a share of GDP (2009)	50.8%
Gross payments to EU (2009)	€0.9 billion
Net EU payments (2009)	€2.7 billion receipts
Per capita payment (2009)	€265 per head receipt
Ten years' sum variation from EU mean GDP change	20 points
Previous membership of trade groups	COMECON, Visegrad, CEFTA
Estimated additional EU regulatory costs	€3.9 billion
Extrapolated annual EU regulatory burden per capita	€390
Level of inward Foreign Direct Investment from outside the EU (2010)	€400 million
Government's declared political priorities in 2011	Economic governance, EU measures protecting Roma
Referenda held on EU issues	2003 – Accession
Opt outs	No
Voting strength at council of ministers	12/345 (3%)
Voting strength at European Parliament (as at close 2011)	22/753 (3%)
Ongoing border issues	Historic claims and interests involving several neighbouring states, especially over Transylvanian Hungarians
Polling of people with positive view of EU	35%

Ireland

Form of government	**Republic**
Population (2010)	**4.5 million**
Population as a share of EU population	**0.9%**
Date joined Community	**1973**
Key motives for joining	**UK market joining, opportunity to reorientate away from UK**
Eurozone membership	**1999**
GDP (2010)	**€156 billion**
Level of public debt, 2010	**€148 billion (96.2% of GDP)**
Annual budget deficit, 2010	**€49.9 billion (-32.4% of GDP)**
Exports by country (2010)	**US 22.1%, UK 16.1%, Belgium 15.1%, Germany 8.1%, France 5.3%, Switzerland 4.2%**
Total exports to EU (2009)	**€50.8 billion**
Total exports to EU as a share of GDP (2009)	**31.6%**
Gross payments to EU (2009)	**€1.5 billion**
Net EU payments (2009)	**€0.2 billion**
Per capita payment (2009)	**€35 per head**
Ten years' sum variation from EU mean GDP change	**26.3 points**
Previous membership of trade groups	**(Sterling Zone)**
Estimated additional EU regulatory costs	**€6.2 billion**
Extrapolated annual EU regulatory burden per capita	**€1,380**
Level of inward Foreign Direct Investment from outside the EU (2010)	**€21.5 billion**
Government's declared political priorities in 2011	**Slashing deficit**
Referenda held on EU issues	**1972 – Accession, 1987 – Single European Act, 1992 – Maastricht, 1998 – Amsterdam, 2001 – Nice (No), 2002 – Nice, 2008 – Lisbon (No), 2009 – Lisbon**
Opt outs	**Schengen, Some JHA**
Voting strength at council of ministers	**7/345 (2%)**
Voting strength at European Parliament (as at close 2011)	**12/753 (2%)**
Ongoing border issues	**Northern Ireland**
Polling of people with positive view of EU	**54%**

Italy

Form of government	**Republic**
Population (2010)	**60.6 million**
Population as a share of EU population	**12.1%**
Date joined Community	**1952**
Key motives for joining	**Trade for North, credibility**
Eurozone membership	**1999**
GDP (2010)	**€1,549 billion**
Level of public debt (2010)	**€1,843 billion (119% of GDP)**
Annual budget deficit (2010)	**€71.2 billion (-4.6% of GDP)**
Exports by country (2010)	**Germany 13.2%, France 11.7%, Spain 5.9%, US 5.8%, UK 5.4%, Switzerland 4.6%**
Total exports to EU (2009)	**€167 billion**
Total exports to EU as a share of GDP (2009)	**11%**
Gross payments to EU (2009)	**€15.4 billion**
Net EU payments (2009)	**€6.0 billion**
Per capita payment (2009)	**€101 per head**
Ten years' sum variation from EU mean GDP change	**8.4 points**
Previous membership of trade groups	**No**
Estimated additional EU regulatory costs	**€62 billion**
Extrapolated annual EU regulatory burden per capita	**€1,020**
Level of inward Foreign Direct Investment from outside the EU (2010)	**€2.5 billion**
Government's declared political priorities in 2011	**Slashing deficit, working out life after Berlusconi**
Referenda held on EU issues	**No**
Opt outs	**No**
Voting strength at council of ministers	**29/345 (8%)**
Voting strength at European Parliament (as at close 2011)	**73/753 (10%)**
Ongoing border issues	**No**
Polling of people with positive view of EU	**49%**

Latvia

Form of government	**Republic**
Population (2010)	**2.2 million**
Population as a share of EU population	**0.4%**
Date joined Community	**2004**
Key motives for joining	**Split with Soviet past, ongoing Russian issues**
Eurozone membership	**No**
GDP (2010)	**€18 billion**
Level of public debt (2010)	**5.7 billion LVL (44.7% of GDP)**
Annual budget deficit (2010)	**984 million LVL (-7.7% of GDP)**
Exports by country (2010)	**Russia 15.2%, Lithuania 15.2%, Estonia 12.6%, Germany 8.2%, Sweden 5.9%, Poland 4.7%**
Total exports to EU (2009)	**€3.7 billion**
Total exports to EU as a share of GDP (2009)	**20%**
Gross payments to EU (2009)	**€0.2 billion**
Net EU payments (2009)	**€0.5 billion receipts**
Per capita payment (2009)	**€219 per head receipt**
Ten years' sum variation from EU mean GDP change	**66.1 points**
Previous membership of trade groups	**COMECON (as USSR), Baltic Free Trade Agreement**
Estimated additional EU regulatory costs	**€720 million**
Extrapolated annual EU regulatory burden per capita	**€330**
Level of inward Foreign Direct Investment from outside the EU (2010)	**€100 million**
Government's declared political priorities in 2011	**Modernisation and efficiency in government, competitiveness**
Referenda held on EU issues	**2003 – Accession**
Opt outs	**No**
Voting strength at council of ministers	**4/345 (1%)**
Voting strength (at European Parliament (as at close 2011)	**9/753 (1%)**
Ongoing border issues	**With Lithuania over maritime oil deposits**
Polling of people with positive view of EU	**26%**

Lithuania

Form of government	**Republic**
Population (2010)	**3.2 million**
Population as a share of EU population	**0.6%**
Date joined Community	**2004**
Key motives for joining	**Split with Soviet past, ongoing Russian issues**
Eurozone membership	**No**
GDP (2010)	**€27 billion**
Level of public debt, 2010	**36.1 billion LTL (38.2% of GDP)**
Annual budget deficit, 2010	**6.7 billion LTL (-7.1% of GDP)**
Exports by country (2010)	**Russia 15.7%, Germany 10.1%, Latvia 9.8%, Poland 7.9%, Netherlands 5.7%, Belarus 5.2%, Estonia 5.2%, UK 5%**
Total exports to EU (2009)	**€7.6 billion**
Total exports to EU as a share of GDP (2009)	**28.1%**
Gross payments to EU (2009)	**€0.3 billion**
Net EU payments (2009)	**€1.5 billion receipts**
Per capita payment (2009)	**€438 per head receipt**
Ten years' sum variation from EU mean GDP change	**55.8 points**
Previous membership of trade groups	**COMECON (as USSR), Baltic Free Trade Agreement**
Estimated additional EU regulatory costs	**€1.1 billion**
Extrapolated annual EU regulatory burden per capita	**€340**
Level of inward Foreign Direct Investment from outside the EU (2010)	**€100 million**
Government's declared political priorities in 2011	**Unemployment, modernisation, education reform, energy reform**
Referenda held on EU issues	**2003 – Accession**
Opt outs	**No**
Voting strength at council of ministers	**7/345 (2%)**
Voting strength at European Parliament (as at close 2011)	**12/753 (2%)**
Ongoing border issues	**With Latvia over maritime oil deposits. Delineation of Bielorus and Russian borders**
Polling of people with positive view of EU	**42%**

Luxembourg

Form of government	**Constitutional Grand Duchy**
Population (2010)	**0.5 million**
Population as a share of EU population	**0.1%**
Date joined Community	**1952**
Key motives for joining	**Two German occupations, support for significant steel sector**
Eurozone membership	**1999**
GDP (2010)	**€42 billion**
Level of public debt (2010)	**€7.7 billion (18.4% of GDP)**
Annual budget deficit (2010)	**€710 million (-1.7% of GDP)**
Exports by country (2010)	**Germany 22.3%, France 15.5%, Belgium 12.1%, UK 9.2%, Italy 7.2%, Netherlands 4.1%**
Total exports to EU (2009)	**€13.0 billion**
Total exports to EU as a share of GDP (2009)	**34.2%**
Gross payments to EU (2009)	**€0.3 billion**
Net EU payments (2009)	**€1.2 billion receipts**
Per capita payment (2009)	**€2,364 per head receipt**
Ten years' sum variation from EU mean GDP change	**16.2 points**
Previous membership of trade groups	**BENELUX**
Estimated additional EU regulatory costs	**€1.7 billion**
Extrapolated annual EU regulatory burden per capita	**€340**
Level of inward Foreign Direct Investment from outside the EU (2010)	**€47.6 billion**
Government's declared political priorities in 2011	**Avoiding EU taxation and legislation in banking, maintaining a competitive telecoms tax**
Referenda held on EU issues	**2005 – EU Constitution**
Opt outs	**No**
Voting strength at council of ministers	**4/345 (1%)**
Voting strength at European Parliament (as at close 2011)	**6/753 (1%)**
Ongoing border issues	**No**
Polling of people with positive view of EU	**48%**

Malta

Form of government	Republic
Population (2010)	0.4 million
Population as a share of EU population	0.1%
Date joined Community	2004
Key motives for joining	Tiny front line immigration state
Eurozone membership	2008
GDP (2010)	€6 billion
Level of public debt (2010)	€4.2 billion (68% of GDP)
Annual budget deficit (2010)	€226 million (-3.6% of GDP)
Exports by country (2010)	Germany 18.4%, France 15.7%, UK 9.1%, Italy 6.6%, Libya 6%, US 5.7%
Total exports to EU (2009)	€0.6 billion
Total exports to EU as a share of GDP (2009)	10%
Gross payments to EU (2009)	€0.06 billion
Net EU payments (2009)	€0.007 billion receipts
Per capita payment (2009)	€18 per head receipt
Ten years' sum variation from EU mean GDP change	19.5 points
Previous membership of trade groups	(Commonwealth)
Estimated additional EU regulatory costs	€240 million
Extrapolated annual EU regulatory burden per capita	€600
Level of inward Foreign Direct Investment from outside the EU (2010)	€500 million
Government's declared political priorities in 2011	EU support over illegal immigration
Referenda held on EU issues	2003 – Accession
Opt outs	No
Voting strength at council of ministers	3/345 (1%)
Voting strength at European Parliament (as at close 2011)	6/753 (1%)
Ongoing border issues	No
Polling of people with positive view of EU	36%

Netherlands

Form of government	**Constitutional monarchy**
Population (2010)	**16.7 million**
Population as a share of EU population	**3.3%**
Date joined Community	**1952**
Key motives for joining	**German occupation during WWII, trade**
Eurozone membership	**1999**
GDP (2010)	**€591 billion**
Level of public debt (2010)	**€371.0 billion (62.7% of GDP)**
Annual budget deficit (2010)	**€32.0 billion (-5.4% of GDP)**
Exports by country (2010)	**Germany 26%, Belgium 13%, France 9.2%, UK 7.7%, Italy 4.9%**
Total exports to EU (2009)	**€276.2 billion**
Total exports to EU as a share of GDP (2009)	**48.3% (Note, this figure is skewed by the Rotterdam effect, counting re-exports through the port originating from elsewhere.)**
Gross payments to EU (2009)	**€3.3 billion**
Net EU payments (2009)	**€1.5 billion**
Per capita payment (2009)	**€90 per head**
Ten years' sum variation from EU mean GDP change	**6.7 points**
Previous membership of trade groups	**BENELUX**
Estimated additional EU regulatory costs	**€23.6 billion**
Extrapolated annual EU regulatory burden per capita	**€1,410**
Level of inward Foreign Direct Investment from outside the EU (2010)	**€5.3 billion disinvestment**
Government's declared political priorities in 2011	**Eurozone**
Referenda held on EU issues	**2005 – EU Constitution (No)**
Opt outs	**No**
Voting strength at council of ministers	**13/345 (4%)**
Voting strength at European Parliament (as at close 2011)	**26/753 (3%)**
Ongoing border issues	**No**
Polling of people with positive view of EU	**38%**

Poland

Form of government	**Republic**
Population (2010)	**38.2 million**
Population as a share of EU population	**7.6%**
Date joined Community	**2004**
Key motives for joining	**Reorientate trade, de-Sovietise**
Eurozone membership	**No**
GDP (2010)	**€354 billion**
Level of public debt (2010)	**778.2 billion PLN (55% of GDP)**
Annual budget deficit (2010)	**111.2 billion PLN (-7.9% of GDP)**
Exports by country (2010)	**Germany 26.9%, France 7.1%, UK 6.4%, Italy 6.3%, Czech Republic 6.2%, Netherlands 4.3%, Russia 4.1%**
Total exports to EU (2009)	**€76.4 billion**
Total exports to EU as a share of GDP (2009)	**25%**
Gross payments to EU (2009)	**€3.1 billion**
Net EU payments (2009)	**€6.1 billion receipts**
Per capita payment (2009)	**€160 per head receipt**
Ten years' sum variation from EU mean GDP change	**27.2 points**
Previous membership of trade groups	**COMECON, Visegrad, CEFTA**
Estimated additional EU regulatory costs	**€14.2 billion**
Extrapolated annual EU regulatory burden per capita	**€370**
Level of inward Foreign Direct Investment from outside the EU (2010)	**€1.3 billion**
Government's declared political priorities in 2011	**The internet in the Single Market, new rules on economic governance, developing a multiannual EU budget**
Referenda held on EU issues	**2003 – Accession**
Opt outs	**Application of Fundamental Rights**
Voting strength at council of ministers	**27/345 (8%)**
Voting strength at European Parliament (as at close 2011)	**51/753 (7%)**
Ongoing border issues	**Minor dispute with Czech Republic**
Polling of people with positive view of EU	**48%**

Portugal

Form of government	**Republic**
Population (2010)	**10.6 million**
Population as a share of EU population	**2.1%**
Date joined Community	**1986**
Key motives for joining	**Resolve post-Salazar and post-Revolution issues**
Eurozone membership	**1999**
GDP (2010)	**€173 billion**
Level of public debt (2010)	**€160.5 billion (93% of GDP)**
Annual budget deficit (2010)	**€15.8 billion (-9.1% of GDP)**
Exports by country (2010)	**Spain 26.8%, Germany 13.1%, France 11.9%, UK 5.5%, Angola 5.2%**
Total exports to EU (2009)	**€23.3 billion**
Total exports to EU as a share of GDP (2009)	**13.8%**
Gross payments to EU (2009)	**€1.6 billion**
Net EU payments (2009)	**€2.1 billion receipts**
Per capita payment (2009)	**€160 per head receipt**
Ten years' sum variation from EU mean GDP change	**27.2 points**
Previous membership of trade groups	**EFTA**
Estimated additional EU regulatory costs	**€6.9 billion**
Extrapolated annual EU regulatory burden per capita	**€650**
Level of inward Foreign Direct Investment from outside the EU (2010)	**€1.1 billion**
Government's declared political priorities in 2011	**Deficit reduction**
Referenda held on EU issues	**No**
Opt outs	**No**
Voting strength at council of ministers	**12/345 (3%)**
Voting strength at European Parliament (as at close 2011)	**22/753 (3%)**
Ongoing border issues	**Spanish town of Olivenza**
Polling of people with positive view of EU	**35%**

Romania

Form of government	Republic
Population (2010)	21.4 million
Population as a share of EU population	4.3%
Date joined Community	2007
Key motives for joining	Aid, Soviet-era border issues
Eurozone membership	No
GDP (2010)	€122 billion
Level of public debt (2010)	158.0 billion RON (30.8% of GDP)
Annual budget deficit (2010)	33.1 billion RON (-6.4% of GDP)
Exports by country (2010)	Germany 18.4%, Italy 14.1%, France 8.5%, Turkey 6.9%, Hungary 4.9%
Total exports to EU (2009)	€21.6 billion
Total exports to EU as a share of GDP (2009)	18.5%
Gross payments to EU (2009)	€1.3 billion
Net EU payments (2009)	€1.6 billion receipts
Per capita payment (2009)	€75 per head receipt
Ten years' sum variation from EU mean GDP change	41.3 points
Previous membership of trade groups	COMECON, CEFTA
Estimated additional EU regulatory costs	€4.9 billion
Extrapolated annual EU regulatory burden per capita	€230
Level of inward Foreign Direct Investment from outside the EU (2010)	€300 million disinvestment
Government's declared political priorities in 2011	R&D, administrative reform, Schengen accession
Referenda held on EU issues	No
Opt outs	No
Voting strength at council of ministers	14/345 (4%)
Voting strength at European Parliament (as at close 2011)	33/753 (4%)
Ongoing border issues	Moldovan issues, significant ethnic Hungarian population
Polling of people with positive view of EU	56%

Slovakia

Form of government	**Republic**
Population (2010)	**5.4 million**
Population as a share of EU population	**1.1%**
Date joined Community	**2004**
Key motives for joining	**Reorientate trade, de-Sovietise**
Eurozone membership	**2009**
GDP (2010)	**€66 billion**
Level of public debt (2010)	**€27.0 billion (41% of GDP)**
Annual budget deficit (2010)	**€5.2 billion (-7.9% of GDP)**
Exports by country (2010)	**Germany 20.1%, Czech Republic 14.8%, Poland 7.9%, Hungary 7.3%, France 7.2%, Austria 7.1%, Italy 5.8%**
Total exports to EU (2009)	**€34.4 billion**
Total exports to EU as a share of GDP (2009)	**54.6%**
Gross payments to EU (2009)	**€0.7 billion**
Net EU payments (2009)	**€0.5 billion receipts**
Per capita payment (2009)	**€89 per head receipt**
Ten years' sum variation from EU mean GDP change	**36.6 points**
Previous membership of trade groups	**COMECON (as Czechoslovakia), Visegrad, CEFTA**
Estimated additional EU regulatory costs	**€2.6 billion**
Extrapolated annual EU regulatory burden per capita	**€480**
Level of inward Foreign Direct Investment from outside the EU (2010)	**€200 million disinvestment**
Government's declared political priorities in 2011	**Eurozone crisis, resulting in the fall of the government**
Referenda held on EU issues	**2003 – Accession**
Opt outs	**No**
Voting strength at council of ministers	**7/345 (2%)**
Voting strength at European Parliament (as at close 2011)	**13/753 (2%)**
Ongoing border issues	**No**
Polling of people with positive view of EU	**47%**

Slovenia

Form of government	**Republic**
Population (2010)	**2.1 million**
Population as a share of EU population	**0.4%**
Date joined Community	**2004**
Key motives for joining	**Trade importance with the West, clean break with Yugoslav past**
Eurozone membership	**2007**
GDP (2010)	**€36 billion**
Level of public debt, 2010	**€13.7 billion (38% of GDP)**
Annual budget deficit, 2010	**€2.0 billion (-5.6% of GDP)**
Exports by country (2010)	**Germany 19.2%, Italy 12.5%, Austria 7.4%, France 6.8%, Croatia 6.4%, Hungary 4.4%**
Total exports to EU (2009)	**€13 billion**
Total exports to EU as a share of GDP (2009)	**37.1%**
Gross payments to EU (2009)	**€0.4 billion**
Net EU payments (2009)	**€0.2 billion receipts**
Per capita payment (2009)	**€93 per head receipt**
Ten years' sum variation from EU mean GDP change	**24.5 points**
Previous membership of trade groups	**COMECON (associate status only, as Yugoslavia), CEFTA**
Estimated additional EU regulatory costs	**€1.4 billion**
Extrapolated annual EU regulatory burden per capita	**€670**
Level of inward Foreign Direct Investment from outside the EU (2010)	**€200 million**
Government's declared political priorities in 2011	**Enlargement, sustainable agriculture, central role within the EU institutions**
Referenda held on EU issues	**2003 – Accession**
Opt outs	**No**
Voting strength at council of ministers	**4/345 (1%)**
Voting strength at European Parliament (as at close 2011)	**8/753 (1%)**
Ongoing border issues	**Threatened to veto Croatian accession over a small bay**
Polling of people with positive view of EU	**41%**

Spain

Form of government	Federal constitutional monarchy
Population (2010)	46.2 million
Population as a share of EU population	9.2%
Date joined Community	1986
Key motives for joining	Reorientation after Franco era, bolster democracy, fisheries
Eurozone membership	1999
GDP (2010)	€1,063 billion
Level of public debt (2010)	€638.9 billion (60.1% of GDP)
Annual budget deficit (2010)	€98.2 billion (-9.2% of GDP)
Exports by country (2010)	France 18.7%, Germany 10.7%, Portugal 9.1%, Italy 9%, UK 6.3%
Total exports to EU (2009)	107.8 billion
Total exports to EU as a share of GDP (2009)	10.2%
Gross payments to EU (2009)	€11.2 billion
Net EU payments (2009)	€0.4 billion receipts
Per capita payment (2009)	€10 per head receipt
Ten years' sum variation from EU mean GDP change	11.4 points
Previous membership of trade groups	No
Estimated additional EU regulatory costs	€42.5 billion
Extrapolated annual EU regulatory burden per capita	€920
Level of inward Foreign Direct Investment from outside the EU (2010)	€5.6 billion
Government's declared political priorities in 2011	Economic stringency
Referenda held on EU issues	2005 – EU Constitution
Opt outs	No
Voting strength at council of ministers	27/345 (8%)
Voting strength at European Parliament (as at close 2011)	53/753 (7%)
Ongoing border issues	Gibraltar
Polling of people with positive view of EU	40%

Sweden

Form of government	**Constitutional monarchy**
Population (2010)	**9.4 million**
Population as a share of EU population	**1.9%**
Date joined Community	**1995**
Key motives for joining	**Trade (weakened EFTA)**
Eurozone membership	**No**
GDP (2010)	**€347 billion**
Level of public debt (2010)	**1,313 billion SEK (39.8% of GDP)**
Annual budget deficit (2010)	**1.2 billion SEK (just over 0% of GDP)**
Exports by country (2010)	**Germany 10.5%, Norway 9.8%, UK 7.8%, Denmark 6.9%, Finland 6.5%, US 6.4%, Netherlands 5.2%, France 5.2%, Belgium 4.3%**
Total exports to EU (2009)	**€55 billion**
Total exports to EU as a share of GDP (2009)	**18.9%**
Gross payments to EU (2009)	**€1.9 billion**
Net EU payments (2009)	**€0.4 billion**
Per capita payment (2009)	**€44 per head**
Ten years' sum variation from EU mean GDP change	**12.9 points**
Previous membership of trade groups	**EFTA, Nordic Council**
Estimated additional EU regulatory costs	**€13.9 billion**
Extrapolated annual EU regulatory burden per capita	**€1,480**
Level of inward Foreign Direct Investment from outside the EU (2010)	**€5.5 billion disinvestment**
Government's declared political priorities in 2011	**Growth with welfare, environment**
Referenda held on EU issues	**1994 – Accession, 2003 – euro (No)**
Opt outs	**No**
Voting strength at council of ministers	**10/345 (3%)**
Voting strength at European Parliament (as at close 2011)	**20/753 (3%)**
Ongoing border issues	**Interests in the Åland islands**
Polling of people with positive view of EU	**33%**

United Kingdom

Form of government	**Constitutional monarchy**
Population (2010)	**62.4 million**
Population as a share of EU population	**12.4%**
Date joined Community	**1973**
Key motives for joining	**Idealist PM, lack of confidence, slow EFTA tariff reductions**
Eurozone membership	**No**
GDP (2010)	**€1,697 billion**
Level of public debt (2010)	**£1,163 billion (80% of GDP)**
Annual budget deficit (2010)	**£151 billion (-10.4% of GDP)**
Exports by country (2010)	**US 11.4%, Germany 11.2%, Netherlands 8.5%, France 7.7%, Ireland 6.8%, Belgium 5.4%**
Total exports to EU (2009)	**€139.5 billion**
Total exports to EU as a share of GDP (2009)	**8.9%**
Gross payments to EU (2009)	**€10.1 billion**
Net EU payments (2009)	**€3.9 billion**
Per capita payment (2009)	**€63 per head**
Ten years' sum variation from EU mean GDP change	**8 points**
Previous membership of trade groups	**EFTA (Commonwealth)**
Estimated additional EU regulatory costs	**€67.9 billion**
Extrapolated annual EU regulatory burden per capita	**€1,090**
Level of inward Foreign Direct Investment from outside the EU (2010)	**€28.5 billion**
Government's declared political priorities in 2011	**Protecting banking sector from EU measures, encouraging increased eurozone integration**
Referenda held on EU issues	**1975 – Continued membership**
Opt outs	**Schengen, EMU, application of Fundamental Rights**
Voting strength at council of ministers	**29/345 (8%)**
Voting strength at European Parliament (as at close 2011)	**73/753 (10%)**
Ongoing border issues	**Northern Ireland**
Polling of people with positive view of EU	**22%**

Is EU membership a positive? A look at analyses already made

In a nutshell...

Studies have been undertaken about the consequences of EU membership. These are, incidentally, in countries that were reviewing whether to join and decided to stay out. Two of the countries (Norway, Iceland) are geographically peripheral while the third (Switzerland) is at the heart of the continent. All three studies concluded that current trading arrangements were better than fuller EU membership.

THE ICELAND CASE

Report by the EFTA Secretariat for the Icelandic Foreign Ministry, 2005

Report of the Alþingis All-Party Committee on Europe, 2007

6.5%

Number of EU regulations, directives and decisions to 2005 that also applied to the EEA Agreement

2,527

Total number of these EU laws that therefore applied to the EEA, over 11 years

101

End number of EU laws that required a change to domestic Icelandic law

1,656

Number of laws passed by the
Icelandic Parliament, 1992-2006

285

Number of laws ascribed directly
to EEA membership

17.2%

Number of Iceland's laws over this
period arising directly from EEA
membership

21.6%

Number of indirectly EEA-related
laws are also included in that tally

A TENTH

Number of EEA acts that were
adopted as laws, as opposed to
Statutory Instruments

77

Number of those laws that related
to commerce

24/33

Number of chapters (areas) in
which the Icelandic government
has tended to choose to co-operate

EXAMPLES OF DEROGATIONS OBTAINED BY ICELAND
★ House heating
★ Electricity
★ Rural waste disposal

 *It should also be mentioned that the EFTA Surveillance authority
(ESA) has been known for interpreting EU laws more narrowly
than its counterparts in the Commission who also take political
views into account while ESA solely focuses on the strictly legal side
of the matter."*

EIRIKUR BERGMANN

760,000 KM²

Iceland's fishing zone, currently outside the CFP

12%

GDP from fisheries

40%

Share of all export value that is due to fish

5%

Workforce employed in the industry

4.7%

Iceland's GDP growth rate in the fourth quarter of 2011. The country allowed its banks to fail instead of fully nationalising them, resulting in a front-ended but contained recession as the value of the currency crashed.

EXPORT PARTNERS (2010)

Netherlands 33.9%, Germany 14.1%, UK 10.1%, Spain 4.7%, US 4.5%, Norway 4.3%

97.2%

Trade as a share of GDP

€3.2 BILLION

EU investment in Iceland stocks (2008)

€1.34 BILLION

Value of EU exports to Iceland in 2009

€6.5 BILLION

Iceland investment in EU stocks

€2.17 BILLION

Value of Iceland's exports to the EU

120%

GDP per capita as compared to the EU average

THE NORWAY CASE

Parliamentary questions

Research commissioned by anti-membership campaign group Nei til EU, 2010

11,511	2,129
Items of legislation adopted by the EU, 1997-2003	Items which fell under the EEA agreement
18.5%	8.9%
Volume of EU legislation that carried across into the EEA agreement	Volume of agreed EU legislation that became Norwegian law, 2000-2009

55%

Foreign trade as a share of GDP

EXPORT PARTNERS (2010)

UK 26.7%, Netherlands 12.1%, Germany 11.4%, Sweden 7%, France 6.6%, US 5%

75%

Amount of Norwegian trade that is with the EU

€284 MILLION

Annual Cohesion fund 'tithe' paid by Norway, primarily for recent EU entrants (Poland gets half), but also including Spain, Portugal and Greece. The fund is not properly a requirement of the EEA but was bolted on by the Commission while Norway's government (as the key EEA economy) was briefly pro-EU.

2008

Canada-EFTA Free trade
Agreement signed

91%

Proportion of scallops imported
to Norway that originate in North
America

95%

Amount of Norway's own seafood
that is globally exported

6TH

Norway's world ranking as an
export market for EU goods

DIFFERENCES WITH EU
BORDERS

★ Free entry for almost all
products from developing
countries

★ Most agricultural goods enter
with no or low tariffs

★ Some distinct protective tariffs

★ Bilateral FTAs through EFTA

2ND

Ranking of personal GDP in the EEA

× 35

Comparative value of oil exports over fish exports

60%

EU imports of alloy sources that come from Norway

€9.9 BILLION

Norwegian exports to EU (2009)

€17.1 BILLION

Norwegian imports from the EU (2009)

THE SWITZERLAND CASE

Europe Report, federal government

120

Number of EU-Switzerland
bilaterals

27

Number of joint committees
covering EU agreements and
generating technical decisions

557 MILLION SWISS FRANCS

Official estimate of the cost of
maintaining the bilateral
agreement

3.4 BILLION SWISS FRANCS

Official estimate of the net cost of
Switzerland joining the EU

4.94 BILLION SWISS FRANCS

Official estimate of the gross cost
of Switzerland joining the EU

737 MILLION SWISS FRANCS

Official estimate of the cost of
Switzerland gaining EEA terms

SWISS EXPORT PARTNERS,
2010

Germany 19.2%, US 10.2%, Italy
7.9%, France 7.7%, UK 5.9%

€67 BILLION

EU's exports to Switzerland (2008)

€47.2 BILLION

EU's imports from Switzerland
(2008)

5.2%

Swiss share of total imports by the
EU

900,000

Number of EU citizens living and working in Switzerland

50.3%

No vote in the referendum to join the EEA (1992)

67.2%

Yes vote endorsing the EU bilateral treaty (2000)

76.7%

No vote on EU membership (2001)

54.6%

Yes vote to join Schengen (2005)

56%

Yes vote on the free movement protocol (2005)

2.7%

Amount of say Switzerland would get at the EP and Council of Ministers if it decided to fully integrate into the EU

157%

Swiss GDP per capita compared with the eurozone (2004)

How to conduct your own analysis of EU membership

In a nutshell...

It is possible to assess for yourself whether a given country gets a good deal from EU membership.

Some aspects are clearly assessable from statistics. Other aspects are a matter of psychological need, democratic debate and recent history, and are therefore more subjective.

The key formula set out below offsets on the top row the benefits of EU membership for any country. The bottom row shows the costs. If overall the five sets of benefits offset the five lots of costs, then EU membership is a positive. And if not, it's not.

STARTING PRINCIPLE

$$a = \frac{b}{c}$$

a: the level of advantage or disadvantage arising from EU membership

b: the benefits gained

c: the costs attached

If **a>1**, then countries gain from EU membership overall

THE KEY FORMULA

$$5a = \frac{f_1+f_2+f_3}{f_4+f_5+f_6} + \frac{s_1}{s_2} + \frac{w}{d+f_7} + \frac{p_1}{p_2+t} + \frac{f_8}{f_9}$$

PART 1	PART 2	PART 3	PART 4	PART 5
Financial	Sovereignty	Superstate	Peace in Europe	Alternatives

★ ★ ★ ★ ★ ★ ★ ★ ★ ★ ★

PART 1: THE FINANCIAL ASPECT

Positives

f1 Increased trade stimulated by membership of the trading bloc, especially from tariff reduction

f2 Production advantages arising from standardisation

f3 Administrative benefits from cutting red tape, especially at borders

Negatives

f4 Net membership costs (with grants this may be a net positive)

f5 Red tape costs and costs of administering policies, plus secondary consumer, business or community impact costs (e.g. decline of ports because of the CFP)

f6 Benefits that would be gained from WTO or other agreements if the EU didn't exist anyway

PART 2: SOVEREIGNTY AND POOLING

The beneficial aspect of pooling sovereignty by making joint and binding decisions, versus the negative impact of the loss of sovereignty. This can be more clearly expressed in the following terms:

e / i1+i2

Positives

e Value added by the country surrendering decision making to QMV to get things done in Brussels

Negatives

i1 Ongoing desire to maintain the veto to protect national interests (democratic will)

i2 Ongoing need to maintain the veto to protect national interests (strategic imperative)

PART 3: STRATEGIC PICTURE
Positives

w ('omega') The end vision of the EU that is aspired to

Negatives

d Democratic alienation arising from the creation of a superstate

f7 The waste and fraud that this alienation may generate (lack of accountability in *spending other peoples' money*)

PART 4: PEACE IN EUROPE
Positives

p1 The extent to which European integration guarantees peace and stability for the country

Negatives

p2 Other factors that brought peace to the country

t The passage of time since the second world war, or whichever crisis attracted the country towards EU membership (i.e. an increasing track record of peace and stability)

f8 and **f9** The costs versus the benefits that would arise from withdrawing from the EU

IN PLAIN ENGLISH

The value of EU membership can be judged by assessing the following:

★ Does it cost more being in or out?

★ Do countries achieve their national interests by QMV, or get outvoted?

★ Do politicians and, more importantly, the public feel comfortable with living in a federal Europe?

★ Does EU membership bring stability and peace to the country?

★ Can a better trade deal be found elsewhere?

Case studies: Germany and Estonia

In a nutshell...

Germany and Estonia joined the EU at different times, for different reasons. Their vastly different economies, circumstances and experiences provide distinct motivations. Germany historically has done well out of membership, since it has been motivated by economic drive and is intrinsically a federal structure. Estonia, as a newly liberalised and high-tech economy, has potentially a great deal to lose, but has taken a geopolitical decision. In both cases, the costs of eurozone membership (which Estonia recently adopted as a sign of faith) have already tipped the economic balance.

GERMANY

9

Countries neighbouring Germany

45,000

Number of foreign businesses that have invested in the country

2ND LARGEST

Germany's status as an exporting nation

GERMANY IS THE LARGEST...

★ Economy in the EU

★ Population in the EU

★ Exporter of goods to other countries in the EU

Germany's economy is approximately equal in weight to the 20 smallest EU economies combined, or approaching one and a half times the scale of its nearest EU competitor

3.6 MILLION
Number of SMEs in Germany

VOLKSWAGEN
Largest company in terms of sales

SIEMANS AG
Largest employer

AN ONGOING BILL

€80 BILLION
Amount annually transferred to East Germany since reunification – around 3% of GDP

€53.4 BILLION
Amount spent by German companies on R&D in 2007. German is the largest European spender on private sector research.

30%
Amount of this spent on developing new cars

20%
Amount spent on electronics

6.3 MILLION
Number of members of the country's largest trades union association, Deutsche Gewerkschaftsbund (DGB)

€82 BILLION
Value of goods and services exported to France, its lead trading partner, in 2009

10%
Amount of German exports that are now sent to new accession EU states

A DISPROPORTIONATE GEOGRAPHICAL ADVANTAGE, A DISPROPORTIONATE FINANCIAL COST

Predicted trade benefits arising from a Visegrad expansion of the EU

★ 4 billion ECU – Germany

★ 3 billion ECU – France and UK combined

★ 3 billion ECU – the other EU countries

★ 3 billion ECU – the joining countries

Net budgetary cost in the process

★ 17 billion ECU

Source: Baldwin/Francois/Portes, 1997

63%

Volume of German exports that go to EU countries

14%

Volume of German exports that go to Asia, its second biggest market. Germany has been China's biggest investor since 1999

1 IN 8

Adults with a university degree

1973

Year the two Germanies joined the UN

EUROPEAN COMMISSION'S SUMMARY OF RECENT GERMAN ECONOMIC HISTORY

"By 1992, tight monetary policy by the Bundesbank had contained inflation, but high labour costs and taxes contributed to stagnating growth in western Germany, which slowed from over 4.6% in 1990 to around 2% for the rest of the decade, reaching a nadir of 0.75% in the first five years of the 21st century. Understandably, the reunification process brought forward a severe bout of economic indigestion – but the German economy then took extended sick leave to recover.

"Following a period of excessive wage increases up to the mid-1990s, economic recovery relied heavily on a decade of strong wage moderation. As a result, since 1995, German unit labour costs have fallen by around 20% compared with its major trading partners. However, until price competitiveness was fully restored, high unemployment persisted and job creation was weak, driving widening government deficits. In response, the government reined back expenditure, but also cut taxes in the hope of stimulating domestic demand.

"However, rising social security contributions to pay unemployment and other welfare benefits squeezed industry, which responded by underinvesting, shedding more labour, and even relocating operations overseas. Moreover, in view of low wage rises, fear of unemployment and doubts about the sustainability of the welfare system, domestic consumers simply did not want to spend. So, with industry and consumers both disinclined to kick-start a demand-led recovery, and a shrinking, post-boom construction sector, the economy remained stuck in a low-growth-low-expectations trap until well into 2005 – despite the restoration of price competitiveness.

"As a consequence, the government deficit rose above the '3% of GDP' ceiling set in the Stability and Growth Pact, meaning Germany was placed in the 'excessive deficit procedure' for four consecutive years (2002-2005)."

★ ★ ★ ★ ★ ★ ★ ★ ★ ★ ★ ★

"THE RELIANCE ON WAGE MODERATION ALONE CANNOT BE REGARDED AS A PROMISING LONG-TERM STRATEGY."

View of Director General of DG ECFIN in 2007

PARIS-BERLIN

The dominant enduring axis of decision-making at the EU

OTHER OCCASIONAL GUEST-STARRING AXES

London-Rome-Madrid/Warsaw

Small countries (when they feel they are being ignored)

London-Scandinavia (EFTA revisited)

London-Berlin (free market, subsidiarity, budget)

London-Dublin (Common Law, borders)

Madrid-Lisbon-Paris (retention of CFP)

Paris-Accession countries (retention of CAP)

Everybody except London (UK rebate)

London-Prague-Warsaw (sovereignty)

London-Copenhagen-Stockholm (Euro)

London-The Hague-Baltic (deregulation)

Lisbon/Madrid/Athens/Dublin (anti-reform of development aid)

Accession countries (more development aid)

---

6 MONTHS

Typical duration of any axis touted as "the new counterpart to Paris-Berlin".

MEANWHILE, IN TALLINN...

THE UK, GERMANY AND THE NORDIC COUNTRIES
Inter-war economic orientation of Estonia

45,000KM²	1.5 MILLION
Size of Estonia	Population

THIRD FROM BOTTOM
Where Estonia fits in terms of relative EU population density, after Finland and Sweden

RECENT FOREIGN OCCUPATION
1940-1941 USSR

1941-1944 Germany

1944-1991 USSR

" *Once the European Union has set the applicants for membership a definite threshold, it is in the interest of Estonia like any other European country to meet those criteria in all respects. We do not need concessions, which would dilute the essence of the Union and make it similar to many impotent world organisations. Estonia, even though she has a taste of blood in her mouth, already meets a lot of legislative and economic requirements set by the European Union."*

Estonian attitudes to the EU, set out by President Meri in 1997

152 MILLION ECU
EU transitional aid given to Estonia 1992-7

 Since 1991 the trade pattern of Estonia has swiftly changed from an almost exclusive orientation towards the CIS to a strong integration with the EU. Following the accession of Finland, Sweden and Austria as well as the entry into force of the Free Trade Agreement between the Community and Estonia, 54% of Estonia's exports were directed to the EU in 1995, while 66% of Estonia's imports originated in the EU."

Commission summary of Estonian trade pattern changes after independence

MACHINERY, ELECTRICAL EQUIPMENT, AGRICULTURAL PRODUCTS AND TEXTILES
Main Estonian imports from the EU at the time of accession

WOOD PRODUCTS AND TEXTILES
Main Estonian exports

ONE-THIRD
Share of Estonian exports which were re-exports of transit goods, or processed locally (hence textiles)

48%
Territory covered in forest

35%
Percentage of non-Estonians in Estonia

* 28% Russian
* 2.7% Ukrainian
* 1.5% Belorussian

A MATTER OF OBVIOUS CONCERN

95%

Population of non-ethnic
Estonians living in the region of
Narva – a twin city that sits on
the Russian border

23%

Number of non-Estonian nationals
at the time of accession who did
not have Estonian nationality

A PROBLEM SENT FROM MOSCOW

Proportions of nationality as they changed during the Soviet policy of
Russification

1934 CENSUS

88.2% Estonian and 8.2%
Russian

1959 CENSUS

74.6% Estonian and 20.1%
Russian

1979 CENSUS

64.7% Estonian and 27.9%
Russian

THE PROCESS OF NATURALISATION

From a law of 1995, applicants could sit an exam on Estonian language,
history and institutions.

Nationality could be acquired if you passed. It also made you eligible for
military service.

The pass rate was 80%-90%.

2007

Date of Russian cyber attacks on Estonia, following riots after a
Soviet-era memorial was removed.

2008

Cyber Defence Centre of Excellence set up in Tallinn by NATO

2010

Memorandum of Understanding signed between NATO and Estonia
(and other states) for co-operation during future cyber attacks

23%

Estonian GDP per head as a
proportion of the EU average in
1995, in purchasing power terms

48%

GDP per head in Greece when it
joined, as a comparison

179 ECUS

Average Estonian monthly salary in 1995

SPEEDY PRIVATISATION

70%

Share of the economy in private hands by mid-1996

ZERO

Tariff levels Estonia applied to agriculture after independence,
notwithstanding food processing contributing a third of gross industrial
output.

This had to change on entering the CAP

60%

Drop in industrial production over 1992-4 as Russia imposed protectionist tariff barriers, requiring a change in target markets

> *"One of the most liberal trade regimes in the world."*

FURS

Total list of items on which import duties were levied

CARS, MOTORCYCLES, BICYCLES AND RECREATIONAL BOATS

The items on which excise taxes were levied

This had to change on joining the Single Market

ESTONIA'S ECONOMIC CONSENSUS, AS REPORTED BY THE COMMISSION

★ Priorities of modernisation and integration in the European and world economy

★ Authorities voluntarily give up discretionary control of the money supply

★ Exchange rate pegged to the Deutsche Mark

★ Increase in base money fully matched by an increase in foreign exchange reserves

★ Neither local authorities nor the central government can borrow from the central bank

★ Central bank lending to commercial banks is restricted to emergency situations

	1994	1995	1996
Real GDP growth rate (%)	-1.8	4.3	4.0
Inflation rate, annual average (%)	47.7	29.0	23.1
Unemployment rate, end-year (%)	7.6	NA	10.2
General government budget balance as a percentage of GDP	1.3	-0.8	-1.6
Current account balance as a percentage of GDP	-7.1	-5.1	-10.2
Debt/export ratio (%)	9.1	10.3	8.8
FDI inflow as a percentage of GDP	9.2	5.6	1.6

INFLATION

A concern pre-accession thanks to the fixed DM link, owing to inflation being higher than in the countries exported to

ONE-THIRD

Number of pre-accession Estonian firms dependent on foreign capital

65%

Average foreign capital in these firms

TEXTILES, CLOTHING PRODUCTS, FOOD

Examples of key areas where Estonia had to re-impose higher tariffs on joining the EU

3.6%

Average level of tariffs that needed to be imposed across industrial products

4%

Foreseen annual level of EU structural grants as a share of GNP

ESTONIA'S GDP BY PURCHASING POWER PARITY
2001 – $14.6 billion
2008 – $27.7 billion

Source: OECD

6.7%

Estonia's debt-to-GDP prior to joining the eurozone

X3

Comparative figure for the next lowest EU country, Luxembourg

85.3%

Average level of national debt for eurozone countries

"THE INDEPENDENCE AND SOVEREIGNTY OF ESTONIA ARE TIMELESS AND INALIENABLE."

Article 1 of the Estonian constitution

"THERE IS NO POINT SAILING AGAINST THE WIND."

An Estonian voter's point of view during the referendum accession

BIG PICTURE MATHS

Changing world share of global output in purchasing power terms

	1980	2015
EU 25	26%	17%
US	20%	19%
Japan	7%	5%
India	3%	8%
China	3%	19%
Brazil	3%	3%
Russia	4%	2%
Other	34%	27%

Source: Gordon Brown, *Global Europe*

THAT COST-BENEFIT EQUATION AGAIN

★ Does it cost more being in or out?

★ Do countries achieve their national interests by QMV, or get outvoted?

★ Do politicians and, more importantly, the public feel comfortable with living in a federal Europe?

★ Does EU membership bring stability and peace to the country?

★ Can a better trade deal be found elsewhere?

The statistics suggest that Estonia's rush towards the EU was an understandable initial (pre-NATO) geopolitical decision given the Russian dynamic and when considered as a reaction to a collapse in its established export markets, but, it came at a high price with respect to its long-term competiveness. Its decision to join the euro was an attempt to maintain geostrategic support in Brussels and a marker of ongoing commitment to being economically pegged to Germany. However, there is a strong risk of this now undoing many of the benefits gained from painful economic reform.

Verdict: A trade shift was understandable, but dropping the free trade advantages that had been attained could well have been a step too far.

Germany's persistence with the EEC, despite high net costs, has meanwhile been rewarded through a secure market – it is the dominant exporter with a persistent and very large trade surplus. It enjoys a preeminent political position in Brussels, sometimes but not always masked by its association with France. As EU and German economic ambitions and interests become increasingly politically indistinguishable, Germany and the EU risk becoming synonymous in the public eye, which would paradoxically defeat one of the key reasons why Germany was meant to be submerged into a European entity in the first place.

Verdict: Depends now if Germany or failed eurozone states themselves end up having to pay up for their mistakes. One or other of Berlin's political or economic aspirations with the EU will take a hit.

An economic sea change – the growing pains of the eurozone

In a nutshell...

Notwithstanding the trade benefits and costs arising from the Single Market, eurozone membership has added a massive extra deficit to the economies that adopted the single currency. This of itself shifts the balance heavily into the negative, for as long as the crisis continues, and for many countries that will need ultimately to leave the euro.

1962

Marjolin Memorandum of 24 October 1962 in which the Commission called for the customs union to lead to an economic union by the end of the 1960s, with irrevocably fixed exchange rates between the member states' currencies.

1964

Committee of Governors of the central banks of the Member States of the EEC (the Committee of Governors) established. The Committee of Governors complemented a Monetary Committee.

1969

Barre Plan proposes distinct monetary identity in the Community.

1970

Werner Report (PM of Luxembourg) sets out a phased introduction.

1971

member states agree to an economic and monetary union.

1972

Community system for the progressive narrowing of the fluctuation margins of the members' currencies (the *snake*) set up.

1973

European Monetary Cooperation Fund (EMCF) established as the nucleus of a future Community organisation of central banks.

1974

Council Decision on the attainment of a high degree of convergence, and a directive on stability, growth and full employment. The system went no further owing to economic shocks and lack of political interest.

1979

European Monetary System (EMS) launched, with the European Currency Unit (ECU) – a basket of fixed quantities of the currencies of the member states.

1988

The European Council confirmed the objective of the progressive realisation of economic and monetary union. Delors tasked with heading up a committee to set about it.

1990

Intergovernmental conference (IGC) explores EMU in parallel with the political proposals.

EMU PHASES

Stage One was to focus on completing the internal market, reducing disparities between member states' economic policies, removing all obstacles to financial integration and intensifying monetary co-operation.

Stage Two was a period of transition to the final stage, setting up the basic organs and organisational structure of EMU and strengthening economic convergence. Achieved primarily through the establishment of a European Monetary Institute (later the Central Bank).

Stage Three sees exchange rates locked irrevocably and the various Community institutions and bodies assigned their full monetary and economic responsibilities. Denmark and UK had an opt out from this stage.

HOW THEY ONCE WERE

The rate at which currencies were locked to the Euro

€ 1

= **40.3399** Belgian francs

= **1.95583** Deutsche Mark

= **340.750** Greek drachmas

= **166.386** Spanish pesetas

= **6.55957** French francs

= **0.787564** Irish pounds

= **1,936.27** Italian lire

= **40.3399** Luxembourg francs

= **2.20371** Dutch guilders

= **13.7603** Austrian schillings

= **200.482** Portuguese escudos

= **5.94573** Finnish markkas

COMMITTEES AND BODIES

★ The **Accounting and Monetary Income Committee (AMICO)** advises on all intra-Eurosystem issues relating to accounting, financial reporting and the allocation of monetary income

★ The **Banknote Committee (BANCO)** promotes intra-Eurosystem co-operation in the production, issue and post-issue handling of euro banknotes

★ The **External Communications Committee (ECCO)** assists the ECB in its communication policy, particularly on issues related to multilingual publications

★ The **Information Technology Committee (ITC)** assists in the development, implementation and maintenance of IT networks and communications infrastructure which support the joint operational systems

★ The **Internal Auditors Committee (IAC)** develops common standards for auditing Eurosystem operations and audits joint projects and operational systems at the Eurosystem/ESCB level

★ The **International Relations Committee (IRC)** assists the ECB in performing its statutory tasks relating to international co-operation and acts as a forum for exchanging views on matters of common interest in this field

★ The **Legal Committee (LEGCO)** provides advice on all legal issues relating to the ECB's statutory tasks

★ The **Market Operations Committee (MOC)** assists the Eurosystem in carrying out monetary policy operations and foreign exchange transactions, and in managing the ECB's foreign reserves and the operation of ERM II

★ The **Monetary Policy Committee (MPC)** advises mainly on strategic and longer-term issues relating to the formulation of the monetary and exchange rate policy and is responsible for the regular Eurosystem staff projections of macroeconomic developments in the euro area

★ The **Payment and Settlement Systems Committee (PSSC)** advises on the operation and maintenance of TARGET, general payment systems policy and oversight issues, and issues of interest for central banks in the field of securities clearing and settlement

★ The **Statistics Committee (STC)** advises on the design and compilation of statistical information collected by the ECB and NCBs (national central banks)

★ ECB recommendations are the instruments by which the ECB may formally initiate Community legislation.

★ ECB recommendations confusingly are also the instruments by which the ECB provides general suggestions.

★ The ECB shares with the European Commission the right to initiate secondary Community legislation complementary to, or amending, the Statute of the ESCB.

★ These areas mainly concern the limits and conditions under which the ECB may require credit institutions to hold minimum reserves, collect statistics, exercise its regulatory powers, increase its capital, or make further calls on foreign reserve assets. The EU Council adopted such legislation at the start of Stage Three of EMU.

★ The Commission may also submit proposals in all the areas where the ECB may make recommendations, but so far it has in general not done so.

★ The party that does not exercise its right of initiative is to be consulted by the EU Council.

1%	0.5%
Supposed medium-term margins of error for countries to remain within EMU debt bandwidths, under the 1997 agreement	Maximum authorised structural deficit permitted under the new 2011 eurozone terms, to be placed into national law by all eurozone countries

WHAT CHANCE OF HARMONISATION IF...?

SOME NATIONAL VARIANTS OF SPELLINGS OF THE 'EURO'

Lithuania – *euras*

Latvia – *eira* (official) or *eiro* (popular)

Slovenia – *evro*

Malta – *ewro*

6

Number of spellings in Slovakia, thanks to declining nouns

JUST USE EURO OR ευρώ

The ECB's position, unsympathetic to issues of grammar.

Bulgaria continues to fight for acceptance of its own Cyrillic variant

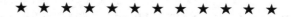

European System of Central Banks (ESCB): the **ECB** and the NCBs of all member states

Eurosystem: the **ECB** and the NCBs of the member states that have adopted the **euro**

European Monetary System (EMS): an exchange rate regime created in 1979

At the start of **Stage Three** of **EMU**, the EMS was superseded by **ERM II** (a 15% bandwidth, as opposed to the narrow one that triggered Black Wednesday)

Bank for International Settlements (BIS): established in 1930 by Belgium, Germany, France, Italy, Japan, the United Kingdom and the United States, the BIS is the world's oldest international financial organisation.

It fosters international monetary and financial co-operation and serves as a bank for central banks.

The BIS acts as: (i) a forum to promote discussion and facilitate decision-making processes; (ii) a centre for economic and monetary research; (iii) a prime counterparty for central banks in their financial transactions; and (iv) an agent or trustee in connection with international financial operations.

Based in Basel with offices in Hong Kong and Mexico City.

Broad Economic Policy Guidelines (BEPGs): the EU treaties oblige member states to coordinate their economic policies within the EU Council.

The BEPGs contain recommendations to policy-makers on macroeconomic and structural policies and assessment.

EUREPO: the rate at which one prime bank offers funds in **euro** to another prime bank in exchange for collateral consisting exclusively of government bonds and bills issued by Euro-area countries. The EUREPO's calculation methodology is similar to that of the **EURIBOR**, but it is representative of rates in the secured markets (repo markets). The panel of banks is also different.

EURIBOR (Euro Interbank Offered Rate): the rate at which a prime bank is willing to lend funds in **euro** to another prime bank, computed daily for interbank deposits with a maturity of up to 12 months. Unlike the EUREPO, the EURIBOR reflects conditions in the unsecured market.

ODD LOGIC

> *As a nation, we owe our gratitude for the adoption of the euro to many.*
>
> *First and foremost to the Slovenian tolar: it was a solid currency, and we bid it farewell with good feelings. It remains an indelible part of Slovenia history, self-confidence and Slovenia's success story. It is precisely because the tolar was a success story that we could adopt the euro; it is precisely because it was so good that its lifespan was so short."*

Speech by the Slovenian Prime Minister on why the country was dropping its national currency, which had existed since Slovenia had dropped the common Yugoslav currency.

ARCHITECTURE

The uncontroversial theme of euro banknote design, thus avoiding political controversies

```
COUNTRIES PRINTING EURO BANKNOTES
            IN 2012
     €5 – BE, ES, FR, IT, AT
     €10 – DE, GR, FR, IE, PT
€20 – CY, EE, FR, IT, MT, LU, NL, SI, SK, FI
     €50 – BE, DE, ES, IT
         €100 – DE
         €200 – DE
        €500 – none
```

Printing euro banknotes takes place in different countries and varies from year to year. However, as this affects the range of notes in circulation, this also makes it impractical to simply swap the notes from a country leaving the euro for a print run of any new national currency.

HEBBEN SIE EURO

Countries that have printed the two largest value euro bank notes over the years

> *Germany*
> *Austria*
> *Luxembourg*

70%

Bundesbank estimate of the proportion of euro notes printed in Germany that in 2009 were outside the country, *the lion's share* being outside the eurozone. The growth in the volume of German euro banknotes in circulation is therefore almost exclusively driven by foreign demand.

IDENTIFYING THE ISSUING COUNTRY BY THE INDIVIDUAL BANKNOTE CODE

X – *Germany*	G – *Cyprus*
Y – *Greece*	1 – *Luxembourg*
V – *Spain*	F – *Malta*
U – *France*	P – *Netherlands*
T – *Ireland*	N – *Austria*
M – *Portugal*	H – *Slovenia*
S – *Italy*	E – *Slovakia*
Z – *Belgium*	L – *Finland*

Source: ThisisMoney.co.uk

SEIGNIORAGE

"Because coins are now issued only as token money for domestic purposes, they no longer need possess a high intrinsic value, and low-standard silver or certain base-metal alloys provide all the qualities required. A substantial margin usually exists between the cost of producing a coin and its statutory currency value; this margin, or profit, is known as seigniorage."

Source: *Encyclopaedia Britannica*

8%

Euro seigniorage, allocated since 2002 to the ECB as a proportion of all notes in circulation

€45 BILLION

Value as at end 2005

THE LATEST AVAILABLE MARGINAL RATE OF THE EUROSYSTEM'S MAIN REFINANCING OPERATIONS

Rate at which this money bears interest, distributed to the NCBs separately at the end of the year. It is distributed in full unless the income earned on euro banknotes in circulation exceeds costs, at which point these are first deducted.

3%

Maastricht criteria for limit of breach of deficit

60%

Maastricht criteria for limit of debt to GDP ratio

2003

Year France and Germany both broke the Stability and Growth Pact rules, inevitably avoiding punitive fines from the Commission – and thus encouraging other states to do the same

12

Number of eurozone countries in breach of the 60% limit in 2010, according to Eurostat

MEDITERRANEAN BLUES

Greece and Italy were estimated at over 100% in debt, i.e. owing more than the country earns in a year

80%

The level both France and Germany had now breached

BIG BAZOOKA

Metaphor for deployment of massive state bailouts. An unfortunate choice given the alternative street slang meaning of the plural phrase.

Properly speaking, it is largely reliant on German money so it should in any event be called a *grosse Panzerfaust*.

€500 BILLION	€700 BILLION
Old bail-out fund for eurozone countries	Larger bail-out fund authorised as part of the new emerging European Stability Mechanism, putatively agreed in November 2011
UNANIMITY	85%
Former decision making process over these loans	New QMV threshold for deciding whether to use these bail-out funds

WHAT CAMERON VETO?

Declared ambitions of the Eurogroup Working Group:

> *Some of the measures described above can be decided through secondary legislation. The euro area Heads of State or Government consider that the other measures should be contained in primary legislation. Considering the absence of unanimity among the EU Member States, they decided to adopt them through an international agreement to be signed in March [2012] or at an earlier date. The objective remains to incorporate these provisions into the treaties of the Union as soon as possible."*

A PARLIAMENTARY BLOCK

The premiers of:

Bulgaria, Czech Republic, Denmark, Hungary, Latvia, Lithuania, Poland, Romania and Sweden

placed a scrutiny reserve in this 2011 meeting, saying that they needed to consult Parliament before signing up to the new bail-out system and eurozone rules.

O

Liabilities for countries that remain outside of this grouping, excepting loans provided through other agencies (the EU main budget and the IMF)

RESULT

A large number of EU countries (predominantly those of the eurozone) now have massive debt fault lines running through their economies.

There is a risk of costs being added to these by increasing the interest paid on state loans, because these are seen as riskier for lenders.

In turn, these higher borrowing costs mean less money can be spent by these governments on standard expenditure (such as schools and hospitals) and more money needs to be taken from businesses to service the debts, making the country both poorer and less competitive.

Most eurozone countries have already had their sovereign credit rating dropped, or are at risk of losing it.

Although they are harder to assess, there are also the costs arising from domestic policy measures taken to restore confidence in the euro – such as having to raise taxes, in turn hitting business competitiveness and investment.

Furthermore, there is the serious impact of fixing interest rates at a level that may suit the core Rhenish economy but not the more peripheral economies such as Ireland. Membership of the euro is high risk for these states.

These additional costs would need to be factored into any assessment of EU costs for those countries.

WHERE THE EURO LEAVES THE COMPONENT PARTS TODAY
OVER/UNDERVALUATION AGAINST THE USD

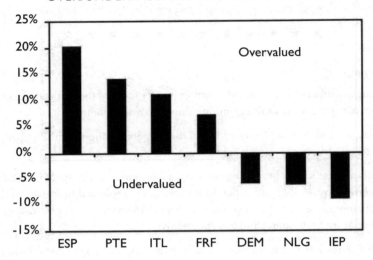

Source: Bank of America Merill Lynch, referenced by Jeremy Warner,
Daily Telegraph, November 2011

Meaning

These are long-term assessments predicting long-term changes. Spain, Italy, Portugal and France are considered overvalued against the US Dollar while within the eurozone. If they left and their new currency floated, their currencies would drop in value against the USD – creating huge problems for Euro-denominated debts, but great opportunities for exports to the US. Ireland would appreciate, which would be bad for exports to the States and also for inward investment from there, but good for absorbing debts denominated in euro. So leaving the eurozone, however the new national currency reacts, carries both opportunities and considerable risks.

Case study: the United Kingdom

£63 BILLION

UK tax take from the financial services sector in 2011, excluding the new bank levy

12.1%

Share of total UK tax take that comes from the sector

Source: City of London

1.1 MILLION

UK workforce in financial services, increasingly subject to EU regulations

3.9%

Share of total UK workforce

Source: City of London

92%

Proportion of total UK trade deficit in the last five years that has been with the EU

Source: Milne notes on *The Pink Book 2011*

19

Number of EU trading partners with whom the UK was in deficit in 2010

3%

Drop in UK exports outside the EU during the recession

A QUARTER

Drop in UK exports to the EU during the recession

Source: Milne notes on *The Pink Book 2011*

43%

Share of UK exports of Goods (*visibles*) as a proportion of all UK exports worldwide in 2010.

57%

Invisibles (Services, Income & Transfers) share

Source: Milne notes on *The Pink Book 2011*

£20 BILLION

Suggested UK structural trade surplus with the US

UK CONTRIBUTION TO THE EU BUDGET, CALENDAR YEAR 2010

UK Gross Contribution
£18,455 million

UK Receipts from EU Institutions
£8,141 million

UK Net Contribution
£10,314 million

Source: Milne notes on *The Pink Book 2011*

£7.3 BILLION

The UK government's official estimate of its net EU contribution for 2010.

This, however, only takes into account funding delivered via the Treasury and not by other departments, for instance for the EU Aid budget.

Equally, the EU budget also pays some accounts directly and this makes the end receipts figure in *The Pink Book* larger than the Treasury statistics.

> ### TREASURY'S OWN NET FORECAST OF THE UK CONTRIBUTION
>
> 2011/12 – **£7.6 billion**
> 2012/13 – **£7.6 billion**
> 2013/14 – **£8.6 billion**
> 2014/15 – **£9.5 billion**

£238 BILLION

UK's gross contribution to the EU budget since joining (Treasury figures)

£170 BILLION

The figure after the rebate

£72 BILLION

The end net Treasury figure

X 7

Per capita gross contribution of UK to the EU budget in 2009, seven times larger per capita than made by the EFTA members combined

3.5 MILLION

Jobs the Department for Business claim as being at risk if the UK left the EU

> *There is no a priori reason to suppose that many of these jobs, if any, would be lost permanently if Britain were to leave the EU."*
>
> *"No reason to suppose that unemployment would rise significantly if the UK were to withdraw from the EU."*
>
> *"But foreign investment would fall, meaning a drop in GDP of 2.25%."*

Key findings of Pain and Young's analysis, 2000

57%	21%
Inward investment attracted by oil and gas plus financial services, strongly unlikely to be affected by any change in EU membership	Value of industries involving inward investment that generically could be affected

Source: Global Britain

PAIN AND YOUNG SUMMARISED BY THE TREASURY

COSTS

Reduction in stock of inward investment:

★ **1%** fall reduces technical progress by **0.32%**
★ **10%** fall reduces export volume by **0.75%**

Increased trade barriers with the EU:

★ Tariffs of **6.7%** plus customs paperwork (approx **2%** of transaction value) will hike relative price of all UK exports by **5%**

BENEFITS

★ Fiscal windfall: Net public expenditure is **£3 billion** lower
★ Lower food prices: Aggregate prices of non-manufacturing imports drop by **5.25%**

28%

Implicit costs of EU membership as a share of GDP, from a study undertaken from within the Treasury – but not intended as a cost-benefit analysis

Source: Global Britain

HOW THAT FIGURE OF 28% ARISES

- ★ EU Protectionism – **7%** of GDP
- ★ Competition gap with US – **12%** of GDP
- ★ EU Over-regulation – **6%** of GDP
- ★ Transatlantic barriers to trade – **3%** of GDP

Note there is no indication of the extent to which there is cost overlap

AUTHOR OF THE REPORT

The Chancellor, Gordon Brown

4%

Estimate of the amount of British exports mislabelled as being to the EU as they are only in transit via Antwerp and Rotterdam

£2.5 BILLION

Estimated costs to the UK of the changes made to the Pregnant Workers' Directive

Source: EP FEMM Committee Impact Assessment

£20 BILLION

Department of Business's estimate of the potential cost of any future loss of the UK opt out to the Working Time Directive

48%

Official government estimate of EU holdings as a share of UK total FDI earnings in 2008

THE NETHERLANDS DISTORTION

Statistical aberration that boosts this statistic from its true figure, since investments are sometimes channelled through Dutch holding companies.

BUSINESS PROBLEMS TRADING IN THE EU

31% – legal and regulatory barriers

25% – getting the right contacts

20% – domestic bias

15% – cultural barriers

45% BELOW POTENTIAL

Estimate of current status of the Single Market. If it were ever achieved, it would be worth $57 billion

62% TO 24%

Share of Respondents in a 2011 poll who agreed with rather than disagreed with the statement that they expected the costs of the Single Market to outweigh the benefits for the City of London over the next five years. A majority also believes that there has been a deficit over the past two decades

Source: Open Europe/ComRes

TREASURY'S "ILLUSTRATIVE" VIEW OF THE VARIABLE IMPACT OF THE EU ACROSS BRITISH BUSINESSES

★ Agriculture
  - CAP has been harmful to UK producers and consumers
★ Low value-added manufacturing (e.g. textiles)
  - In long-term decline, but transition probably cushioned by trade protection and structural adjustment funds
★ High-tech manufacturing (e.g. electronics/automotive sectors)
  - Likely to be most affected because of tradeability across EU
  - Estimated that 40 out of 120 manufacturing sectors affected by single market (around 12% to 18% of EU GDP)
★ Low value-added services (e.g. retail/distribution)
  - Little observable benefit from Single Market programme to date (hence need for new directive!) but possibly additional regulatory burdens
★ High value-added services (e.g. financial services)
  - Increased export opportunities for UK firms offset by rising regulatory burden

From a 2005 PowerPoint presentation

263

Number of pages in the Minford/Mahambare/Nowell/Elgar cost-benefit analysis, probably the most comprehensive review to date

DISPARATE ECONOMIES

1.4%	16%
UK workforce in agriculture in 2001, representing **0.6%** of GDP	Comparative figure for Greece, at **6.7%** of GDP

VOCABULARY OF PROTECTIONISM

Tariffs – entry taxes

Tariff escalation – tariffs on finished products but not on raw goods, encouraging domestic production

Quotas – limits on volume of imports

Tariff rate quota – limited access to a reduced entry rate, surplus to which is taxed at a higher rate

Anti-dumping duties – reciprocal action against (real or imagined) subsidising of exports

State aid – subsidising uncompetitive industries, including the use of tax breaks

---

BOUND TARIFF
Official rate of tariffs

APPLIED TARIFF
Actual rate of tariffs

"WATER"
The difference between the two

MFN: Most Favoured Nations. Post-war system of applying external tariffs set at a common rate to WTO members.

GSP: Generalised System of Preferences. A more recent development allowing for preferential treatment, at the risk of endorsing protectionism through tariff escalation.

REGULATORY AND MARKET ENVIRONMENT IN 1998

Scale 0–6 from least to most restrictive

	Britain	Rest of EU	US	EU minima	EU maxima
Air passenger transport	2.2	3.8	1.2	2.2	5.5
Road freight	1.3	2.8	1.5	1.3	4.6
Mobile telephony	0	2.9	n.a.	0	4.6
Fixed telephony	1	3.1	0.3	0.4	6
Electricity	0	4.1	4.3	0	6.
Railways	3	5.1	1.5	3	6
Retail distribution	2.5	2.7	n.a.	1.2	4.7
Average	1.4	3.4	1.7	1.4	4.5

Source: Minford quoting Messerlin (2001)

BRITISH-BOUGHT BENEFITS, BRITISH-BORNE COSTS?

"As the UK has been a significant driver for openness and reform within the EU, it is quite possible that if the UK had not been a member, the Single Market may have evolved differently – potentially less successfully."

Treasury Paper on EU Membership and Trade

 That country having no written Constitution, who can tell when its Constitution is changed?"

De Tocqueville on England
(arguments on democratic accountability are also in play)

63

Number of clauses in Magna Carta

1320

Declaration of Arbroath affirms Scottish sovereignty

1628

Torture, a restricted practice, outlawed in England

1689

Bill of Rights

1708

Torture outlawed in Scotland

1734-1812

The major continental European states ban torture (and in Spain's case the Inquisition as well)

ACCOUNTABILITY

1:864,800

Average ratio of MEP to voter (mid-2010)

1:95,800

Average ratio of MP to voter

ELECTORAL DISTANCE?

WAYS OF CHOOSING MEPS

D'Hondt (current method)

Used in list system to allocate seats; uses a series of divisors (1, 2, 3, 4, etc.) to ensure that next candidate to be elected is from the party with highest average vote.

First-Past-the-Post (previously)

Candidate with largest number of votes wins, whether absolute majority or not.

Source: House of Commons Library

THE EU IN A NUTSHELL

WHAT IS THE VALUE OF THE SINGLE MARKET?

VIEW ONE

★ EU GDP in 2002 is 1.8 percentage points or €164.5 billion higher thanks to the Internal Market. **European Commission**

★ About 2.5 million jobs have been created in the EU since 1992 that would not have been created without the opening up of frontiers. **European Commission**

★ The Single Market may be responsible for income gains in the UK between 2% and 6%, that is between £1,100 and £3,300 a year per British household. **Department for Business**

★ Over 1992-2006, EU GDP assessed to have risen by 2.2% thanks to the Single Market. **European Commission Report, 2007**

★ Assuming that gains were distributed evenly across EU member states then 2.2% of additional GDP translates into roughly £25 billion of gains to the UK over the period 1992-2006. **Classified – but now released – Treasury report**

★ EU countries trade twice as much with each other as they would do in the absence of the single market programme. Given that, according to the OECD, a 10 percentage point increase in trade exposure is associated with a 4% rise in income per capita, increased trade in Europe since the early 1980s may be responsible for around 6% higher income per capita in the UK. **Department for Business, 2010**

VIEW TWO

★ These benefits need to be compared with the estimated red tape costs, which the Commission has assessed as two to three times higher (see Part Six).

★ They also need to be compared with the benefits in tariff reduction that today currently exist in parallel through the liberalisation of world trade, regardless of the EU.

★ **This means the benefits to the UK today are restricted to a limited number of industries that fare better under the Single Market, but the significant costs are spread out across the whole economy.**

★ The benefits listed above are, moreover, misleading. FDI and competitiveness in Britain were both boosted by domestic reforms in the 1980s.

★ EU growth occurred as a consequence of UK, Dutch and German-led reforms that these countries were already unilaterally implementing in their own national markets. The Single Market therefore only affected growth in their EU export market, not their national markets. Britain's EU export share being less than that of its free market allies, it did not get comparatively so much out of the changes.

★ Single Market processes have since the 1990s increasingly generated Social Market costs and a recurring trend of protectionism.

★ Consequently, the benefits of the Single Market for the UK are considerably overrated.

A DEPARTMENT THAT'S STILL HOLDING OUT

Enthusiasm for the EU within the Department for Business (as opposed to some other departments) is partly explained by optimism that eventually more trade barriers will drop in the EU. Their assessment is that this could mean:

★ 0.5% to 1% of EU GDP with progress on services

★ 1.1% on financial markets

★ 0.6% to 0.8% on energy

★ 0.2% on tax co-operation

Other studies the department cite estimate that full implementation of the Services Directive could raise UK GDP by 0.4% to 0.6% (£4-£6 billion).

2.5%

Commission's estimate of the value of production affected by non-tariff barriers within the Single Market

BETWEEN 13.4% AND 45%

Rather broad-ranging but bigger assessment from a 2009 World Bank paper assessing EU barriers

A PRO-EUROPEAN'S VIEW

"My answer to why we need a European Union today – and of course we do – is this. We need to go back to first principles and see what's changed. The founding fathers had seven reasons for setting up the Community:

1. *The need for constraints on the nation states, after two devastating world wars*

2. *No faith that the United Nations could make states conform to rules of civilised behaviour*

3. *The emergence of Stalin's aggressive empire, then monolithic and extending over the whole Communist world, including China*

4. *Europe's need to come together and work together if it wanted to pull its weight in the world*

5. *Europe's need to end protectionism in order to achieve economic health*

6. *The need to anchor a recovering Germany within a democratic framework*

7. *The perception that inter-governmentalism was a totally inadequate response to these challenges"*

Sir Christopher Audland, who hand-wrote the UK's second application to join the EEC, interviewed in 1998

Source: EU archives

Is the EU the right answer to developing Britain's trade?

In a nutshell...

The UK is historically a globally trading economy and remains far less linked to the Rhineland economies today than many of its EU counterparts.

As such, the question arises as to whether it would do better reinvigorating those ties, particularly given that the promising markets of the future lie beyond Europe in China, India, South America, and elsewhere, with continuing strength in the North American economy in which British firms have several natural advantages.

These tables are a little heavy on the eyes at first sight, but they do allow you to explore at your leisure the context of the UK's truly global trade.

BRITAIN'S GLOBAL CONTEXT: TRADING NOT JUST WITH ONE CONTINENT

UK exports in hard times (Goods, Services, Income, Transfers) 2006 to 2010 (not adjusted for the Rotterdam-Antwerp Effect or the Netherlands Distortion)

£bn	2006	2007	2008	2009	2010	Change over 2008 to 2010
Exports to EU-26	310	320	349	283	273	-22%
Exports to Rest of World	326	360	354	300	342	-3%
Exports to whole World	636	681	703	583	614	-13%
Proportion going to the EU	49%	47%	50%	49%	44%	-6%

Source: Global Britain

CUTTING EDGE ECONOMY DEVELOPING NICHE INDUSTRIES
High-tech exports as a percentage of total exports

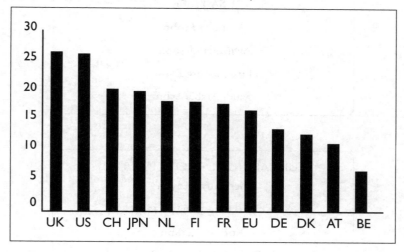

BRITAIN'S GLOBAL COMPETITIVENESS: BIGGER AND BETTER BEYOND EUROPE

UK BALANCE OF TRADE WITH THE REST OF THE EU (2006-2010)
-£142.5bn

THE BALANCE WITH THE REST OF THE WORLD
- £12.2bn

UK TRADE DEFICIT WITH THE EU AS A PROPORTION OF ITS DEFICIT WITH THE REST OF THE WORLD
92%

UK LARGEST SURPLUSES IN 2010
USA **£20bn**

Australia **£10bn**

Switzerland **£6bn**

Luxembourg **£6bn**

Saudi Arabia **£5bn**

UK LARGEST DEFICITS IN 2010
Germany - **£23bn**

China/Hong Kong - **£22bn**

Norway - **£18bn**

EU Institutions - **£10bn**

Spain - **£5bn**

UK EXPORTS TO EU
£273bn

UK IMPORTS FROM EU
£325bn

UK'S EU TRADE DEFICIT
-£52bn

UK EXPORTS TO REST OF THE WORLD
£342bn

UK IMPORTS FROM REST OF THE WORLD
£327bn

UK'S NET TRADE SURPLUS OUTSIDE OF THE EU
£16bn

Source: Global Britain (2010 figures)

THE UK: AN ATTRACTIVE PROPOSITION TO FOREIGN INVESTORS

TOP FIVE INWARD DESTINATIONS OF FDI TO THE EU IN 2010

1. *Luxembourg* (€47.6bn)
2. *UK* (€28.5bn)
3. *Ireland* (€21.5bn)
4. *Germany* (€14.5bn)
5. *France* (€8bn)

Source: Eurostat

TOP FIVE OUTWARD INVESTING EU COUNTRIES IN 2010, EXTRA-EU 27

1. *Luxembourg* (€38.3bn)
2. *Belgium* (€35.9bn)
3. *Germany* (€28.7bn)
4. *France* (€22.7bn)
5. *Sweden* (€16.2bn)

Source: Eurostat

FDI PREFERENCE IS BASED ON ISSUES SUCH AS:

★ Language (especially English)
★ Local investment promotions
★ Tax breaks and other policy incentives
★ Quality of labour
★ Cost of labour
★ Union issues
★ Domestic transport links
★ International transport access
★ Product transport and import/export ease
★ Technology (e.g. broadband)
★ Communications

- ★ Level of corruption
- ★ Red tape
- ★ Crime rate
- ★ Personal interest: social and family environment
- ★ Personal links: historic, education, family or ethnic community
- ★ Hub access beyond Europe

In many of these, the UK over the last 20 years has been highly competitive or enjoyed innate advantages. These are not reliant on EU membership.

WHO INVESTS IN BRITAIN?
Main inward investors into the UK

Measured by earnings, adjusted for the Netherlands Distortion

By Region

USA + Canada	**58%**
EU	**25%**
Rest of World	**17%**

By Country

USA	**55%**
France	**9%**
Germany	**5%**
Switzerland	**4%**
Australia + NZ	**4%**
Canada	**3%**
Belgium/Lux	**2%**
Italy	**2%**
Eire	**2%**
Netherlands	**1%**

Source: Global Britain

PREFERRED PARTNERS: WHERE BRITISH BUSINESSES IN
RETURN LIKE TO INVEST

Main recipients of UK investment overseas

Measured by earnings, adjusted for the Netherlands Distortion

By Region

USA + Canada	**35%**
EU	**22%**
Rest of World	**43%**

By Country

USA	**33%**
Australia	**7%**
Hong Kong	**5%**
Germany	**4%**
Eire	**4%**
France	**4%**
Switzerland	**4%**
Singapore	**3%**
Canada	**2%**
South Africa	**2%**

IS THERE AN ALTERNATIVE TO OUR CURRENT EU ARRANGEMENTS?

MOOTED ALTERNATIVES

0.01%

US International Trade Commission assessment from 2000, on the long-run GDP impact of the UK quitting the EU and being in NAFTA instead

0.12%

Assessed real income rise quoted by the Treasury if the UK stayed in the EEA on leaving the EU

"NAFTA members gain, EU14 lose. Findings are heavily caveated however."

UK Treasury summary

A COMPARISON OF SCENARIOS

Undertaken by Commission staff under the Department for Business rubric

Scenario 2 – UK leaves EU, stays in the EEA

Scenario 3 – UK leaves EU structures entirely

 Given the actual low level of EU external tariffs, the implementation of tariffs between UK and other EU members to the level of actual tariffs between the EU and the rest of the OECD (scenario 3) would have overall very similar consequences than scenario 2."

-0.2 to -0.3 %

Unofficial Commission estimate of the impact on the UK economy of UK leaving the current terms of EU membership (but excluding regulatory burden savings that would also emerge)

Source: BIS 2011 paper

3

Commonwealth countries other than the UK that are in the twenty largest world economies (excluding China's links via Hong Kong)

GDP GROWTH IN 2010

United Kingdom **1.4%**
United States **3%**
Canada **3.2%**
Nigeria **7.9%**
India **8.8%**

Source: World Bank

OPEN FOR BUSINESS? THE TOP 20 OF THE 2012 INDEX OF ECONOMIC FREEDOM, MARKING POSSIBLE OTHER MARKETS FOR EXPANSION (WITH SCORE)

Country	Score
Hong Kong	89.9
Singapore	87.5
Australia	83.1
New Zealand	82.1
Switzerland	81.1
Canada	79.9
Chile	78.3
Mauritius	77
Ireland	76.9
United States	76.3
Denmark	76.2
Bahrain	75.2
Luxembourg	74.5
United Kingdom	74.1
The Netherlands	73.3
Estonia	73.2
Finland	72.3
Taiwan	71.9
Macau	71.8
Cyprus	71.8

Number of EU countries coloured green for 'satisfactory' on the Economic Freedom Heat Map

Source: Heritage Foundation

A BUSINESS STUDY FROM 2000

Impact of EU Membership	Cost to the UK (% of GDP)	Benefit to the UK (% of GDP)
EU budget	0.75	-
CAP	1	-
Customs Union	-	0.5
Single Market	0	0
Social model	1	-
FDI	-	0.5
Total end cost	**Between 1.75 and 3% of GDP**	

Source: Institute of Directors

A MORE RECENT REVIEW FROM 2005

	GDP per year (%)
Net UK financial contribution	0.4
Costs of Common Agricultural Policy	0.3
Manufacturing trade costs	2.5 to 3
Regulation (including harmonisation and social agenda)	6 to 25
Pensions (bail-out/common tax)	2 to 9
Euro membership (not yet applicable)	Doubling of economic volatility
Increased business dynamism	Unquantifiable

Source: Minford/Mahambare/Nowell/Elgar, 2005

In a nutshell...

The UK is a large economy that does get some trade benefits from EU membership, but at significant economic costs in the process. There is also a noted democratic deficit leading to public discontent. Is the cost larger than the benefit? We need to revisit our magic formula.

THAT COST-BENEFIT EQUATION OF OURS AGAIN:

★ Does it cost more being in or out?

★ Do countries achieve their national interests, or get outvoted?

★ Do politicians and, more importantly, the public feel comfortable with living in a federal Europe?

★ Does membership of the EU bring stability and peace to the country?

★ Can a better trade deal be found elsewhere?

THE DATA SUGGESTS THAT EU MEMBERSHIP IS AN ADVANTAGE TO THOSE COUNTRIES WHICH (AMONG OTHER ISSUES):

★ Export heavily to other EU countries, i.e. trade heavily in central Europe

★ Trade lightly with countries worldwide where EU and reciprocal tariffs are an issue

★ Have a high proportion of their GDP as EU exports, i.e. red tape costs are less of a share of total burden on domestic trade

★ Have a history of conflict with Germany or other larger neighbours

★ Have no public confidence in their politicians to run their country

★ Are net recipients of EU dole

★ Have very large and comparatively inefficient agricultural sectors

★ Have infrastructure that requires massive capital input (from the EU) to reach European standards

- ★ Have large fishing fleets rather than fisheries resources
- ★ Have a small number of vital national interests in which Brussels has the competence to legislate, so they can concentrate their lobbying
- ★ Are consistent in their negotiating aims, rather than varying between whichever political party is in power
- ★ Support the basic principle of ever-closer political integration at EU level, and thus spend their energies negotiating preferential terms rather than constantly expending political chips on blocking and delaying measures
- ★ Have a limited history in operating as a free and independent country
- ★ Have capable diplomats acting as negotiators
- ★ Occupy common ground with both Paris and Berlin on matters of vital national interest
- ★ Enjoy a not totally insignificant voting strength in the institutions
- ★ Share identical national interests with a number of other states
- ★ Send a disproportionate share of staff to the EU civil service
- ★ Possess a limited track record as a functional democracy
- ★ Have a history of belonging to a larger state
- ★ Are insecure, feeling guilt at or fear of their past
- ★ Are domestically traditionally averse to the basic principles of free trade, with a governing class that is less protectionist
- ★ Have kept out of the eurozone, or alternatively anticipate as eurozone members receiving special treatment, i.e. being bailed out
- ★ Have negotiated key opt outs (but ideally, more than any country currently enjoys)
- ★ Avoid gold plating EU laws
- ★ Have a tendency of not implementing EU legislation that they don't like and a track record of getting away with it

No country fills all of these criteria. Several fill so few the disadvantages of membership are overwhelming. Others, particularly the original Rhineland states of the old EEC, come closer to ticking the key boxes.

But overall, from wherever in the EU you hail, much of the maths is personal. It's your country: **you** do the sums and **you** decide!

LET THE PEOPLE DECIDE?

Different historic reasons behind supporting a referendum

- ★ **Tactical**. Belief one side will win
- ★ **Strategic**. Allowing a debate so that an informed public will better support the end decision reached
- ★ **Diplomatic**. To strengthen the negotiating hand if the result needs to be sold to the public, or already carries a mandate
- ★ **Political**. Handing over responsibility to the public directly to preserve party or governmental unity
- ★ **Democratic**. Belief that the people should have a say on a matter of great importance

Some suggested further reading

Sacred Causes and *Earthly Powers* by Professor Michael Burleigh

Two books on European ideologies that set the context for contemporary politics

The Throw that Failed by Lionel Bell

The history of Britain's attempts in the 1960s to join the EEC

Should Britain Leave the EU? by Patrick Minford, Vidya Mahambare and Eric Nowell

A view from a business economics perspective

Europe of Many Circles by Sir Richard Body

Alternative approach to how European co-operation could develop

This Blessed Plot by Hugo Young

Sympathetic yet relatively even-handed historical review of UK attitudes towards European integration

The Castle of Lies by Christopher Booker and Richard North

Strong critique of EU bureaucracy and political direction

Confessions of a Eurosceptic by David Heathcoat-Amory

Political memoirs of a former Europe Minister

The Devil Knew Not by Bill Newton-Dunn

Political thriller written by a Lib Dem MEP that achieves the impossible by making the European Parliament almost interesting

The Rotten Heart of Europe by Bernard Connolly

A Commission whistleblower's inside story on the collapse of the ERM – especially relevant today with the problems around the Euro

Helpful websites

epp.eurostat.ec.europa.eu/portal/page/portal/eurostat/home
Eurostat

www.europarl.europa.eu
European Parliament

euobserver.com
Balanced wide-ranging reporting

en.euabc.com
A very handy A-Z of the EU containing many more facts and figures

ec.europa.eu
European Commission

www.europeanmovement.eu
Campaigners for EU integration

www.fedtrust.co.uk
Research supporting the establishment of a federal Europe

european-convention.eu.int
Convention on the Future of Europe: probably the best location to find a large cross-section of political essays on the EU, predominantly in favour of integration but with some keynote pieces against

www.taxpayersalliance.com
Has a selection of major EU research papers reviewing cost issues

www.brugesgroup.com
Contains many EU-critical papers

www.openeurope.org.uk
Strong on business and City costs

www.freebritain.org.uk
Longstanding opponents of EEC membership, of historic and current interest

Déjà Vu

AN EMAIL JOKE CIRCULATING AROUND THE CITY OF
LONDON IN NOVEMBER 2011

Some years ago a small rural town in Italy twinned with a similar town in Greece.

The Mayor of the Greek town visited the Italian town. When he saw the palatial mansion belonging to the Italian mayor he wondered how he could afford such a house. The Italian said: *"You see that bridge over there? The EU gave us a grant to build a four-lane bridge, but by building a single lane bridge with traffic lights at either end this house could be built."*

The following year the Italian visited the Greek town. He was simply amazed at the Greek mayor's house, with its gold taps and marble floors; it was marvellous.

When he asked how this could be afforded the Greek said: *"You see that bridge over there?"*

The Italian replied: *"No."*